COLLEGE OF ONE

SHEILAH GRAHAM (1904–88) was born Lily Shiel in Leeds, England, the youngest of six children in a desperately poor family of Ukrainian Jews who had fled the pogroms at home. Her father died young, and because of the family's straitened financial circumstances, her mother was forced to place Lily in an orphanage at the age of six. When she left school, she got a job in a department store demonstrating a toothbrush that cleaned only the backs of teeth. At eighteen, she married an older businessman and became a chorus girl, joining the ranks of Cochran's Young Ladies. She based her first newspaper piece, a casual called "The Stage Door Johnnies by a Chorus Girl," on these experiences. In 1933, she moved to the United States to work as a reporter for the *New York Mirror*, and soon was recruited to write a nationally syndicated daily column on Hollywood. For the next thirty-five years, she would be the most powerful Hollywood gossip columnist, carried by more newspapers than Louella Parsons and Hedda Hopper, with her own radio program, and later, a television show. In 1937, she met and fell in love with F. Scott Fitzgerald; they would live together until his death in 1940. Graham's memoir of her time with Fitzgerald, *Beloved Infidel*, was an international bestseller that was made into a movie starring Gregory Peck and Deborah Kerr. She died in Palm Beach, Florida.

WENDY FAIREY is the daughter of Sheilah Graham and the philosopher A. J. Ayers. She teaches English literature and creative writing at Brooklyn College. She is the author of *One of the Family*, a family memoir, and ██████████████████████████████ s.

THE NEVERSINK LIBRARY

I was by no means the only reader of books on board the Neversink. Several other sailors were diligent readers, though their studies did not lie in the way of belles-lettres. Their favourite authors were such as you may find at the book-stalls around Fulton Market; they were slightly physiological in their nature. My book experiences on board of the frigate proved an example of a fact which every book-lover must have experienced before me, namely, that though public libraries have an imposing air, and doubtless contain invaluable volumes, yet, somehow, the books that prove most agreeable, grateful, and companionable, are those we pick up by chance here and there; those which seem put into our hands by Providence; those which pretend to little, but abound in much. —HERMAN MELVILLE, *WHITE JACKET*

COLLEGE OF ONE

THE STORY OF
HOW F. SCOTT FITZGERALD
EDUCATED THE WOMAN HE LOVED

SHEILAH GRAHAM

AFTERWORD BY WENDY FAIREY

MELVILLE HOUSE PUBLISHING
BROOKLYN · LONDON

COLLEGE OF ONE

Copyright © 1966, 1967 by Sheilah Graham

Afterword copyright © 2013 by Wendy Fairey

First Melville House printing: May 2013

A portion of the afterword has been adapted from Wendy Fairey's memoir, *Bookmarked: The Life and Adventures of a Reader of English Fiction*.

Design by Christopher King

Cover photograph: F. Scott Fitzgerald with Sheilah Graham in Los Angeles, courtesy of Princeton University Library

Melville House Publishing
145 Plymouth Street
Brooklyn, NY 11201

and

8 Blackstock Mews
Islington
London N4 2BT

www.mhpbooks.com

ISBN: 978-1-61219-283-3

Manufactured in the United States of America

1 2 3 4 5 6 7 8 9 10

A catalog record for this title is available from the Library of Congress.

For those who hope for an education

ACKNOWLEDGMENTS

I wish to thank Scott's daughter, Mrs. Samuel Lanahan, Jr., for her great generosity always in allowing me to "use anything you like" from the treasures of her father's papers. And my thanks go to Professor John Kuehl for his help before I started to write this book, and for his encouragement and insistence that I could do it; to Scott's secretary, gentle Frances Kroll Ring, who reminded me of several incidents I might have forgotten; and to Princeton University, which I am beginning to love almost as much as did Scott, for permission to quote from all documents relating to Scott. And most of all I wish to thank Mr. Alexander Clark, Curator of Manuscripts in the Department of Rare Books and Special Collections at the Princeton University Library, who with his assistant, Mrs. Randall, was unfailingly helpful on my numerous visits to the Library as I sought the material for this book.

CONTENTS

FOREWORD

In telling the story of *College of One*, it was inevitable that I would have to retrace some of the incidents of *Beloved Infidel*, the first correct account of F. Scott Fitzgerald's last years in Hollywood. The education devised for me by Scott took place during the same period. This new book, however, deals less with our relationship than with the courses of study he planned for me—the teacher and the pupil, our College of One. Where it does become personal—how could I write about Scott without also revealing what I felt for him?—I have tried to be objective, to see the man as he was, viewing him as calmly as possible, rather than as a woman in love with him so long ago.

The book has not been easy to write; and during the past two years I have sometimes wanted to abandon it. There can be few mistakes—none, if possible—in a book that deals primarily with education. I am not used to being so careful and I have found the constant checking of facts, and the remembering, exhausting at times. But each time I decided positively that I would not continue, I felt intensely depressed. *College of One* could not be thrown away. In a sense it is Scott's book—the story had to be told; an unusual man's ideas on what constituted an education had to be preserved. It is a new chapter to add to what is already known about an author who has been microscopically investigated in all the other areas of his life.

This is the last book I shall write about Scott Fitzgerald. My next book will be a novel, for which I already have the theme and title. When I write it, I will try to remember—as I have tried with this book—what Scott taught me about writing, not to use the first thought, or even the second, but to go deep inside the mind, to the third and fourth layer, so that what is translated into words is the best of which the writer is capable.

S.G.

COLLEGE OF ONE

CHAPTER ONE
THE LOSING AND THE FINDING OF COLLEGE OF ONE

THE CURRICULUM FOR MY COLLEGE OF ONE WAS lost. I discovered its disappearance in 1954 when a magazine editor visited me in Beverly Hills and suggested I write the story of my life. He knows, I thought. "What you really want," I said, "is an account of my time with Scott Fitzgerald." In recent years editors had approached me about this, and my answer had always been "No." "We want to know about *you*," this one assured me, "an English girl who came to America. Why did you come and did you find what you came for? Of course"—casually—"anything you'd write about Fitzgerald would be interesting." I would think about it, I promised.

I had been thinking about it ever since I had read Arthur Mizener's biography of Scott, *The Far Side of Paradise*, and Budd Schulberg's unsympathetic portrait in his novel *The Disenchanted*. It seemed to me that both books had given the wrong impression of Scott as I knew him in Hollywood. Perhaps the time had come to tell my story.

When the editor left, I went into my garage, lifted the lid of the trunk, and for the first time since I had placed it there in June of 1941 I held the bulging brown manuscript envelope marked SCOTT. It contained the visible fragments of the three and a half years we had spent almost continuously together, until his fatal heart attack in my Hollywood apartment on December 21, 1940. I carried the package to my desk, untied the thin brown ribbon that barely held the flaps together, and, with some apprehension but more curiosity, sifted at random through the material. Ah, here were the two acts and the prologue of our unproduced play, *Dame Rumor*. His letters and poems to me. I had forgotten how beautiful they were. Scraps of paper with scribbled messages in his loose straight-up handwriting. The recording he had made one evening of "Ode to a Nightingale." Some short stories I had written, my fictional account of our meeting and falling in love. I had titled it *Beloved Infidel* after his poem to me. I had forgotten the story and his severe editing. Here was the entire lecture he had written for me. He was on the wagon, or so I thought, when I made the tour, and I had kept the telegrams he had sent to the various cities, humorous but also intended to reassure me that I was capable of lecturing and to convince me he was sober.

But where was the detailed curriculum we had called my College of One, the twenty-odd closely typewritten pages that had absorbed us and given us so much satisfaction in the last two years of his life? I searched through the envelope again. I went back to the trunk to see if they had fallen out. Incredibly they were missing.

Everything else was there, but the education that had widened all my horizons and enriched my life was gone. Papers don't vanish. I must have put them somewhere else. I called Pat Duff, the tall dark-haired girl from Montana who had been my secretary before and after Scott's death.

She remembered that I had placed everything concerning Mr. Fitzgerald in the big envelope marked SCOTT. She had typed the name, she recalled, and pasted it on the folder. I called Scott's secretary, Frances Kroll. She was sympathetic when I cried, "My education, it's lost. I can't find it anywhere." She tried to think where it might be. She knew how much this project had meant to me. She remembered Mr. Fitzgerald's giving me the pages she had typed, but it was fifteen years ago and she could not recall specifically what they were except that they were courses in poetry, history, politics, literature, art, and music. She remembered most about the music because her brother, Nathan Kroll, had drawn up the lists for Mr. Fitzgerald, who hadn't known too much on the subject and had wanted an expert to choose the best of Beethoven, Brahms, Chopin, and all the great composers. Had she made copies of the lists? I asked Frances. He made copies of everything, even his letters to his daughter, Scottie. The lists had been typed, I remembered; there must have been copies. Frances thought so, but wasn't sure. They had been changed and retyped so often. If I could remember what the lists looked like, she suggested, perhaps I could write to Scott's daughter to ask if they had turned up with his papers and books. Frances had sent them all to Judge John Biggs, his executor, who had given them to Scottie.

After Scott died, I told Frances, I had deliberately erased him from my memory, with everything that had concerned us. It was the only way to survive the shock and the dreadful loss. "All I can remember is that they were lists of titles, but the order and the method I have forgotten." I still had most of the books—about two hundred for the two-year course—and the comments he had written in them to help me understand or to make me smile. I would always have those. I had never stopped reading them. I had read all of Proust twice again, I told Frances, when I was expecting each of my two children. The long volumes had helped to pass the times of pregnancy.

The nagging disappointment of losing the curriculum increased after the publication of my autobiography, *Beloved Infidel*, in 1958, when I received many letters asking, What was the education Scott Fitzgerald prepared for you? Why don't you publish it? Perhaps you could help others. I strained my mind to the utmost trying to remember where, as the lists were not in the folder, where else they could be. Scottie might have them; they could have been with the papers sent by Frances to Judge Biggs. But these were *my* lists. Scott had given them to *me*. As I did not have them, they might be irrevocably lost.

Scottie and I had kept in contact after her father's death. She had invited me to her graduation from Vassar in June of 1942 and to her wartime marriage to Lieutenant Samuel Lanahan, Jr. It had given me enormous pleasure to buy her wedding gown. She was my daughter Wendy's godmother. I was godmother to her son Timothy, born three years later. In recent years we had not seen each other. Her life was in Washington, mine in Hollywood. If I had known better how to describe the papers, I might have written to Scottie to ask whether she had come across them, although I was somewhat apprehensive of her reaction to another book about her father. I had heard that she had sent most of her father's papers, books, and scrapbooks to Princeton. I wrote to the university, to some of the professors who had written articles and pamphlets on Scott. But there was nothing resembling my vague description—titles of books,

I repeated endlessly. The papers had to be somewhere. Could they have been stolen? If so, by whom and why?

Among my acquaintances were two kleptomaniacs, a man and a woman. They both had had access to the garage on several occasions. One winter afternoon when it was raining, I had asked the man to bring in some logs from the garage. He had taken so long I had gone outside to call him. His car was in the driveway and, glancing inside it, I saw the back seat and floor piled with my wood. Perhaps he had also dipped into the unlocked trunk and taken the curriculum, with the notion that it might be valuable. In spite of his failing, I liked him and found it impossible to demand bluntly, "Did you take these papers?" He would have denied it in any case. I thought of a method to produce the papers, if he had them. "I'll pay five hundred dollars if you find them for me," I told him, after informing him of my loss. He was very interested and promised to do his best.

The woman was no longer a friend, and I had not communicated with her for several years. The more I thought of it, the more convinced I was that she had taken the papers. She was always puttering around in the garage. Also there had been a mysterious telephone call to a mutual acquaintance, when she had said, "I have something that belongs to Sheilah. What should I do?" "Give it to her," was the obvious reply, but she had not. I thought of breaking into her home to search for the curriculum—it's not stealing to take what is yours—but I could have been caught and arrested. I queried several people she knew, and one telephoned me with great news. "She admits to having them"—but before I could get too excited: "She says she sent them East to her family for a book she plans to write on Fitzgerald." She was a pathological liar, but the possibility that she might have my College of One haunted me. Early one morning in January 1964 I telephoned her and demanded, "Do you have the papers?" To my astonishment, she replied, "Yes, I have." I asked a few questions and came to the conclusion that she was lying. Perfunctorily I advised her that if she really had them, she should send them to Princeton, where they belonged with the rest of the Fitzgerald material. "They have enough already," she retorted. "Any big magazine will pay me a million dollars for them." I hung up. Princeton. I must go to Princeton.

It may be difficult to understand why I had not gone immediately to Princeton when I realized that I had lost my College of One. There was some feeling of not wanting to bother the great university. Also I had not been married to Scott—a woman from his past suddenly appearing and demanding some mysterious lists. Chiefly I was worried that in going through the papers I would find something derogatory about me. *Collier's* magazine in 1949 had published Scott's short story "The Last Kiss," originally titled "Pink and Silver Frost," which I recognized as a hostile version of Kathleen in *The Last Tycoon*. He had written it when we were quarreling about his drinking. When Scott drank, he sometimes wrote or made punishing remarks. He had written a shattering sentence on the back of my photograph during a drinking period. After his death I had taken it out of the frame to put away, and there, in writing twice the normal size, the jarring slap from the dead man. What else had he written about me in the times when he was like an angry imp trying to hurt everyone? There might be dozens of nasty remarks on paper for everyone to read. This is the main reason I did not go to Princeton before or during the writing of *Beloved Infidel*. As long as

I did not see anything cruel, I could imagine it did not exist.

I knew I was being absurd. He had loved me. Arthur Mizener had written in 1948, when he asked me for information on Scott for his biography, that he had realized in going through Scott's papers at Princeton the extent on which he had depended on me. Dan Piper, another Fitzgerald biographer, had asked about our play. In the letter he also mentioned finding a note with abbreviated descriptions by Scott of some of the people he knew: "Don (O.S.) the Red, Ted (P.) the Pink, Rogers (C.) the Fink, and Bud, the UnTalented." "Nothing about you," he had assured me. Could I be sure? I was not sure, but it was time to go to Princeton. Whatever I would find must be faced.

There were forty boxes awaiting my search in the Rare Books Department. Mr. Alexander Clark, Curator of Manuscripts at the Princeton University Library, had placed them on two large tables. He was respectful, kind, hovering in the background ready to help. I should not have worried. Scott himself had taught me that in the boundless sphere of the intellect there is no prudishness, no shockability. There is only evaluation of facts, and a morality founded on truth. It was foolish of me not to have come before.

I worked fast. "Not here. Not here," I repeated with mounting depression as I scanned the descriptive labels on thirty-eight boxes. "When I have more time, I will come back and read it all," I said to Mr. Clark, somewhat embarrassed. He opened Box 39 and said quietly, "If it is anywhere, it will be here." I turned over the mass of papers, some in Scott's handwriting, some typed. Long sheets of yellowing manuscript and torn scraps with just a few scribbled words. "No. No." And then, my eyes afraid to believe what they saw, the precious curriculum, page after page. I had found my education. It had been among Scott's papers given to the university by Scottie, and no one had known what all the titles were about. Scott had kept the original. Since I finished the music course after Scott's death, I must have had a copy. It must have been lost or stolen. For me, this was the most priceless treasure in the universe. I laughed and was incoherent as I tried to explain to Mr. Clark just how much the discovery meant to me. I hugged the papers to my bosom and in the sedate library at Princeton, while Mr. Clark and his assistant, Mrs. Randall, smiled, I danced a fairly wild jig. I had found Scott's legacy to me, his most important gift, my College of One, long pages with detailed courses in history; poetry; English, American, French, and Russian literature; music; art; philosophy—the two-year liberal arts education conceived by my self-appointed professor.

CHAPTER TWO
THE MEETING OF PROFESSOR AND PUPIL

FROM *THE LAST TYCOON*, KATHLEEN TO STAHR: "... the man I told you about knew everything and he had a passion for educating me. He made out schedules ... He wanted me to read Spengler—everything was for that. All the history and philosophy and harmony, was all so I could read Spengler, and then I left him before we got to Spengler ... It was just in place of babies ... But it's so endless—the more you know the more there is just beyond, and it keeps on coming ..."

"But you were in love with him."

"Oh, yes—with all my heart."

"The man" in *The Last Tycoon* was an ex-king. Kathleen was based a great deal on me. Stahr was a combination of Irving Thalberg, the producer who had been the boy wonder of Hollywood, and Scott Fitzgerald, the former boy wonder of American literature—but he was mostly Scott, and it was Scott who had "a passion for educating me."

Soon after we started my education, Scott told me he would write a book "one day" about how to make learning interesting, to make the student eager to continue after high-school graduation or the college degree, to prove that even for the least brilliant scholar education need not be a boring headache, something to go through for the precious diploma. It could be stimulating and lasting—for the rest of one's life. With the enthusiastic involvement he brought to every project, he planned our College of One, a two-year course in which I was to be the sole pupil. It worked so well that he tried to enroll his daughter, Scottie, three thousand miles away. Almost every letter he wrote her at this time was packed with advice for her reading, with tricky questions for her to answer on pain of losing her allowance. "A mere skim of the poems all at once will not possibly answer the questions asked," he noted in pencil at the beginning of a typed list of twenty-eight poems. And, planning another scholastic trap: "Obscure lines, obscure characters. Different bks. On what poem of Keats (obscure). Something only I and she know. Family history. What character reminds her of etc. What question in beginning of book is like answer at end." Scott and his daughter were not on good terms then, and she was understandably outraged. She was at Vassar, she reminded him tartly, and was already getting an education.

But mine had stopped at the age of fourteen. In the field of learning I was a raw beginner. I presented a fascinating challenge for my gifted amateur when he decided to instruct me. Scott Fitzgerald had a lifelong habit of taking people over, trying to improve what they were, hoping to imbue them with his enthusiasms. He could never resist a new project or problem. It was a way of life for him. The extent of his involvement depended on how much he liked you; as Scottie discovered, to her irritation, he really was attending Vassar with her. Even with new acquaintances he would go out of his way to help them. He especially enjoyed discovering and even creating new writers. After reading *Miss Lonelyhearts* by Nathanael West, he had written enthusiastically about him to his publisher, Maxwell Perkins, at Scribner's. He had helped Ernest Hemingway at the beginning of his career in Paris during the twenties, as he encouraged Budd Schulberg in the late thirties. Donald Ogden Stewart told me recently in London that he first met Scott in St. Paul, Minnesota. "He showed me a shoe box filled with loose pages—his novel *The Romantic Egotist*, which later became *This Side of Paradise*. I was working for an insurance company, but wanted to be a writer. He gave me letters of introduction to Dorothy Parker and Robert Benchley, who were with *Vanity Fair*, and I became a writer." He helped Zelda with her writing as he helped me with mine.

Scott was a flame, warming, illuminating, burning, until the fire was extinguished by his death at the age of forty-four. He never had any lasting doubt about his own position as a writer and a teacher, in spite of some of the letters he wrote when he was depressed. He knew he would live in literature. He was as careful with his letters and the ideas he expressed in them as he was with a story. He felt that whatever he wrote would be read again in the future. The day before he died, the *Hollywood Reporter* quoted Erich Pommer's definition of a Hollywood intellectual as "a fugitive from the F. Scott Fitzgerald era." "You see, you are an era," I teased him. He nodded thoughtfully. It was anguish for him to be out of print. "There is very little of what has been written in the past twenty years that does not bear my stamp," he wrote Mr. Perkins in 1940, when begging for a reprint of *The Great Gatsby*.

Scott Fitzgerald was forty years old when I first saw him in Robert Benchley's apartment at the Garden of Allah,

Bastille Day, July 14, 1937. I didn't know it then, but he had come to Hollywood in a final attempt to conquer the film industry and at the same time pay his debts, which amounted to approximately $40,000. I had just become engaged to the Marquess of Donegall and was planning to give up my column in Hollywood for the life of a peeress in London. The last thing either Scott or I wanted was to fall in love. But we did, and, looking back, I know it was the best thing that could possibly have happened for us both. We were to help each other for the rest of our respective lives.

During our three and a half years together Scott seemed, from my vantage point, to be extremely well educated. His reading of history, politics, poetry, and the novel was enormous and never-ending. He possessed about four hundred books in his Hollywood library, another two thousand in storage, and he knew them intimately. He had an open mind for every subject, spoken or written, although this was still a secret to some of his critics and admirers. In *The New Republic*, February 17, 1941, soon after Scott's death, Glenway Wescott wrote: "Aside from his literary genius ... I think Fitzgerald must have been the worst educated man in the world." Wescott believed that Princeton, where Scott had learned to appreciate good authors, had not managed to give him confidence about his own merit as a writer. "He never knew his own strength ... When he was a freshman, did the seniors teach him a manly technique of drinking ...? If they had it might never have excited him as a vague, fatal moral issue." In 1951, Malcolm Cowley, editing *The Stories of F. Scott Fitzgerald*, stated, "He was not a student for all the books he read, not a theoretician, not a thinker." In 1925, five years after the publication of *This Side of Paradise*, Edmund Wilson wrote, "He has been given imagination, without intellectual control of it." However, soon after Scott's death, Wilson as editor of the unfinished novel, *The Last Tycoon*, stated in the Foreword: "Monroe Stahr is really created from within at the same time that he is criticized by an intelligence that has now become sure of itself." Scott would have been pleased that Wilson, his "literary conscience," was accepting him on his own high level.

Scott's own evaluation of his scholastic standing was written shortly before we met, "How I Would Grade My Knowledge at 40." He had been almost as harsh on himself as his critics.

Literature and attendant arts	B+
History and biography	B+
Philosophy	B−
Psychiatry	C
Military Tactics & Strategy	D+
Languages	D
Architecture	D
Art	D
Marxian Economics	D

Everything else way below educated average, including *all* science, natural history, music, politics, business, handicrafts, etc. etc. save for some specialized sport knowledge—boxing, football, women, etc.

Today there is less skepticism of Scott's wide range of intellectual interests. With each new book about or by him, especially *The Letters of F. Scott Fitzgerald*, there is the realization that he knew a great deal about many things. He had learned to theorize, to think, although he was always less interested in the dissection of his reading than in the enjoyment he received. In the last years of his life he had learned to make mature decisions privately and quietly. He no longer felt impelled to boast about what he knew.

It is true he was ignorant in his youth. It was hard for him to get into Princeton and harder for him to stay there. He had to repeat part of his junior year—contrary to printed reports, he did not actually flunk—and went into the Army in his senior year before he could graduate. Scott's excuse for his academic incompetence was that he suffered from periodic tuberculosis. It seems to me that he was interested in too many extracurricular projects—getting into a good club, writing for The Triangle Club, the *Nassau Lit.* "I want to pull strings," says Amory Blaine in *This Side of Paradise*, "even for somebody else—or be *Princetonian* Chairman or Triangle President. I want to be admired." Scott wanted to be admired, to be a leader—except in the classroom, where he was too impatient with the slow process of learning. The plodding and minute dissection were not for him. He wanted the successful end without the grinding application.

"There was a need for more contact between professor and pupil," Scott believed—another explanation of his academic failure. I was luckier. I had an enthusiastic teacher who was never too busy or too tired—and God knows he was a tired, busy man—to explain, discuss, and render fascinating everything he had taught himself from books.

Our project gave Scott enormous satisfaction. He was doing something valuable. He was saving at least one sheep from the abyss of ignorance. Later he would put it

all in a book and save the others. He was a stern professor. I worked hard. When the going was rough, he would
comfort me: "Never mind, most college graduates are just
as ignorant." He jeered at me once. I can't remember the
provocation, only his irritated remark, "*Everyone* knows
that." But when I sighed, "I'm so vulnerable," he apologized,
and it never happened again. He devoted hours a day for
nearly two years—time he could not afford—to our experi-
ment in education.

Scanning the lists of titles, I am sure that if Scott were
planning the courses today, some of the books would be
eliminated, others certainly added. In the late thirties
Communism and "the Revolution" were the burning top-
ics. Near the beginning of *The Last Tycoon* the stewardess
tells Cecilia of a young actress who had appeared to be con-
templating a jump from the plane—"she was not afraid of
poverty, but only of revolution." "I know what Mother and
I are going to do," she confided to the stewardess. "We're
coming out to the Yellowstone and we're just going to live
simply until it all blows over." Cecilia tells the stewardess of
the lawyer and the director who have their plans all ready
for the revolution. "The lawyer had a boat hidden in the
Sacramento River and he was going to row upstream for
a few months and then come back, because they always
needed lawyers after a revolution to straighten out the le-
gal side." The director "had an old suit, shirt and shoes in
waiting and he was going to Disappear into the Crowd."
"But they'll look at your hands. They'll know you haven't
done any manual work for years . . . and they'll ask for your
union card." Scott told me this conversation had actually
taken place with a director we both knew. It would have
been interesting to have his impressions on the segregation

problems, which may one day be as old-fashioned as yesterday's "revolution." Scott knew the South well through
Zelda. It is hard to imagine that he would not have written
a novel on the racial turmoil of the last decade.

So much has happened since Scott's death. I remember
saying with a sigh, "And Scott doesn't know," when Hitler
in 1941 marched against Russia instead of invading England as we had expected in 1940. Television had been invented before Scott died, but the war had postponed its
use in this country. The long-playing record appeared after
Scott's death, and this would have changed my course in
music. The best writers, critics, and historians of the forties, fifties, and sixties would undoubtedly have appeared
on my curriculum.

Scott imagined a Diamond as Big as the Ritz. What
would he have done with the atom bomb and the gigantic
flights into outer space; the alarming expansion of population, the murder of the Jews in Europe? Korea, Vietnam?
I would give ten of my remaining years to hear Scott ex-
pound on these matters. However, I believe that for the
most part he set down in his lists for me that which will
endure. The best that any education can do is to add understanding of the past and present, to gird one for the future,
to sharpen the intelligence, to enable one to evaluate whatever comes along, to listen, to learn, to question, to be interested in what is going on, to be involved, to believe "this
concerns me," above all *to keep the mind alive*. This is what
I believe Scott Fitzgerald did for me in his College of One.

CHAPTER THREE
WHY AN EDUCATION WAS SO IMPORTANT TO ME

A STRANGER LOOKING AT THE WOMAN I WAS IN the summer of 1937 might have wondered why an education was so important to me. I had a good job. I wrote a column for the North American Newspaper Alliance then as now, and the important people of the film industry bowed low before me. I had many friends in Robert Benchley's set, which comprised some of the most interesting people in Hollywood. I didn't know too much about the events of the day, or about anything, but no one seemed to care. I listened without interrupting when Bob and his friends discussed books and politics, and was careful to nod with a practiced look of intelligence during the pauses. I could have settled happily into my role of pleasant scenery, but I wanted to be more like them. I wanted to know as much as they did. I was like a balloon filled with air, smooth and soft to the touch, but God help me if anyone flicked a pin. I was afraid someone would expose me as a fake and there would be laughter at my stupidity and lack of learning. It was lonely always being on the outside. I was usually on edge, always vaguely guilty.

Perhaps the guilt had started at the London orphanage

to which my ailing and widowed mother had dispatched me at the age of six (my father had died when I was a baby). If I had been a valuable person, I thought to myself, why would my mother banish me to such a dreadful place? Why were the children I read about in books living at home with their parents? Was it because I was homely and afflicted with an eczema rash? I was sullen, unfriendly, and my hair, like that of the other girls, was cropped to the skull and would remain so until I was twelve. Obviously I was the kind of child who could not be loved in a home. As far back as I can remember, there was a sense of apprehension, the waiting for an ax to fall.

I was surprised when I evolved into the brightest student at the orphanage. Sometimes my mind would take fascinating leaps. I could usually solve arithmetic problems as fast as they were written on the blackboard. But on days when I was unhappy there was a numbness that terrified me. All I had was a brain, and if it did not function there was no reason at all to admire me.

The school system of the orphanage depended on the City of London for support and followed the standard curriculum for County Council grade schools—what we call in America public schools. Today in England you cannot leave school until you are fifteen. In my time at the orphanage, we left at fourteen, accompanied by a wooden box containing a coat, a skirt, two blouses, two calico nightgowns, and two changes of underwear. I had something extra, three books—prizes.

Looking back, I suppose I probably learned more at the orphanage than I would have learned at home in the East End of London. It was better than playing in the streets. Our education and recreation took place where we lived.

We depended upon one another. Cheeky newcomers were soon brought into line. We developed a double code of ethics, for ourselves and for the bullying teachers. It was important to me to be admired. Other girls were popular because they were outgoing or pretty. I could earn admiration by my prowess in the classroom.

Books were the breath of my existence. *David Copperfield* was my favorite—the first part. His childhood was worse than mine. My Mr. Murdstone was the headmaster, but he was a remote dragon, except for the terrifying times when I happened to pass him and he would for no apparent reason give me a whack across the back to speed me on my way. Charles Kingsley's delightful story *Water Babies*, in which the children attended school under water, enthralled me. They were spanked when naughty, but always lovingly. Bernard Shaw has written that children will accept being smacked by their parents as long as they know the parents love them. When we were beaten at the orphanage, there was a lack of interest which made the blows more painful. I longed to meet someone like the hero of *Daddy Longlegs*, my second favorite book. The heroine had been adopted by a handsome trustee of her orphanage and sent to a good school where parents or guardians paid for the privilege and the children went home for the "hols." I devoured stories like *The Girls at Hadley Hall*. It was the next best thing to going there. When I was Head Prefect, I tried to follow the same impossibly high code of conduct. Those girls were proud of their school, and I tried to be proud of mine.

I thrilled to epic songs and poems, the rousing Welsh song "Men of Harlech," "Rule, Britannia." I dreamed of performing acts of heroism, like Boadicea, the British warrior queen at war with the Romans, who

> Rushed to battle, fought and died,
> Dying, hurled them at the foe:
> Ruffians, pitiless as proud,
> Heaven awards the vengeance due.
> Empire is on *us* bestowed
> Shame and ruin wait for you.

And there was the brave Sir Richard Grenville—

> At Flores in the Azores, Sir Richard Grenville lay,
> And a pinnace, like a flutter'd bird, came flying from
>   far away.
> "Spanish ships of war at sea! We have sighted fifty-
>   three!" ...
> Then sware Lord Thomas Howard, " 'Fore God I am
>   no coward."

He wanted to flee because they were six to fifty-three, but
Sir Richard wouldn't hear of it. They went down, of course,
but were patriotic to the last gurgle of water. I wept for
them and was proud of being British, as I was in the poem
I wrote at the orphanage on the Battle of the Somme:

> We came out victorious
> As Englishmen always do,
> But still we were precautious
> And so were our allies too.

This wasn't much worse than my play *Dame Rumor*, written in 1938 under the supervision of Scott Fitzgerald and
abandoned after the second act. At twelve I wrote an essay
titled "The Night" that began, "When twilight visits the

earth, and the world is shrouded in a thick mist of darkness." Not very good, but it was considered brilliant at the orphanage, and I was made to recite it to the assembled school. I knew it by heart and afterward repeated every word over and over, remembering all the eyes fixed admiringly on me. We put on a revue for the teachers, and, wearing a soldier's cap and a cane with the drab school uniform, I marched up and down on a stage made of long dining tables and sang:

> "I'm Burlington Bertie,
> I rise at ten-thirty ...
> I stroll down the Strand
> With my gloves on my hand,
> And when I come back they are off ...
> I'm Bert, Bert,
> And royalty's hurt,
> When they ask me to dine I say no.
> I've just had a banana
> With Lady Diana.
> I'm Burlington Bertie from Bow."

Another girl, a blond cherub, sang:

> "I'm Pierre de Bon Ton de Paris, de Paris.
> I drink to ze wine, eau de vie, eau de vie.
> When I walk in ze park
> All my friends zey remark,
> 'He's Pierre de Bon Ton de Paris, de Paris.' "

I would have preferred to sing that one because of the French.

I can never forget the songs of the orphanage.

Here, a sheer hulk, lies poor Tom Bowling,
The darling of our crew-oo;
No more he'll hear the tempest howling,
For death has broached him to.

Some of the words don't make sense, but that is what I sang. And "Where the bee sucks, there suck I." And "Night of love and night of stars," from *Tales of Hoffmann*, and from where I don't know, "Buddha made the harvest and made the winds to blow, Sitting at the doorway of a day of long ago." I could sing you the rest but I can hear my daughter saying firmly, "No, Mother. No."

After being clumsy as a child, I became well coordinated simply because I longed to be. I had to shine in all areas of endeavor, and sports were important. In my last year I was appointed captain of the girls' cricket team—the only team at the school ever to beat the boys. How proud I was of that. I can still hear them calling, "Lily Shiel [my real name], are you ready?" And me drawing a deep breath and replying, "I am ready."

There were debates at the orphanage. One I remember: Monarchy versus a Republic. The headmaster called my name unexpectedly to lead the side for the Republic. I was thirteen and, beneath the cocksure exterior, full of uncertainty and shyness. My cheeks burned. I looked wildly for escape. There was none. Everybody was looking at me, waiting. My mind has always worked fast when I am in danger. Like a shaft of heavenly light, the sudden memory came to me from a Bible class that God had been very much against the children of Israel having a king. He had insisted that a God was enough. They wanted a king and had crowned Saul and after him David and all the others. But disaster had followed, and now look where we all were. I was complimented by several teachers for making such a good case. I could not stop repeating what I had said. As later, when Constance Bennett called me the biggest bitch in Hollywood and I replied quickly, "Not the biggest bitch, Connie, the second biggest bitch." Saying it over and over, weeping, as I drove home. I sometimes think I have a record-player in my head.

In the winter of my thirteenth year I decided to teach myself French. I had found a small French dictionary, and I can see myself after a supper of two slices of gray-white bread covered with rancid margarine, and a watery mixture they called cocoa, sitting on the lukewarm heating pipes that spanned the classroom floor and memorizing French words but not knowing how to pronounce them. French was the language of the well-educated young ladies at Hadley Hall. In the other exclusive schools I read about, the girls all struggled with French. Even then I wanted to be as good as the best. I was trying to create my own College of One.

I was two classes ahead of my closest rival, and it was suggested to my mother that I try for a scholarship that would ultimately take me to a university where I would be trained to teach. I wanted to go to college, although the idea of taking the examinations alarmed me. What if my brain had one of its numb periods and the fallibility of my scholastic prowess was exposed? My genuine disappointment was mixed with relief when my mother informed the headmaster that the scholarship was not possible. She needed me at home to do the housework and look after her. She was dying of cancer. If things had been different, I might have had my education then. I probably would not have come to America, halfway round the world to Hollywood and Scott Fitzgerald.

And then, as if rocketing to another planet, I was blasted from my warm place as the best student at school, admired by my contemporaries, revered by the smaller girls, a big figure on the sports field, debating on this and that, reading the poems of the nineteenth-century social reformer Elizabeth Fry in an impassioned voice and dreaming of conquering the magical world outside—to the reality of scrubbing floors, waiting my turn at the food shops, scraping fish, cooking, washing dishes, washing clothes, and looking after my poor uncomplaining mother.

My education froze at the point of leaving the orphanage. I had a fair amount of English history, including the First World War, a faint smattering of European history and ancient Rome—I would never forget Pope Gregory the Great's comment on the blond blue-eyed English slaves, "Angels, not Angles"—nothing of American history except a brief chapter on the war of 1776. Later, when my College of One professor mentioned the War of 1812, I didn't know what he was talking about. The mowing down of the British at the Battle of New Orleans was absent from my history books at the orphanage. My arithmetic had reached: "If Farmer John's 15 chickens lay 30 eggs in 4 days, how many chickens would be required to lay 72 eggs in 6 days?" This problem was always difficult for me to solve even when my brain was racing. Songs, but no knowledge of music. No art at all, although we drew some still lifes, flowers and an occasional apple or orange. I had no talent for painting and envied the girls whose daffodils and fruit were recognizable. My handwriting is poor to this day. The subjects taught were simple history, geography, arithmetic, and English—very little grammar, and mine has always been weak. I understand verbs because Scott Fitzgerald explained they were essential to good writing, but I still sometimes have to be reminded of what a pronoun is, and I have never quite conquered the "I" and "me" puzzle. This is what I learned during my childhood. It wasn't bad, considering the circumstances, but it wasn't much and it stopped too soon.

At home in the East End, I lived only to visit the nearby dance halls, where my new prettiness (my skin had emerged petal-smooth from the years of eczema) brought me the same kind of attention from the Cockney seventeen- and eighteen-year-old boys that my excellence as a student had given me at the orphanage. Perhaps my looks would be a door of escape from the drudgery at home. I dreamed of "Young Lochinvar"—a favorite poem at the orphanage— who would come out of the West, lift me onto his white charger, and away we would go. I never quite knew where, but it would be a place where people were admired without the pressure of having to be the brightest scholar. I couldn't guess that Young Lochinvar would be an exhausted, married, middle-aged American author.

In the East End no one cared that I could recite poetry by the yard and that I knew all the dates of the English kings. Having a smart line with boys was more important. Dancing. Hokey-Pokies (ice-cream sandwiches) afterward. Pressing hard against the boy. Kissing passionately in doorways. Reading the *News of the World*. Wondering about the girls who, according to the newspaper, were raped or who vanished mysteriously in the alarming business of white slave traffic. You must never go off with a stranger. He or she might be an agent. You would vanish into a brothel in South America and be cast out when you were twenty-five, old and broken. It was safer to tease the boys to the limit and remain technically pure for the knight who would carry you off to his castle and marry you.

We were all in the same boat in the East End. We had all left our schoolbooks at the age of fourteen. No one asked embarrassing questions, nor did many persons ask them later in my "society" period—for different reasons. The poor didn't know. The well-educated were so sure of their position that there was no necessity to discuss what they had learned at Eton, Harrow, Oxford, Cambridge, or the smart finishing schools in Paris or Lausanne.

If my mother had not died when I was seventeen, I might have married one of my ardent dance partners and lived ignorant ever afterward. I would certainly not have met my first husband, Major John Graham Gillam D.S.O., and, at his urging, emigrated to America. However, it is a probability that I would have left the East End. From the time I had been taken with my class at the orphanage to the Tower of London, an expedition that culminated in the West End with tea and currant buns at Selfridge's on Oxford Street, I had dreamed of revisiting that dazzling community. While my friends in Stepney and Bow were content with the movie palaces in the neighborhood—if you went alone, as I sometimes did in the afternoon, you were likely to find a male hand halfway up your clothes— Saturday night would usually find me in the gallery queue for a musical comedy in the West End. If I could not get anyone to go with me, I went alone. From the top tier of the Vaudeville Theatre in the Strand I saw the first *Charlot's*

Revue, with Beatrice Lillie and Gertrude Lawrence. I have never forgotten Miss Lillie's monotone rendition of "I've got ten baby fingers and ten baby toes, waiting there for me, down in Tennessee." When we sang it together not long ago, I knew the words better than she did.

I sometimes wonder how I jumped the barrier. In England your accent is the straitjacket that holds you securely in the class to which you are born—with some exceptions now. If you can sing and play a guitar, and come from Liverpool, you might go pretty far. It's easier in America, where ambition, success, or merely the desire can erase the class and poverty lines.

After my mother died and I obtained a job selling toothbrushes at Gamage's store in Holborn, halfway between the East End and West End, I decided to go all the way and live in a boarding house in Sussex Gardens, a brisk five-minute walk from Oxford Street and Selfridge's. I was immediately aware that Major Gillam was "class" when he bought a toothbrush from me and at the same time offered me a job. He had the voice and manner I remembered from the trustees at the orphanage. He was a gentleman. I knew that even before he said, "By Jove!" which I imagined was standard conversation for majors. He was in his early forties, very handsome, and I fell in love with him.

Major Gillam, an agent for iron and steel foundries on the Continent, with a soft-goods department—lamps, laces, clocks, Turkish delight—on the side, had two girl secretaries and a young man assistant, who whenever he deigned to notice me was scornful, or so I thought. While the two secretaries were less class-conscious, one in particular made no attempt to hide her amusement at my mispronunciation of the French words that sometimes came up in the letters I was delegated to close and stamp. Major Gillam had written a book, *A Gallipoli Diary*, and was engaged on another that necessitated frequent visits to the British Museum. When he asked me to go with him, I hastily invented an excuse. He would be aware at once that I was extremely ignorant. I have learned since that time that men who are in love are not interested in whether the girl knows an A from a B at the beginning of the relationship. Afterward they usually try to improve her.

My manners were on a par with my level of learning, and they were more noticeable. When I ate, I stuffed my mouth to capacity and tried to guzzle things down as though fearful they would be grabbed away if I didn't. Bits of food from my mouth dribbled all over my clothes. I had only a faint idea of the function of a knife and fork. There was a grab-all, snatch-all system to my eating. The first time we ate a meal together at the Mars, a Greek restaurant in Soho, Johnny watched me in friendly amazement as I plowed through the seven courses. For three shillings and sixpence—a carafe of wine was a shilling extra—they gave you hors d'oeuvres, soup, a small sole and salad, followed by a somewhat hairy chicken with two vegetables and tiny roast potatoes. Vanilla ice cream for dessert. Then cheese and crackers, fruit and nuts, and coffee. I was like a runner who couldn't wait for the starting pistol. I devoured everything in sight and it was as though a locust had dined. Johnny in his kind manner showed me how to fold my hands on my lap between bites and to place my knife and fork side by side on the plate when I was finished. In England, if you want to be mistaken for a swell, you never shake salt directly on the food. "You pour it on the side of your plate," said Johnny. I have never seen the sense of this.

My table manners are much better today, although I still eat as though every meal were my last.

When Johnny married me and asked me to break the news to the sister and brother-in-law who were financing him in his business, I realized from their distress that Johnny had made a very bad match indeed. A girl from the East End with a Cockney voice! How awful. The brother they loved could have married a girl with a good education, and to waste himself on someone whose vowels were so atrocious! I could understand their chagrin.

With the lack of family assistance after our marriage, Johnny's business failed. I hesitantly suggested that perhaps he should get a job where his experience could be useful. He became angry and told me I didn't know what I was talking about. I didn't. But it made no sense to me to be in business on your own when there was no money and no business. I soon concluded that Johnny and Mr. Micawber in *David Copperfield* had a great deal in common. The fortune to be made was just around the corner, tomorrow, meanwhile lend me a fiver today. With his sister unyielding, Johnny turned to the moneylenders. It was a nightmare: the gas and the electricity discontinued, the telephone suspended, the threat of eviction from the small flat on Wigmore Street (W.1.) that I had begged him to rent after a succession of dreary boarding houses, some of them worse than that of my first adventure in living alone.

Johnny had acted as an amateur with the Birmingham Repertory Company, and he was convinced that my accent could be cured by stage experience. He used some of the moneylenders' cash to enroll me at the Royal Academy of Dramatic Art, where I suffered the humiliations of an outsider. I had nothing in common with the other students.

They always seemed in a hurry when I made attempts at conversation. And what could I say to the woman who sat next to me in most of my classes, a twenty-eight-year-old graduate of Girton College, Cambridge? Charles Laughton, bored with his father's hardware business up north, had enrolled on the same day I had, but while his accent was strictly Yorkshire, no one dared laugh at him. His startling talent was aristocracy enough. He spoke French like a native and starred in all the French plays.

I was determined to learn French. Shortly before our marriage Johnny had sent me to Paris for two weeks, hoping the experience would widen my horizon and make me less awkward. I was tremendously excited and had written to a finishing school for girls at Neuilly. To my delight it accepted me. But when the principal learned that I had only two weeks in which to be finished, he said in English, "It would take two years at least to make a lady out of you"—and, in an aside, something about its being impossible to turn a sow's ear into a silk purse, which made the girls at the round dining table giggle while my cheeks burned with shame. A sow's ear. Would I always be so low?

When my isolation at RADA became unbearable and Johnny's desperate situation with the moneylenders made it difficult for me to stay there, I used my low rating at the end of the first term as an excuse to leave. I would never be a Shakespearean actress. I might have done better if I had dared to let go, but I was always on guard and miserable about my vowels, which one of my teachers mercilessly exposed to the grinning class. I was fairly good at miming, but too self-conscious to go far. At the end of the term my class put on a Cockney play for friends and relatives. I was so carried away by the applause (mostly from

Johnny's corner) that, completely ignorant of my lapse of etiquette, I stepped forward and took the bow for the entire cast, Laughton included.

I told Johnny that a student had said rather conde-scendingly, "With your face and figure, you really should go in for musical comedy." Johnny thought it was a good idea, and we could use the money. He found the cash for singing and dancing lessons and after about six weeks of intensive training believed I was ready to explode on the West End. With his sublime faith and my desperate deter-mination, I landed in the final weeks of *The Punch Bowl* at the Vaudeville Theatre, then into Charles B. Cochran's chorus at the London Pavilion in Piccadilly Circus, where I was an unexpected success.

I became the ewe lamb for a group of lively wolves that included an equerry to the Prince of Wales and one of his friends, a rich fiftyish baronet, Sir Richard, who wanted to fulfill my childhood dream by adopting me. It was too late for that, which was fortunate, as he proved to be a masoch-ist. One day after an exquisitely cooked luncheon in his elegant home in Belgravia, he suddenly bared his chest and excitedly asked me to pinch his nipples—"hard." It was my first experience of this sort of thing, and I was shocked. I hesitantly touched one of Sir Richard's nipples. "Harder," he begged. I made an excuse about "a rehearsal" and fled.

Johnny, far from being upset by all this—I told him nearly everything—encouraged my seeing these men. He was deeply involved with the moneylenders and hoped that one of my admirers would rescue him from his financial troubles. In fact, one married man, a Catholic, to whom I was introduced by Mr. Cochran—a man who prayed for his wife to die so that he could marry me, while I prayed that she would live so he couldn't—gave Johnny a job in one of his companies. The reason, Johnny convinced himself, for allowing me so much freedom with other men was that they were "gentlemen," had all been to good universities, and some of it might brush off on me. Unfortunately, culture is not catching, although you can acquire a veneer if you are observant and possess a talent for mimicry. I was soon saying "gel" for girl and "orf" for off; but I was still Lily Shiel, a sow's ear although I wore silk, courtesy of the enamored Catholic. Poor Johnny. Like Scott, he was always desperate for money. How could he survive except through me?

I hated the stage with its glaring tinsel, the straining ambition, the exhaustion, although I smiled and went through my paces because there was no escape. I was riding in Rolls Royces with men who admired me, this year's pretty thing. There would be a new one next year. I was the girl I had envied a few years ago on my trips to the West End to savor how the rich lived, but I wanted to shout at the smug men, "You have made a mistake about me. I am not a tart and never could be." If Johnny was awake when I came in, he would take me to bed with gentle teeth on the nape of my neck as a mother cat transports her kittens, and there we slept in platonic harmony. His money worries and my late hours—the stage at night, the suppers afterward—and the tiring dancing lessons by day had soon destroyed the husband and wife relationship. He became my child, although he was old enough to be my father, for which he was often mistaken. He was an oasis where it was falsely peaceful. The problems were there, but we ignored them. One night I awakened to find him sprawled across the bed.

He had suffered a mild heart attack. "When I came to and saw you, I thought I was in heaven with an angel," he said. And yet I sometimes wondered, "Would he turn me in to the highest bidder?" I did not judge him. He was as helpless as my mother had been when she had been forced to send me to the orphanage—and as Scott was when he had to work on trashy films in Hollywood. I am different. I am afraid sometimes, but I am not helpless. All my life I have found solutions to situations I dislike. I had the gifts for seizing a lucky moment, the energy to follow through on an opportunity. In his notes on Kathleen for *The Last Tycoon*, Scott wrote, "This girl had a life—it was very seldom that he met anyone whose life did not depend in some way on him or hope to depend on him." I had learned early to depend on myself.

The first glimpse into a different life—and I was aware of its importance—was when I wrote a brief article about the stage and it was accepted by the *Daily Express*. From my brain, atrophied though it had been, the putting of an idea on paper had earned me ten dollars. It was exciting. To be an author. To be on a different plane, not just a pretty girl. It was also worrying. You had to be clever to be a writer. You must be more educated than I was. Full of the fervor of being in print, I called at King's College in the Strand, which is part of London University. I realized, I told the young man at the information desk, that I could not attend the regular classes. I did not have the proper background for that—how I envied the young men and women casually strolling around the campus accepting the miracle of being there as an ordinary thing—but were there professors who gave private lessons in English literature? There were.

There are always teachers who need money. It would be a guinea a lesson. The money I had earned from the article would pay for two sessions.

A thin-faced young teacher sat opposite me across the table in a small room at the college. I showed him my article, explaining, "I want to be a good writer. I used to write well in school." I didn't mention the orphanage. He gave me Sterne's *Tristram Shandy* and asked me to come back the following week with a report. It was a struggle reading the book, and I didn't know where to start with the report. At the next session he gave me *Moll Flanders*. After reading it, I asked my tutor, "Are you sure it's good literature?" It was pornographic—a word I didn't know then—but I liked it. After a week with *Tom Jones*, which I also enjoyed, though I couldn't imagine how it would turn me into a good modern writer, we dropped the lessons. My small joust with English literature affected my journalistic style, and it took several weeks before I was able to return to the salable mediocrity of my articles about the stage. The few pieces in the *Express* and the *Daily Mail* made me something of a celebrity in the Cochran chorus. They set me apart from the other girls, and I enjoyed the distinction as I had been proud to be the best student in the orphanage. I *was* different. I was not content to be what I was, where I was.

It was only indigestion, I am convinced now, but the Queen's doctor, called by my titled admirer, ordered "an immediate operation." I didn't know it then, but my stage career was over. Recuperating in the South of France with a carefree Johnny, staying at the expensive Hotel Eden at Cap d'Ail, I decided to go all out for a career in journalism. It would be less agonizing than the stage, the late evenings with officers in the Guards, the undergraduates who drank too much, and the strain of pretending to enjoy the suppers at Ciro's and the Embassy Club with the sex-hungry, tongue-tied, frustrated young bloods who wanted a night on the town with a real actress, who fumbled inexpertly and sometimes couldn't control themselves. I hadn't the faintest idea what to say to them. It was easier to let them kiss me in the taxi taking me home to Johnny, who would sometimes awaken briefly to ask, "Did you have a good time?" It seems incredible that such a marriage could exist. Not only did it exist, but even with the divorce in 1937, after I had packed up and gone to the United States, the father-daughter, mother-son love we had for each other lasted until his death in January 1965.

Through his uncle, Captain the Honorable Jack Mitford, I met Tom Mitford. Jack had married a princess of the Krupp munitions dynasty shortly before the First World War. The princess had dissolved the marriage during the war at the insistence of the German government. Jack, a loyal Englishman, had fought against the Germans with his regiment in the Life Guards, as Tom (who had admired Hitler with his sisters Unity and Diana) fought the Germans in the Second World War. Tom was killed on the very last day of the war—blown up by a land mine, his cousin Randolph Churchill told me later in Hollywood.

Randolph and Tom were the first visible intellectuals among the people I had met through a society girl, Judith Hurt, who lived in Scotland with her family. During the London season they occupied the apartment above ours in Wigmore Street, and we had become friendly after meeting several times on the stairs. I had gone ice skating with

Judith and she had introduced me on the rink to Captain Mitford. At this time I also met young Bill Astor, whom Randolph detested. He despised him along with all the "Cliveden set," believing they were Nazi sympathizers. He sneered at Bill's "American mother," although his own grandmother was American.

I hadn't any idea of what being a Nazi meant, though I had been enamored of a blond blue-eyed Bavarian I had met with Johnny in Garmisch-Partenkirchen near Munich early in 1931. Over his garage door he had proudly painted "Eustace the Nazi." Tom and Randolph were the best-looking men I had ever seen, and I was flattered that they seemed to enjoy my company. They were young and detested the bluestocking type. I was decorative, safely married, and my role was to listen while they settled the affairs of the world. Tom was a brilliant pianist, and I was uncomfortable while he played the works of composers whose names I didn't dare pronounce—Chopin, for instance, I would have called Chopp-in. I was afraid he might draw me into a conversation about music, but he never did. He read Christopher Marlowe's *Doctor Faustus* to me. I liked the line, "Sweet Helen, make me immortal with a kiss," but I did not understand much of the rest and would not have dared to ask for an explanation. Tom probably knew where I stood in the realm of education, but would never have embarrassed me with a direct question. Randolph recited poetry and quoted from books I had never heard of. I smiled while squirming at the possibility he might want me to comment on the readings, but he was too enraptured with the sound of his beautiful voice. The glow lingered on his handsome face in the silence afterward. Randolph, like his father, Winston Churchill, was passionately interested in politics. His father was considered too impetuous politically at this time and had been rejected by the electorate. His son would pound the air and talk vehemently of "when my father returns to power." His good friend Brendan Bracken was sometimes along. They were always planning to bring the senior Churchill back to his rightful place in the government.

To keep up with the events of the day, I read the *Daily Telegraph*; the *Times* was too much for me, although I joined the Times Book Shop on Wigmore Street. I have always loved books, always enjoyed touching good bindings and found pleasure in expensive paper and good print. After my marriage I spent many afternoons staring at the rare books in the Bond Street shop windows, regretting I could not own them. The books I read were mostly biographies of famous people. A reviewer of Lady Asquith's autobiography, *Margot*, stated that other women could learn from the book. I rushed to buy it and was disappointed at not being turned overnight into an intellectual. Later, in America, I heard that Dorothy Parker, reviewing the book, had quipped, "The affair between Margot Asquith and Margot Asquith will live as one of the prettiest love stories in all literature." During the war, after Scott's death, when I wrote about the women's effort in England for my syndicate, I decided to interview Lady Asquith, whose husband had been Prime Minister at the beginning of the First World War when I was an ugly duckling at the orphanage. She suggested we lunch at the Savoy. "I hope you're rich," she said, "because the food here is very expensive." I was fascinated at the way she polished it off. She told me her husband had left her only three hundred pounds. I wondered how she managed the big car, the chauffeur, and a house in Scotland. She kept calling me up, trying to get another lunch or dinner.

In those earlier days it became essential for me to learn French. It didn't matter about German. Not too many of the English people at the winter sports in St. Moritz spoke German, although the Mitfords, with whom I went, used it as easily as they did English. But they all knew French, and lack of this language could betray my lack of education. Johnny learned of a Catholic order near London where unmarried French girls came to hide from the scandal of motherhood. They were allowed to stay a year and usually lived with a family to teach the children French. I applied for an unmarried mother, and the prettiest young lady rang my bell one day, with a suitcase, ready to stay. She had been engaged to a count and all the lingerie in her trousseau had been embroidered with her new initials, but he had abandoned her a week before the wedding. The baby boy "*avec ses yeux si gros*" was with her embarrassed mother in Paris.

My friends were not as enraptured with Raimonde as I thought they would be. I kept her secret, of course, but while the men understood French, most of them preferred to speak English with English girls. When I had sufficient mastery of the French language, I brought Raimonde with me on the weekends in country homes. I'm fast at languages, as my daughter is, and I jabbered happily with Raimonde, convinced that I sounded like a girl who had actually attended a finishing school in Paris or Switzerland. Raimonde had her own insecurities and wanted to belong to these charming people as much as I did. One weekend in the country, she insisted on riding a frisky horse with us. Johnny had had me taught to ride at the Cadogan Riding School in Belgravia, and I sat my horse well, although I was afraid and expected the beast to throw me off, which it did frequently. Raimonde had never been on a horse before, as I realized at once. The horse went into a wild gallop, and she fell off, and broke her two front teeth. To this day I can hear her wailing, "*Mes dents! Mes dents!*"

I was moderately successful as a free-lance journalist, but my horizon was limited. I had met A. P. Herbert at a charity matinee and he had advised me, "Write only about what you know." My articles were about a young girl married to a middle-aged husband—I was paid eight guineas for that one—or about the young society people I knew and what an enchanting life theirs seemed to be. Which was preferable, a baby or a car? I was quite a celebrity in my circle, a blonde who had brains enough to write. Sometimes I wondered what these confident boys and girls had learned at their schools and universities. It was considered bad form to flaunt too much knowledge, and so I was able to participate in the conversations and the parties and the tennis. Johnny had me taught tennis and squash at the Queen's Club. I became so expert at squash that I was number three on the team of five women who played for the International Sportsmen's Club. At this time I met the Marquess of Donegall, who captained the men's squash team.

The surface of my life was delightful, but, a notch below, there was always great anxiety. I was afraid that in my present life I could be exposed at any time as someone who didn't belong. When I had interviewed Viscountess Rhondda for *The Sunday Chronicle*, she had asked sharp questions that I was unable to answer. I felt undressed, all my ignorance revealed. I wanted to be the brightest girl in the school again. I was exhausted from the continual worry. America was a new country. It had something called syndication. You wrote an article and it appeared in hundreds of newspapers. With Johnny's urging and blessing, I made my first trip to New York in 1931 with what I thought at first was resounding success.

CHAPTER FOUR
SWIMMING UPSTREAM

JOHN WHEELER OF THE NORTH AMERICAN Newspaper Alliance liked my articles. He signed a letter stating we would share in the proceeds from them. Elated, I sent cables to my friends in England with the news that from now on I would be making a hundred dollars a week—I had asked a newspaperman how much I could earn from syndication. I had to keep impressing people with my cleverness. What else did I have to offer? Only Johnny believed there was something more than a pretty face. But I didn't believe in Johnny.

Until I met Fitzgerald, no one had cared to probe far enough to learn how much I was suffering because of my inadequacies. Johnny was concerned only with my social behavior; otherwise he considered me perfect. It did not occur to him that what I needed most in the world into which he had plunged me was to return to school. To him it was more important for me to *look* as though I belonged and to be able to function in the realistic world of earning money.

Before Johnny, I had not cared about being anything but what I was, a girl from the East End who found delight in looking at the West End but who could never be part of

it. Now it was all jumbled, and I didn't seem to belong anywhere, certainly not with the new batch of society people
in New York—the Astors, the McAdoos, the Bakers, the
Donahues, the Cosdens, the Lawrences—to whom I had
letters of introduction and who invited me for weekends
to their country homes, where I felt out of place and uncomfortable. I preferred my visits to Judge Smith's family,
who lived on the Philadelphia Main Line. I had met Sam
Smith in England; he had been at Oxford with my friends
the Ian Bowaters. Sam's brother Ludlow Smith was married
to Katharine Hepburn, but I didn't meet her then because
she was in a play in New York. The Smiths had colored servants, and this enchanted me. Biscuits were called cookies.
I liked that. Sam's mother, a gracious lady, took me to lunch
at the home of a friend who collected rare manuscripts,
chiefly of Doctor Samuel Johnson. They were in glass cases
and on stands and must be handled with the utmost care.
While I was in Philadelphia, I visited the *Philadelphia Ledger* and sold them a story for their Sunday magazine comparing English and American society girls, I who was an
impostor with both. I went to the offices of *The Saturday
Evening Post* and received a tentative commission to write
a piece on Lord Beaverbrook, but nothing came of it except
meeting him.

I loved New York. Half the people I met had been millionaires before the 1929 crash and were now broke; the
Josh Cosdens had been worth two hundred million dollars.
They still had the penthouse overlooking the East River,
but when they had entertained the Prince of Wales the
servants went on strike in the middle of dinner for their
unpaid wages. Lee Orwell had been vice-president of the
National City Bank. All he had left was his beautiful New

York town house, which he was desperately trying to sell. Gerry Dahl, who had been the head of the Brooklyn Manhattan Transit Corporation, a New York subway company, didn't have a dime to his name. "Brother, Can You Spare a Dime?" was the popular song of the day. Men were selling apples on all the street corners, it seemed. Tim Durant, married to the daughter of Marjorie Post, took me to Wall Street and talked of the stockbrokers who had been wiped out overnight. It was all on such a big scale that I found it oddly exciting. In 1931 the depression was worse than ever, but people were still saying, "It will soon be over." When I returned in 1933, they were reconciled to it.

I had hoped to find a rescuer in New York, in what I had first imagined was a city of millionaires. But the millionaires were poor and the rescuer had not materialized. I left New York in the evening, which made it more depressing. Two acquaintances with whom I had dined at the Plaza dropped me off at the boat when they discovered I was going alone. From my cabin on the *Aquitania* I could hear the gay parties and happy shouts. On deck Rosa Ponselle was singing "The Star Spangled Banner"; then came her cry, "To the next President of the United States!" Governor Franklin D. Roosevelt was on board with his son Elliott. They were going to Paris to visit his mother. I was full of self-pity and wept uncontrollably.

In London I was more restless and dissatisfied than I had ever been. Waiting impatiently for sales and checks from John Wheeler, I decided to write a book, the story of my life as fiction. The title, *Shadow Leaves*, was from a poem by Edith Sitwell. (Scott's first story at Princeton was titled "Shadow Laurels," one of the many coincidences of our lives.) I had met Miss Sitwell briefly on a country weekend and my hostess had given me her new book of poems. In the verses of "Shadow Leaves," whenever the wind blew the leaves shifted to a different pattern. My life had been like that, changing with every wind. In the part of the book concerning my marriage, the husband was a weakling. Johnny recognized himself, and it made him unhappy.

My friends knew I was writing a book. The chief reason for doing it was to impress them. Always when we met they would say, "How is the book coming along?" As time passed, they wanted to know when it would be published. To retain their admiration, I gave a date of publication even before I submitted *Shadow Leaves* to the first publisher. It was winter, then spring, then summer, then winter and spring and summer again. I imagined they were beginning to doubt whether I really had written a book, especially as I always had time for tennis, squash, and weekends in the country. Finally, it was finished.

"The grammar will have to be corrected," said Johnny. "Otherwise it's brilliant. I just wish I could have been a better husband, and then Buchanan"—my name for him in the book; there was Tom Buchanan in *The Great Gatsby*—"would not have been so dreadful." I assured Johnny that he was not like Buchanan.

A dozen publishers refused the book and now I avoided my friends, who had thought I was a "clever puss." And then, as always in my life, it seems, I was saved from exposure. Mr. Cowan, of the new publishing house of Rich and Cowan, wrote asking to see me. Johnny and I were wild with excitement when his letter came. Obviously he was planning to publish *Shadow Leaves*.

I trembled, sitting across the desk from the pleasantly plump, balding man who was tapping the table with my manuscript. His first words deflated the balloon. "Your book shows promise, but . . ."

How I always dread the "but." I cannot bear suspense; I always had to read the last page of a book first until Scott cured me. Rushing to the dreaded point, I asked, "Are you going to publish it?"

"No," he replied, "but I think you have a talent for writing." What good would it do me? I thought. Some good, it seemed. "*Shadow Leaves*," he continued, "is obviously the story of your life."

I had written of the orphanage, the stage, society. "Oh, no," I lied.

"Every author's first book is an autobiography," he told me flatly. "I doubt whether this book would sell six copies."

"What *does* sell?" I asked him miserably.

"Mystery stories, murder stories, detective stories," he replied. "Why don't you write one for us?"

I agreed reluctantly. I *had* to produce a book. Rich and Cowan advanced me twenty-five pounds, and I used the money to rent an office overlooking Trafalgar Square, where I could write twelve hours a day without interruption. I called the book *Gentleman Crook*. It was finished in two months, and, oh, the relief when it was accepted by Mr. Cowan. I still have the postcard with my photograph used by the publisher to advertise the book. The text, in tiny print:

If the nineteenth-century Haddingtons had not been heavy gamblers and drinkers, David Haddington might have lived a peaceful existence at Stonehurst, the home of his ancestors for the past four hundred years. When, as the result of an aeroplane crash, his mother is killed, and David is thrown on the world, he determines to seek adventure and a fortune by any means legitimate or otherwise.

His search leads him to the homes of an international financier, a crooked millionaire newspaper owner, and the casino at Monte Carlo. How he eventually finds happiness is told in a manner that makes this first novel by a well-known journalist, an entertaining and exciting story.

The "Excerpts [also printed on the postcard] from some of the many Press reviews received" were just as deceptively optimistic:

"The author has no opinion of high so-called finance, and her book should make a big appeal to those who like revelations of this kind." *Morning Post*.

"A thriller that is always entertaining." *L'p'l Evening Express*.

"A very adroit piece of journeyman work." *Glasgow Herald*.

It was early 1933. *Gentleman Crook* would be published in August. The expected elation was absent. Again I wondered why it had been necessary to impress a handful of people who would not have cared whether I wrote a book or not.

It was Johnny who advised me to go to New York again. "This time you will go as the author of a book," he said proudly. Nothing had come of my signed letter from the North American Newspaper Alliance. My Catholic admirer had died, and Johnny had lost his job. "John Wheeler will sell your articles when he knows you are having a book published," he was sure. Johnny was positive it would be a best-seller. I was not. In actual fact, the twenty-five pounds' advance was all I received.

I decided to go to New York *before* the book was published. I could be more confident as an author with a book *about* to appear than as one whose novel had failed. I sailed on the *Aquitania* in June. "I'll send for you when I get settled," I promised Johnny. But we both knew the marriage was over. He loved me and he told me years afterward he had prayed for my happiness in America.

I would work hard, I vowed, as the ship slid into the dock, guided by the busy tugboats. I too would find a secure harbor. It was 96 degrees, the sun was blazing, and I sweated in my dark green velvet suit with its glimpse of an orange silk blouse. I barely noticed the heat, with too much else to worry about. There could be no turning back. There was no one and nowhere to turn back to.

Mr. Wheeler did not sell my articles, but I landed a reporting job on the *New York Mirror*, then overlapped it with another job on the *New York Journal*. I was charged with determination and a flood of energy, writing a column for the women's page, interviewing convicted murderers, the mother of President Roosevelt (she was full of anecdotes about "my son Franklin"), movie stars who came to New York (Carole Lombard, Merle Oberon, Leslie Howard, Claudette Colbert), the chief executioner at Sing Sing. I covered the Hauptmann trial, a murder trial in Massachusetts of three students from MIT, and Mrs. Gloria

Vanderbilt's fight for the custody of her daughter. I wrote for magazines—*Vogue*, *The Delineator*. I earned between three and five hundred dollars a week. I could afford to be generous to Johnny.

There were new friends and acquaintances: Quentin Reynolds, Steve Hannagan, Deems Taylor, Ruth Hale, Heywood Broun, the Gene Tunneys, Clare Boothe, who was not yet Mrs. Henry Luce, A. C. Blumenthal, the promoter, and Mario Braggiotti, the pianist, who lived in my apartment house, the Beaux Arts. Mario and his family, I was told, had been the inspiration for the book and play *The Constant Nymph*.

I had vowed I would not feel inferior to anyone again. But Americans were not like the British. They delighted in talking about what they knew, whether it was politics, poetry, painting, books, or music. They were always having discussions, and I would sit silent and strained, not knowing quite what to say, where to look. I remember a conversation introduced by Clare Boothe at John Wheeler's apartment: Which of these celebrities would get the most newspaper coverage if all of them died on the same day: the Pope, President Roosevelt, the Prince of Wales, or Charlie Chaplin? John thought the President; Mrs. Boothe, Charlie Chaplin. Everyone but me had an opinion.

World affairs and education in America were in the open. The Americans did not know more than the British, I was sure, but they discussed more. If only I had not wasted those years with the charming society people in England, but had employed someone to teach me about these things. Who was Einstein? And was it Froude or Freud and what was the difference?

Mario Braggiotti asked me with a small group of his

friends to hear him play. When it was my turn for a favorite piece, I was embarrassed until I remembered a song I
had learned at the orphanage. I hummed it to Mario and
it turned out to be Brahms' "Cradle Song." An intellectual-
sounding composer. I was pleased. I sang it for them rather
quaveringly.

> Angels whisper good night in silvery light,
> To watch over you, the whole night through,
> And to bear you above, to the dreamland of love,
> And to bear you above, to the dreamland of love.

The lullaby was always my "favorite piece." I met Mario
again recently, but he had forgotten. I can never forget my
discomfort and anxiousness as I watched his fingers flying
up and down the keyboard, careful to avoid his face, hoping he would not ask for another piece.

When John Wheeler offered me the N.A.N.A. column
in Hollywood, I jumped at the chance. Hollywood was no-
torious even in London for the ignorance of the people
who made the films. I would be comfortable there. No one
could embarrass me with erudite conversation. Most of the
men who ran the film industry had not gone to college, but
had sold newspapers, or had been furriers or glove sales-
men before becoming movie tycoons. Irving Thalberg, still
called the boy genius, had dropped out of high school and
taken a business course. He had worked as a secretary for
Carl Laemmle, Sr., who brought him to Hollywood. If a boy
without much education was regarded as a genius, I knew
I could interview him without embarrassment. I would be
comfortable with the uneducated people in Hollywood.

But it was in Hollywood, unexpectedly, that my

ignorance on most subjects was most noticeable. Mr.
Wheeler had given me a letter of introduction to Robert
Benchley, who was then acting in the numerous shorts
he wrote for the Metro-Goldwyn-Mayer Studio. Through
Bob, who was sophisticated and looked like a happy wal-
rus, I met Marc Connelly, the playwright of *Green Pastures*; John O'Hara, who had been acclaimed in 1934 for
his first novel, *Appointment in Samarra*; Dorothy Parker,
who always called Bob *Mr.* Benchley; Edwin Justus Mayer,
whose play on Cellini, *The Firebrand*, had resulted in a Hollywood contract to write screenplays for Marlene Dietrich
and Gary Cooper; Sam Behrman; John Huston; millionaire
Jock Whitney; John Barrymore; Roland Young; Donald
Ogden Stewart; Charlie Butterworth, Bob's close drinking
companion. And Scott Fitzgerald.

They had known each other casually in New York during the early days of the *Smart Set* and *Vanity Fair*. Bob,
who was not particularly fond of Scott, told me of the incident in the South of France when Scott, tipsy, had taken a
flying football kick at an old woman vender's tray and sent
the sweetmeats flying. He had paid for the candy, but it
was dreadful. Scott told me later that he believed Bob was
jealous of his early fame. There had been a cocktail party
for Scott in New York. "Everyone was struggling to talk to
me. I saw Bob on the fringe of the crowd watching me, and
there was real animosity on his face."

Writers were almost outcasts in Hollywood. They clung
together even when they did not like each other. Learning
from Miss Parker that Scott was living in one of the bun-
galows at the Garden of Allah where writers from the East
stayed to save themselves the bother of a long lease and
housekeeping, Benchley asked him to stop by for the party

he was giving to celebrate my engagement to the Marquess of Donegall. In *The Last Tycoon*, Scott transposed our first encounter to have Kathleen and her friend Edna float onto the back lot of the studio on top of the huge detached head of the god Siva during an earthquake. The hero, Stahr, believed Kathleen was wearing a belt with cut-out stars. It was the other woman who wore the belt, he discovered after finding her. When Bob realized that Scott had left the party, he called asking him to come back. "Who is still there?" Scott asked cautiously. He was not drinking, and he found the merrymakers hard to take when he was sober. There were not many left, but among others Bob described Tala Birell, a blond actress. The name and description seemed to fit the girl Scott had observed sitting quietly amid the noise and the swirling gaiety. He had noticed her belt with small stars cut in the leather. She was the only person besides himself who was not drinking. He returned but excused himself quickly when he realized his mistake. Miss Birell was wearing the belt, but she was not the girl.

I had been aware of him, wondering about the man under the lamp in shades of palest blue who was so detached from everyone there—a face emerging from the smoke of his cigarette. When I looked again, the chair was empty. I saw him a few evenings later at the Anti-Nazi League dinner at the Cocoanut Grove chaired by Dorothy Parker. Scott was one of her guests at the long table facing mine, at which Marc Connelly was host. Everyone else was dancing. We smiled as we recognized each other. Before going off with Donegall, I had asked Bob who the man was who had vanished so abruptly. When he replied, "F. Scott Fitzgerald," I was interested. I had heard of him; he was the man who wrote of the flaming youth of the twenties. I was sorry he had gone. He would have been worth a paragraph for my column. And now here he was, seeming so pleased to see me.

"I like you," he said.

"I like you," I replied. I was flirting and should have felt guilty, but did not. That very day Don had flown back to London to tell his mother, the Marchioness of Donegall, of our engagement. "Let's dance," I suggested.

But the people were coming back through the looking glass, as Scott described this encounter between Kathleen and Stahr in *The Last Tycoon*, and we had to meet a third time before we danced and fell in love.

I had planned to go to the Hollywood Bowl with Jonah Ruddy, the Hollywood correspondent for the *London Daily Mail*. He was already at the house when Eddie Mayer called and invited me to dine with him and Scott Fitzgerald. Jonah grumbled at the waste of tickets but came with me. While Scott and I danced at the Clover Club, Eddie and Jonah seemed faraway murals on a wall. "We ought to go back to them," I said after each dance, but we did not. We danced or stood waiting for the music to start again while Scott asked questions about me and my forthcoming marriage to Lord Donegall and he held me close while my "dark gold" hair tickled his chin. "Is it getting in your mouth?" I asked coquettishly. He swung me out, or walked loosely around me, then close again, and I was having a wonderful time. There was no one there with second sight to tell me, "Here is the person for whom you have been searching so desperately, who will give you comfort and love and anguish, and the education for which you have longed."

CHAPTER FIVE
THE BEGINNING OF COLLEGE OF ONE

SCOTT FITZGERALD WAS A BORN TEACHER. HE WAS happiest discussing a book he had just read or expounding on the politics of Hollywood and the world, theorizing about the battles of history—if this had not happened, this would have, and now it was all happening again in Europe. He was the first person I ever heard scorn the impregnable Maginot Line. "The Germans will bypass it with their tanks," he was sure.

World War II was inevitable, he told me two years before it started. England, America, and France were burying their logic in a quicksand they called "Peace in our time." In 1938 he advised Scottie to take a trip with a group of students to Europe. "It will be your last chance to see the France we know."

During 1938 and 1939 we listened on the big old-fashioned radio in his living room at Malibu to Hitler's rantings and the terrifying roar of "Heil Hitler," "Heil Hitler," against the Wagnerian thunder of waves crashing on the Malibu beach. Scott was amazed when I told him that Tom Mitford, who had met Hitler in Munich during 1932, thought he was a great man with a magnetic voice. "My God, they're so blind," he cried. Why couldn't they see that

Hitler was the Pied Piper who would drown the democracies? The Spanish Civil War was a rehearsal for the coming holocaust. They were all practicing for the bigger stage. He disliked Mussolini and informed me that the Italians were cowards; "They are brave when they are twenty to one." A gang of policemen had beaten Scott in Rome and then flung him into jail. He reinforced his argument by giving me Ernest Hemingway's *A Farewell to Arms* to read.

The absorbing topic in Hollywood when Scott came in 1937 was the fighting in Spain. Almost as important were the maneuverings of the left and right wings of the Screen Writers Guild to gain control of the highly paid authors. I read the newspapers and knew what they were talking about but could not understand why they were so concerned. I had never bothered about these vague matters. I looked up the words "radical" and "reactionary" to see what they meant—but radical or reactionary, the result seemed to be the same, no matter who was in power. The world for me was a place where some people were confident, rich and/or of "good family," and this entitled them to all the privileges; even Scott preferred his father, from an old Baltimore family, to his mother, whose father as a boy had migrated with his parents to America from Ireland during the potato famine of the 1840s. The larger percentage of the people were poor, worked hard to live, while the bosses took all the profits.

Like so many of the ignorant poor of England, I was a stanch conservative, a devout follower of tradition. Ours not to question why, ours but to work and die. Authority was always right; this had been pummeled into me at the orphanage. God Save Our Gracious King, God Save All Our Gracious Kings. Those terrible Russian anarchists.

There were some in England, and as an adolescent I had prayed that I would never get in the way of their bombs. The comic papers I read in the East End of London had shown men with sprouty whiskers whose names usually ended in "vitch" or "ski," blowing up factories and not caring that children might be working in them. Older members of my family had worked in factories when they were twelve, from six in the morning until late at night. And yet, unions were something to avoid. A relative as a young man had led an abortive strike for more pay. He had been fired. "What a fool!" they said.

And now to hear such educated writers as Donald Ogden Stewart (Yale), Eddie Mayer (Columbia), Frances Hackett, and Mary McCall (both Vassar), all of whom earned thousands of dollars a week, concerning themselves so passionately with the plight of the rank and file simply did not make sense to me. They're fakes, I thought. Eddie told me how stingy Charlie Chaplin was; he was born poor, but now, rich and liberal, he made "comrade" speeches. Ask him for money, and he would close up like an anemone at the beach when you poked it in the middle with a stick.

"I cannot understand how a rich man can be a liberal," I said one day during a pause in a conversation at the home of Salka Viertel, Garbo's friend and writer. We were there to listen to a man recently returned from the International Brigade in Spain. He was in Hollywood to raise money from the rich "pinkos," as Scott called them. From the general look of surprise, I realized I had made a *faux pas.* Scott had written of the rich and beautiful. But he was more vehement than any of them in his concern for the poor and his hatred of Hitler, Mussolini, and Franco. Most of the writers I met were anti-fascist, and if they did not have the stomach or were too old to fight in Spain, as David Lardner had done, or to write about it as Hemingway was doing for John Wheeler's syndicate, they gave their money to buy guns for the Loyalists and signed published petitions to help the children of Spain who were being slaughtered indiscriminately on both sides. In such an atmosphere, it was becoming difficult to retain the comfortable philosophy of "This has nothing to do with me."

It is hard to pinpoint the actual beginning of the College of One. The barren soil is only slightly disturbed with the planting of a seed. But before you know it, there is something pushing through. Things germinate for a long time before you see them. The Second World War, for instance. It had started, Scott explained to me, in 1934, when Japan annexed Manchuria from China, which had disturbed Russia—"And even before that, at the peace tables of Versailles." I had never thought of it like that. Didn't the conqueror always annihilate the loser? We had won. We came out victorious, as Englishmen always do—shame and ruin wait for *them*. In my history books at school the winners had burned the homes of the vanquished, they had robbed them of their women and taken the children as slaves. That was how it was. It was important to be on the winning side. It kept you safe. The wicked Kaiser with his ridiculous mustachios and his goose-stepping soldiers who raped the terrified women holding babies in their arms on the war posters—they deserved to be impoverished. "But that is how you breed another war," Scott explained. The Romans had built roads and walls in England after the conquest. They had given the savage natives rules to live by. Because of this they had ruled for many centuries. Napoleon was important not for his victories but for his clemency and the laws he gave the vanquished. But Napoleon was an ogre in English history books; he deserved to die in disgrace on St. Helena. Scott would smile and shake his head. It was confusing to me. How could I be sure who was right?

I remained silent during the discussions. If I were asked a direct question it was evaded with a firm "I never discuss politics or religion." If only they would confine the conversation to what had happened at the studios. That was an area in which I was comfortable. I could laugh when Marc Connelly told of Dorothy Parker and her husband, Alan Campbell—they worked as a team—beating on their office window, which overlooked the cemetery at the MGM Studio, and shouting, "What's it like in the outside world?" I enjoyed hearing about the hilarious exploits of Ben Hecht and Charlie MacArthur, who were always up to something, always disappearing without telling their producers, while the faithful accounting department mailed their checks regularly. They all seemed to despise the people who paid them so well. It didn't seem fair, and I was scornful of them sometimes. If I were paid all that money, I would try to like the people who paid me—although Louis B. Mayer was dreadful, if the stories were all true; Louis B. Merde, one of the writers called him. They also detested Irving Thalberg. He was opposed to their union, and for the first time I heard the word paternalism. It was used disparagingly, although I thought it had a nice sound.

Sometimes, hearing them bounce from topic to topic, I did not realize, until I saw the deep marks, that I had been pressing my nails hard into the palms of my clenched fists in my lap. The tension was exhausting. It was all right when Scott and I were alone, but at the beginning, before our

withdrawal from the people we knew, before we started
the College of One, we dined frequently with his friends—
Dorothy, Alan, Frances and Albert Hackett, the Ira Gershwins, the Herman Mankiewiczes, Helen Hayes, Charlie
MacArthur, the Ted Paramores, the Ogden Nashes, and
the Nathanael Wests. Scott had written Nat a glowing letter
of praise after the publication of *Miss Lonelyhearts*, and we
saw a great deal of him with his wife, Eileen, in Hollywood.
(The Wests were killed in a car accident the day after Scott
died, and I remember a feeling akin to jealousy that they
had gone with him.) I wanted so much to be a part of the
group, to get excited in the arguments, to know what they
were talking about. Scott was aware of my distress and,
when it was possible, brought me into the conversation by
telling of something that had happened at the studio. We
laughed when he told us of informing Joan Crawford that
he was working on *Infidelity*, her next movie. "Write hard,"
she had replied fervently. Scott cautioned me not to use
any of these stories in my column, which further deflated
me. Even *he* could not talk freely to me. It made me more
of an outsider in their magic land of expressed ideas and
opinions. I never dared voice a contrary opinion. "Yes, of
course," I would mumble.

A chance remark by Eddie Mayer about Swann and
Odette, in Proust's *Remembrance of Things Past*, sent me
speeding to Martindale's Book Shop in Beverly Hills: "He
was insanely in love with her. He ruined himself for her
and when it was all over he said, 'And she was not even my
type.' " I had told Eddie that I could not understand why
Scott was in love with me, because from what I had heard
of his interest in rich, confident girls, I was not his type.
Proust could be important. It might be valuable to discover

Odette's secret; perhaps it could be applied to Scott. I was dismayed that Proust's *Remembrance* comprised seven lengthy volumes. I would try to plow through them. Perhaps then I would know as much as the others did, and Scott would have reason to be proud of me.

When Scott saw me with Proust, he was immediately interested. Until then—it was about nine months from the time we had met—I doubt whether he cared about the books I read. He was content that I was his girl. He was married, with no hope of a divorce, an author whose books were not in demand. He often drank to excess. There were not too many women who could be happy with these circumstances. Scott knew I was popular with the Benchley set; I did not give them up completely in those early months. Sometimes I dined with Eddie, John O'Hara, or Bob, or visited the Ronald Colmans with Oscar Levant. Scott suffered when I was unavailable, but at first he accepted the situation. He was not sure how far he wanted our relationship to go. He knew I had recently divorced Johnny in order to marry Lord Donegall. He was pleased that I was no longer engaged to Don—"Although I don't have the right to monopolize you. You know I can never abandon my poor lost Zelda." His health was not good. He suffered from exhausting insomnia and took several strong sleeping pills at night, then Benzedrine in the morning to wake up properly and work.

"A girl like you can have any man she wants," he would say. He was not entirely reassured when I protested, "But I only want to be with you." It was his nature to be jealous and he worried when I told him—it was October 1937—that I was dining with Arthur Kober. Arthur was unmarried and doing well with his "Bella" stories in *The New Yorker* and as a screenwriter in Hollywood. Scott was so distressed that I promised to be home by eleven-thirty—"And you can telephone me," he said. I was a few minutes late; Arthur told an interminable story while I waited for him to open the door of the car, and that delayed me fifteen minutes. It was enough to set Scott off on his first drinking spree since our meeting, although I did not realize then that the hoarseness of his speech was caused by gin and not the cold he said it was. It became simpler to stop seeing other people except with Scott.

In the beginning, I had hoped we could marry. I used to brood about it, punishing him with my silences. In his notes on Kathleen in *The Last Tycoon*, Scott wrote, "He was afraid of her when she thought, knowing that in the part of her most removed from him, there was taking place a tireless ratiocination, the synthesis of which was always a calm sense of the injustice and unsatisfactions of life ... protests that were purely abstract and in which he figured only as an element as driven and succorless as herself. This made him more afraid than if she had said, 'It was your fault,' which she frequently did." But when we started the education, our relationship developed a whole new dimension. The fact that he could never marry me was less important. I was too interested and busy to be depressed, and when he was drunk I was glad we could not marry. The two things I feared most were drunkenness and insanity. With Scott, I had both. I dreamed often of Zelda. She was usually staring at me or raking my face with sharp fingernails. I did not confide those dreams to Scott.

We had our separate homes, but with the education and with few people to distract us, we settled into a comfortable domesticity. I spent weekends at his beach house and later at his home in Encino. Until he rented an apartment on Laurel Avenue in Hollywood on the street next to mine—Hayworth Avenue—he used my spare bedroom when he stayed in town.

"You must not read more than ten pages of Proust a day," Scott warned me. "It is too difficult and you will find it hard to finish if you take on too much." He immediately made a plan for me: ten pages a day until I had completed one-third; then I could go to thirty pages a day, and forty for the last third of *Swann's Way*. He kept the other volumes until I needed them, so that the magnitude of the reading would not scare me.

That was really the beginning of our College of One—plodding through Proust. The formal curriculum materialized six months later at Encino. By that time I was in better health intellectually. The Proust volumes had stretched my capacity to read, to sit still, and I became involved with the characters. The little boy who waited for his mother to kiss him good night. His unhappiness when she had visitors and could not. What a tyrant the boy was, and how his parents indulged him. This was Proust himself as a child, Scott told me, delighted by my interest. I wanted to know what kind of man he was and his method of writing. His family had been rich. He was in society, Jewish, and the Dreyfus case had embarrassed him. The Baron de Charlus was the Marquis de Montesquiou, a well-known society pederast. Proust himself was homosexual and Albertine was really a boy, Albert. The girls at the seaside, the sun that awakened him from his after-lunch nap—our worlds had been so different, but there had been a seaside expedition from the orphanage, and I loved the sun on the water. And in the morning in the dormitory I had drowsily watched the duplication of the iron bars of the windows moving in wavy shadows on the wall. "He worked in a dark room with all the windows closed and held the sheets of paper in the air while he wrote," Scott told me. I wouldn't like to be a genius if I had to work that way, I was sure. When I came to Madame Verdurin, I asked Scott, "Is she laughing or crying when she puts her hand over her face and rocks back and forth?" We tried it, sometimes laughing, sometimes pretending to cry. Later we would act out many of the characters in the books for College of One.

I ate the madeleine and drank the tisane with Proust, and my childhood at the orphanage was revived: the perfume of the sweet peas on the tables of the kindergarten, the lumpy potatoes with the eyes still in them, my ash-blond hair falling like flax at my feet as it was cropped close to my skull.

"You must write your story," said Scott, and that was when he brought me the big black ledger and divided my life into pages, from the age of three months until my arrival in Hollywood. It was to be in seven parts: "Each of 7 parts to have *theme* and dramatic idea, *plot, cast of characters, occupational.* Put it all down," he advised.

He had always committed his thoughts and experiences to paper. Plans and lists were the spine of his life. As a boy, in his Thought Books, he had made lists of girls, which ones had liked him the most, who had kissed him, who had wanted to dance with him. Like Samuel Butler, whom he admired, he had a compulsion to write things down. He catalogued everything. He was the most orderly man in a state of disorder I ever knew. There were lists for every occasion: lists of battles from the beginning of recorded time to

After Brest-Litovsk (Feb 1915):

1918 | Counter-Revolution. The Red Army
     | *1919*   Allies occupy Archangel & Vladivostok
     | PERIOD OF CIVIL WAR
     | *1920*   Big Famine

1921

1922   N.E.P. (New Economic Policy)

1924   Lenin Dies. Stalin all ready to seize power

1926   Trotsky-Stalin Break Open

1927   Trotsky Exiled

1928   FIRST FIVE YEAR PLAN

1929   GREAT FAMINE. Kulaks blamed & liquidated
         (inflow of American engineers after depres-
         sion here)

1932   Litvinov Policy Abroad. Stakhanov speed up

1934   SECOND FIVE YEAR PLAN

1935   Joins League—ALLIANCE OFFER

1936   MOSCOW TRIALS—old Bolshevik Purge

1937   Military Purge (anti-fascist)

1938   SECOND BIG PURGE   MUNICH OFFER

1939   LITVINOV POLICY JUNKED   GERMAN PACT

I thought Scott might have been as great a general as Wellington, with his plans and strategies. As a younger man on the French Riviera, he had collected toy soldiers of every nationality. Children and adults were enthralled with his maneuverings of the warriors and the stories he invented while his men marched to victory.

There were lists of his "fixations," from Marie (Hersey) (1911) to S. (Graham) (1937–40). His total of feminine fixations from the age of fourteen: sixteen persons. "Before that basketball? Nancy, Kitty, Violet? Can I count Cici, Mary R.,

Tommy or Charlie?" There was a list of the meetings with Ernest Hemingway. They had petered out between 1931 and 1937. "Four times in eleven years (1929–40) not *really* friends since '26."

There were lists of the books he had read by the time he was twenty, thirty, forty. Lists of painters and their works at the age of forty. A list of the thirty-six dramatic situations, from "Supplication" to "Loss of Loved Ones," copied from the Georges Polti book, first published in 1916. Lists of plots in the *Saturday Evening Post*. Lists of the prices paid—imitating Butler, who had earned much less than Scott, a total of £62.10.10 from *Erewhon*, and lost £960.17.6 from his thirteen other works. There were lists of the types of stories each studio preferred. Scott asked me to do some research for him on this, and I was delighted to be of use to him. His list of "Story Needs," dated March 1, 1939, stated the requirements of the various studios.

Columbia:	Story for Edward G. Robinson.
	Dramatic vehicle for Edith Fellows.
	Headline and propaganda and exploitation stories; i.e., parents on trial, first offender, child bride, etc.
Paramount:	Jack Benny vehicle on the order of "Get-Rich-Quick Wallingford"
	Story for Martha Raye—Bob Hope
	Story for Lamour—Harlow type
	Story for Gracie Allen
METRO:	Story for Hedy Lamarr
	Outstanding melodramas
	Weingarten looking for "Raffles" type of smart comedy melodrama.

March — Aug '25   Paris
Oct 25 — Feb, 26   Paris
Apr 26 — Oct 26   Riverria
One Day in October '28   } 1 in 2½ yrs

Apr 29 — June 29   Paris

Three or four Meetings in Autumn 1929
One meeting in Oct 1931   ← Two years
One meeting in   1933   ← Two years
Two meetings in   1937   ← Two years
                                    ← Three years

4 Times in 11 years

Four times in eleven years (1929-1940). Not really friends since '26

Mary + R.W.
      fications
Marie 1911
Cleaver 1912 + J.J.
N — 1913
E — 1914
G K — 1915
D.P. — 1916
G.K. — 1917
    Rosealie April at 1917
Z — 1918 — 1919
    Paradise 1919
Z — 1920 — 1924
    Gatsby 1924
M.9.S — 1925 - 1927
M — 1927 - 1931
H.P.S Tender 1932 - 1934
Goethe — 1935 - 1937
S. — 1937 - 1940

Gatsby
Basil
Paradise
                    Cleaver
            Basin   Sammy (Basil)
                    Ella
                    Actress (Rosalie)
            Paradise
                    Sally
                    David
                    Shirlee
                    Haris
                    Fly
                    Ernst
                    Charlie (?etc)

Total from age 14 — Sixteen persons.
Before that Basket ball? Nancy, Kitty, Violet?
Can't count Cici, Mary R., Tommy, or Charlie?

Principal:	Story for Bobbie Breen, with a family touch.
RKO:	Good warm human interest story.
	Bert Gilroy wants inexpensive stories.
	Leo McCarey wants unusual stories for daring picture.
	Leigh Jason wants stories with a message.
	Border Patrol.
	Astaire picture legitimate story.
	Barbara Stanwyck
	Ginger Rogers
	Claudette Colbert
	Irene Dunne
Selznick:	Story for Ronald Colman. No costume but straight romantic or comedy roles.
	Story for Lombard—no nutty comedies
	Story for Colbert—no nutty comedies
20th-Fox:	Wants to put Ritz Brothers in vehicle with famous music.
	Stories for Temple
	Jones family story
	Melodramas for Wurtzel
Universal:	A jungle story.
	Kenneth Goldsmith wants action stories.
	Modern Cavalry story.
	Modern sea story with character on order of "Sea Wolf."
	Peace-time spy story.
	Irene Dunne
	Margaret Sullavan.
	Basil Rathbone

	3 stories for Jackie Cooper and another boy—with heart interest.
	1 human interest story on type of "Over the Hill."
	1 modern adventure drama.
	Newspaper story and current event features.
Warners:	Modern story for Muni, preferably with a timely angle.
	Modern story for Bette Davis.
	Story for six year old Janet Chapman.
	Story for Miriam Hopkins.
	Story for Cagney.
Chas Rogers:	Wants stories for 13 year old girl who can sing popular and operatic songs.
Lou Brock:	Horror story or horror melodramas

Scott listed football plays that were sure to improve the game. He wrote them on anything close at hand, on scraps of paper, in the backs of the books he bought me. When I was at Princeton presenting my Fitzgerald memorabilia (after the publication of *Beloved Infidel*), we stood in a small group while President Goheen related how before nearly every home game in the thirties the coach, Fritz Crisler, or Asa Bushnell, the graduate manager of athletics, received a telephone call from Scott in the early morning with a new football tactic that would surely result in a victory for Princeton, which was doing badly. On one occasion, after an urgent call from Scott in the small hours, Crisler told him he would use the play on one condition, that Scott would take full credit for its success and full credit for its failure, "if any." Perhaps they should hold the system in reserve, Scott had replied.

There were lists of what he was going to do tomorrow, what he had done today. On an undated Tuesday in 1940 he listed: "Things to do—pay bills, dentist, write *Esquire* story. Read Wordsworth in volumes, plot for movie, *Call of the Wild* for Sheilah. *Esquire* letter. Income tax, laundry, $36 to Scottie." Another list: "A Sept Schedule At the End of my 44th Year 1940. Sept 1st-22nd. Sure job. Sept 22nd-Oct 20th. Possible job (to save $2,000). Three days planning novel. Write on it to Dec. 1st possibly *finishing* first draft. *Alternate* Feather Fan if job is not extended. Or play or Philippe. *Not* another story—no stories, radio out and plays." At the bottom of this page, a list of his sleeping pills: the combination of seconal 1½, nembutal 1½; or 2½ nembutals; or seconal 1½, barbitol 5 gr.

Perhaps the lists reassured him that he was alive, that he could still function. He seemed doubtful sometimes. He wrote himself a postcard to the Garden of Allah, asking, "Where are you?" signed Scott. Perhaps this is why he needed an audience, even if it were just his secretary, his maid, or me. He needed the reassurance that he existed and that he still had the old magic.

The plan and the lists for my education were a life-saver for Scott. His contract with Metro had expired. The other studios were not rushing to sign him. There are few secrets in Hollywood, and his drinking bouts were known. College of One distracted him from his failure as a screenwriter. It occupied his mind. He had to be busy even if it meant writing gibberish, which he sometimes did just before passing out completely. It was a lucky chance for us both that I was his girl in those last years of his life, that I was as eager for him to educate me as he was to be my teacher.

And it almost did not happen. "The Story of an

Inebriated Gentleman," I wrote in the big ledger. And underneath: "Living with him was like sitting on top of a volcano—picturesque but uncomfortable." It was often more than that. The eruption was sometimes dangerous.

I was asleep in my Hollywood apartment when the insistent ringing of my telephone brought me sharply awake. Scott had been drinking heavily, and I had decided I would not see him for a while. It made me too unhappy—the sly look on his face, the ether-like smell of alcohol, the subterfuges about the liquor (his favorite hiding place was inside the back of the toilet in his bathroom), the filthy handkerchiefs, the unpressed clothes, the quick anger, the lies, the awful language, although when he was sober he winced if you said "Damn." I always went back when he stopped drinking, after the agonized drying-out period, during which he was looked after by a series of registered nurses, who fed him intravenously because he could not keep food down. He could eat anything while he was drinking—fudge with crab soup was not unusual—but as soon as he stopped, up it all came. On this morning when the telephone awakened me, I glanced at my bedside clock. It was almost five. "I called the doctor," said Scott in his soft appealing voice. "He's getting me the nurse. He gave me a shot and I'm sleepy. Will you come over and wait for her?" Of course I would come.

It was getting light as I drove over Laurel Canyon into the valley. I parked my car in the courtyard of his house on the Edward Everett Horton estate in Encino. It would be another lovely day, as the birds were remarking in a shrieking chorus. The front door was open. Upstairs in his bed, Scott smiled at me impishly like a precocious boy who has pulled off a trick. He had been writing: his wooden board with the blocks on each side to make a writing desk was across his knees; his hair twirled to a point as he twisted it when he was thinking; a pencil in his hand and one behind his ear; yellow typing paper on the bed and on the floor and the air sour with the smell of alcohol. He yawned prodigiously, and I said, "Why don't you go to sleep? I'll wait downstairs for the nurse."

"Okay, baby." I took the desk and the papers and straightened the pillow and the blanket and the sheet. "You won't leave?" He yawned again settling down in the bed.

"I'll be downstairs," I promised. The top drawer of the mahogany chest near the door was open. A soiled handkerchief did not quite cover his gun. On an impulse I took the gun and slipped it quickly inside my coat. In his present state, it might be dangerous.

He was like a tiger leaping. We rolled on the floor while he clawed wildly at my hands. He had always seemed physically weak, but now he was strong. My only thought at first: He must not get the gun. Then I became angry, almost mad with anger. My fingers were numb and bleeding. I could not hold the gun much longer. Let the bastard kill himself, who cared? But I wouldn't stay to see it. I jerked him from me, flung the gun away, and struck his sweating grimly smiling face with all the strength of my open palm and told the son of a bitch to shoot himself and what a good riddance that would be, and then ran down the stairs into my car, swearing and crying.

"Go on, kill yourself," I shouted. It would be a release for us all. He was no good to anyone like this—not to himself, to Scottie, or to me. Zelda needed him, but she had had him for a long time and they had destroyed each other.

But when the morning became afternoon and the anger

had gone, I thought of him with the gun and I was afraid. I did not believe he would kill himself, but it could go off accidentally. At six o'clock I telephoned. "He left for the East this morning," his maid informed me. She was surprised. "Didn't he tell you? He said he's never coming back. I'm to stay on the job until I hear from him." I hung up slowly. Of course, he was going to Zelda. I should not have struck him, I should not have called him dreadful names. He was a proud man and I had humiliated him beyond endurance. But he had not yet sent the maid away. It could mean that he was coming back.

He was away two weeks and returned at the end of April. He had appeared, like a madman, at the sanitarium in Asheville, North Carolina, had ordered Zelda to pack, and had flown with her to Cuba, where she carried a Bible and prayed continuously, attracting further attention with her old-fashioned clothes—the short long-waisted dresses of the twenties, when they were the gayest, most envied couple, when everything was "... bingo bango ... and people would clap when we arose, at her sweet face and my new clothes." He was beaten up at a cockfight, trying to rescue the bird, while he cradled it in his arms, shouting, "You sons of bitches." It was all very confused, but somehow they landed at the Algonquin Hotel in New York and Scott was drinking and Zelda was still praying and Scott was in a fight with a waiter and tried to throw him down the stairs, and Mr. Case, the owner, not knowing what else to do, sent Zelda back to the sanitarium and Scott first to Bellevue, then to Doctors Hospital, where he picked himself up one night and returned to California.

His voice was cold, but if I wanted to see him so badly, he said, I could come, but not yet. He was going into the drying-out period. And then I came and he was blessedly sober. The time was right for a new project. There would be few jobs for him at the film studios until his death, but there would be two projects that would absorb him, that would restore his confidence as a writer: a new novel, about Hollywood—he asked me what I thought of calling it *Stahr*; and the education of Sheilah Graham, born Lily Shiel. It was later than we knew, but there was still time.

With Proust as the beginning, the plan for College of One was committed to paper on a long night in mid-May of 1939. We had been to a film preview. As we often did, we were singing as we drove back to Encino. Scott was teaching me the words of a popular song of the late twenties, "Don't Bring Lulu," written by a brash young man called Billy Rose. We found the words excruciatingly funny and laughed, singing at the top of our voices. Then we were quiet. Scott seemed pensive. In a low voice he started reciting:

> "Fair youth, beneath the trees, thou canst not leave
>   Thy song, nor ever can those trees be bare;
>   Bold Lover, never never canst thou kiss,
>   Though winning near the goal—yet, do not grieve;
>   She cannot fade, though thou hast not thy bliss,
>   For ever wilt thou love, and she be fair!"

He glanced sideways at me to see if I was paying attention. Sometimes I would go off into myself, wondering about us or thinking of my column or a problem with a film star. I was listening. I had never heard this kind of poetry before.

"Who wrote it?" I asked. Scott smiled. He was quoting from his beloved Keats. I knew the name, but only vaguely. There had been short poems by Browning at the orphanage: "Oh, to be in England, now that April's there," and the verse that ends "God's in His Heaven, all's right with the world," which I hadn't believed; one verse of Wordsworth that began "I wandered lonely as a cloud"; and all the heroic poetry. But what Scott had just recited was the best there was. "What is it from?" I asked him. It was the "Ode on a Grecian Urn," he replied happily.

In a famous letter to his daughter dated August 3, 1940, Scott wrote: "Poetry is not something easy to get started on by yourself. You need at the beginning some enthusiast who knows his way around. John Peale Bishop performed that office for me at Princeton ... The Grecian Urn is unbearably beautiful with every note as inevitable as the notes in Beethoven's Ninth Symphony." Bishop had lit the flame for Scott at Princeton, and now he was to pass the torch to me. He would show me the way. He carefully parked the ancient Ford in the courtyard at Encino, and we hurried into the house, to the bookshelves in the living room and his volume of Keats. Sitting close beside me, he read me the whole poem, savoring each word. Delighted by my interest, he then recited Andrew Marvell's "To His Coy Mistress":

> "Had we but world enough, and time ...
> Now, therefore, while the youthful hue
> Sits on thy skin like morning dew,
> And while thy willing soul transpires
> At every pore with instant fires ..."

Then Shelley's "Ode to the West Wind." The door was open.

At last I was to be invited inside. The next morning he gave me the first page of College of One. He had stayed awake far into the night, planning what the courses would be.

CHAPTER SIX
THE MASTER PLAN

THERE WOULD BE NO MATH, BOTANY, BIOLOGY, Latin, or French. This education was for a woman who had to learn in a hurry, who wanted to be familiar with what in a broad sense was taught in a liberal arts college. It would embody Scott Fitzgerald's ideas on what should be taught and his personal method for getting the most from what he considered essential subjects in the shortest possible time. It would take between eighteen months and two years, he estimated. The student would be ready for her diploma in May 1941, after taking written and oral examinations on what she had learned. As the sole graduate of the F. Scott Fitzgerald College of One, class of '41, I would wear blue stockings and a cap and gown, and I would receive a unique scroll presented with due ceremony by the founder himself. It would also be a reeducation for Scott. He would be taking every course with me. We would study history, literature, poetry, philosophy, religion, music, and art. He was as eager to brush up on his own knowledge as I was to learn from the beginning.

The first part of the plan had two sections, a sketchy outline and a detailed list of the books I would actually be reading. The various courses were given to me by Scott one

at a time as the education progressed, and apparently—
unless there really was a copy of the curriculum that was
stolen or lost—I returned each section to him as it was
completed.

The courses were tentative and changed as we went
along, since the main objective at the beginning was to
get the plan on paper, to get started. French Drama (with
some instruction), planned as the first course, to occupy
six weeks, was postponed and then abandoned after some
discussion of Racine. Proust had written about *Phèdre* in
his *Remembrance of Things Past*, and I was anxious to know
what it was about. Scott read me Molière's *Le Bourgeois
Gentilhomme*. But there were other courses I needed more
urgently than I did the French dramatists.

His knowledge of serious music was much greater than
mine, but he needed help for this course. He turned to his
newly acquired secretary, Frances Kroll, a gentle slender
brunette recently out of college. Her brother, Nathan Kroll,
conducted a symphony orchestra, and he decided which
of the great composers I should study. Like all women in
contact with Scott, Frances was speedily under his spell
and was as much his admirer as I was; perhaps she showed
more understanding of him in some respects.

Frances soon became Franny or François. At the beginning, until he was convinced of her complete capitula-
tion, he inconsiderately telephoned her in the middle of
the night to moan, "No one is reading me; what's the point
of all this writing?" Or sometimes he awakened her to explain a change in the courses. Later he sent telegrams or left
notes. Two have survived:

Dear Franny—oh how I regret this. Oh how my heart

bleads, but the arrival of Great Expec threw off page 2 of my poetry schedule. Oh how my heart bleeds and bleeds.

S.

It meant a retyping of the entire poetry course.

Dear François, this is a development of the earlier chart. It will still just go on one big page, that is if the first column (the English stuff) will. Notice it's a little different in categories. Am sleeping.

The time allotment of three weeks only for the Greek and Roman History course surprised me. Scott explained that he was merely giving me a skim-through, a smattering of names, places, and dates. When his daughter was planning to take Greek Civilization and Literature at Vassar, he wrote her: "It seems to me to be a profound waste of time." At Princeton, Scott had written a parody of "Ode on a Grecian Urn" titled "To My Unused Greek Book":

Thou still unravished bride of quietness,
Thou joyless harbinger of future fear,
Garrulous alien, what thou mightest express
Will never fall, please God, upon my ear.

He was more interested in "Medieval History (500–1500)," although the time allowed was also three weeks. In 1935 Scott had made a careful plan for a medieval novel, tentatively titled *Philippe, Count of Darkness*. It was to run to 90,000 words. Later he considered rewriting three Philippe stories into a 30,000-word novelette. "He is one of the best characters I have ever drawn," he wrote Max Perkins in January 1939. Nothing came of it because he decided it would be more profitable for him to write a novel about Hollywood—now tentatively titled *The Last Tycoon*. He might have changed the title, had he lived. He was never quite sure of it. He explained to me why Stahr's first name was Monroe; "Jewish parents often give their sons the names of American Presidents."

Again, Scott allowed three weeks for "History of France 100 B.C. to 1st World War." He wrote a poem, "Lest We Forget (France by Big Shots)," for me to fix the rogues, the rulers, and the *siècles* in my mind, starting with the Gallo-Roman period. I found it a great aid to remembering events and learned it by heart. Among the verses were:

Brennus, amid Roman wails,
Threw his sword into the scales . . .
      Saint Louis was a pious blade
Who vainly led the last crusade . . .
      Henry of Navarre, no ass,
Knew that France was worth a mass.*

Elie Faure's courses on architecture and art were dropped. Instead, I learned about capitals, pediments, and the round Roman arches that evolved into the Gothic architecture of the twelfth century in Prentice's *Heritage of the Cathedral*.

"Decorative Art and Furniture" was to have lasted three weeks, but that too was abandoned, and it is only in the last

---

*For longer excerpts from this poem, see *Beloved Infidel* (New York: Henry Holt and Company, 1958), pages 312–14.

decade that I have known the difference between Shera-
ton, Chippendale, Louis Quatorze, Regency, Victorian, and
Early American furniture.

According to "Possible Lines of Study," there were to
be six weeks of "Readings in Foreign Literature (excluding French and Russian, Greek, Roman, Italian, Spanish,
German)"—what was left? Scott changed the plan later to
include the French and Russian authors—in fact, nearly all
the foreigners.

I cannot remember what happened to "Cushman's Philosophy, with readings," to take twelve weeks. It is not anywhere on the philosophy course. "Spengler and Modern
Philosophers" was to be the culmination of my education,
as it had been for Kathleen and her ex-king in *The Last Tycoon*. "When you have completed Spengler you will know
more of history than Scottie at Vassar," he promised me.
After he explained Spengler to me, I wondered whether I
could ever read him. How could one man know so much
of cultures and civilizations? And how alarming he was,
with his prophecies of wars that would ravage Europe, then
America, and spiral across the Pacific until Asia was master
of the world.

By now I might have forgotten the order of the courses
but for my correspondence with Johnny, in which I gave
detailed accounts of my studies (without ever mention-
ing Scott Fitzgerald, as Scott never wrote of me to Zelda).
Johnny would have been unhappy if he had known of
Scott's importance in my life, as Zelda would have been
if she had known of my existence. I showed Scott all my
letters from Johnny, whom he found enchanting, with
the dreams and hopes that never materialized. He read
me most of the letters from Zelda. They were beautiful, I

thought, with brilliant imagery, although, as Scott pointed out, the unusual prose led to a vast nowhere.

I quote from a letter I wrote to Johnny on March 3, 1940:

I am now reading Ernest Renan's *Life of Jesus*. He debunks the mystical and miraculous part and leaves a good, great and simple personality. I have also re-read the *Gospels of Matthew and Mark*. I have been going to some Art Exhibitions. There is a fine building in Los Angeles called the Huntington Library. In it are most of the 18th Century painters—Gainsborough, Reynolds, Romney and lovely landscapes by Constable and Turner. What a pity the British let them get away. I have been reading books on art as well. As you have probably guessed, I have been trying to make up for my lack of education. My studies are arranged in little courses. I started with History. Course No. 2 is dedicated to Poetry. No. 3 to Religion and Fiction. No. 4 Philosophy, History and Economics. No. 5 is Music, with Spengler to follow. Interrupting each course, when possible, are novels and biographies pertaining to or having a background to the subject.

Another letter to Johnny, dated April 22, 1940: "I am currently reading Morton's *A People's History of England*, which gives the complete story of England from the people's point of view, not from those above looking down. It gives the reasons for the formation of Parliament and the evolution of the bourgeoisie as a class. It is pretty hard going, but I'm learning quite a lot from it." This was only a year after the start of College of One, two years after I had sat silent and anguished while Scott, Eddie Mayer, Buff

Cobb, and her husband, Cameron Rogers, had discussed in detail Marlborough and the Treaty of Utrecht in 1713, which had given wartorn Europe thirty years of peace. It had seemed unbearable that they knew more of European history than I did.

Scott was aware that what I lacked most was a knowledge of history. It was important for me to get a smattering of this inexhaustible subject as quickly as possible. H. G. Wells's *Outline of History* is not hard to understand, and this is why he chose it for me. At the same time, it does give a complete account of the major events of the known world to the time of its publication in 1920—a revised edition takes it to 1931. (After the death of Wells in 1946, the history was brought up to date by Raymond Postgate.)

I was pleased that on the master plan the English section was longer than any of the others. When I had confided to A.P. Herbert my longing to learn French, he had remarked, "Why don't you first learn English?" And now I would read a great deal of English, with a man who was proud of the emphasis his family had placed on education. In the Fitzgerald Section of the Rare Books Department at Princeton, there is the note he wrote for his daughter:

Variety in American Education

You went to Vassar
Your father to Princeton
Your grandfather Fitzgerald to Georgetown
Your   "   Sayre   "   Roanoke College, Va.
Your great grandfather Scott to St. Johns, Annapolis
Your great-great grandfather to Washington College,
      Md.—I have his B.A. Diploma dated 1797

Some of the Keys went to Wm and Mary
And some of the Tylers to the University of Virginia
    but I haven't the data at hand at this moment.
This is apropos of nothing.

But it was apropos of a great deal. Education obviously
meant as much to Scott as it did to me. He was Princeton,
his daughter was Vassar, and I was College of One.

Bleak House, the fifth book in the English section, was,
Scott told me, "Dickens' best novel." I knew he knew better than I did, and for years I would parrot: "*Bleak House*
is Dickens' best novel." I recently reread the two volumes
and found Esther Summerson too good to be real, as I
found most of Dickens' young women, two-dimensional
to the point of mawkishness. I liked Mr. Jarndyce, but is
anyone ever so completely without any vices whatsoever?
In today's world Lady Dedlock would have claimed her
daughter much earlier, without so much groaning on the
grave of her love. *Bleak House* may be Dickens' best book,
but I prefer *A Tale of Two Cities*, although Lucie is almost a
counterpart of Esther. *Great Expectations* rather frightened
me with the terrifying Magwitch, but I loved Pip and was
pleased that the boy had received a good education and
come out all right in the end. Actually the book of Dickens I
have always liked best is *David Copperfield*—especially the
first part, ending with the dirty, tired Copperfield finding
his Aunt Betsy, who took him in and gave him shelter and
love. Nevertheless I still like to read *Bleak House*, chiefly
because of Miss Flite, Lawyer Tulkinghorn, the Jellybys and
their children, the Smallweeds, and the marvelous descriptions of the alleys and the jumbled shops of London.

I realize now that I liked or disliked the characters in

Dickens for the wrong reasons; I have always related to myself. I was not advanced enough in those early days of the education to understand how Dickens had created the characters, or the structure of his novels. I was interested chiefly in the story. I was aware that Dickens was a master of his craft only when Scott told me that he saturated himself in Dickens and Dostoevski before starting a new novel. Before *The Last Tycoon* he also read Froude's *Julius Caesar*.

It seems incredible that before Scott's College of One I had not read *Vanity Fair*, the first of the novels in the curriculum. It was easy to read in the good edition Scott bought me in three volumes with thick paper and strong print. Again my enjoyment was for the simple reason of pleasure. I did not consider the "how" of Becky Sharp. I found her interesting and she was somewhat like me. I much preferred her to the meek Amelia, who was put upon repeatedly without protesting. Becky fought for what she wanted, as I did. Her ambitions had been somewhat different from mine; she had wanted money and position, I had wanted acceptance. Perhaps they are related. The rest of Thackeray I found less absorbing. Even then I realized that *Pendennis* and *The Virginians* were not in the same class with *Vanity Fair*.

I had read *Alice's Adventures in Wonderland* and *Through the Looking-Glass* at the orphanage. As I always dealt in facts, Alice's shrinkages and enlargements were worrying, and I hoped they wouldn't happen to me. I had feared the Duchess, with her strangely wrapped-up head in the Tenniel drawings, and had thought the Cheshire Cat ridiculous. The Mad Hatter's tea party had interested me only because of its connection with food. Alice with Scott was a totally new experience. He explained the satire,

which I had not understood before. I never had much of a
sense of humor. Life had always been a serious matter. In
spite of some dreadful times, it never really had been for
Scott. He laughed at so many things, with a sort of chok-
ing amusement. He was always puncturing the pomposity
of important people and deriding the sheeplike following
of tradition. With Scott I found a way to smile at things
that had seemed solemn or frightening. I went even further
than Scott. I learned to laugh at myself, which he was never
able to do.

Studying the lists of the books I was to read, I saw there
were a few authors with whom I was already familiar. I had
not heard of George Moore, but I knew Arnold Bennett.
I had met him during my stage career. He was a friend
of C.B. Cochran and always came to the opening nights.
I had heard of H.G. Wells but had read nothing by him.
Compton Mackenzie's name was familiar because of the
articles he sometimes wrote for the London newspapers.
The drama and poetry sections might as well have been in
Greek, except for Byron, Browning, and Wordsworth. At
the orphanage I had won sixpence when I was thirteen for
being the first to memorize the segment in Byron's *Childe
Harold*—

There was a sound of revelry by night,
And Belgium's capital had gathered then
Her beauty and her chivalry, and bright
The lamps shone o'er fair women and brave men . . .
And all went merry as a marriage bell,
But hush! hark!

The Shot, then: "On with the dance! let joy be

unconfined." This was on the order of the heroic poems I loved. I remembered Waterloo and Wellington from the history lessons. A line in *Vanity Fair* was marked by Scott: George Osborne killed at Waterloo and, "Amelia was praying for him while George was lying on his face, dead, with a bullet through the heart." "I can never forget this sentence," said Scott.

I had met George Bernard Shaw briefly. Mr. Cochran, who sometimes escorted his "young ladies" to the theater, had taken me to a matinee and Mr. Shaw was sitting immediately in front of us. When I was introduced to the white-bearded satyr he looked at me so fiercely that I was more frightened than thrilled. I knew of Kipling—the *Just So Stories*, "Mandalay," and "If." As for Shakespeare, my knowledge of his work was confined to a few songs from his plays, although at RADA I had stuttered through a scene in *Hamlet* as the Queen to Charles Laughton's King and had been eliminated quickly from the role.

In the other sections, I had read one book by Hemingway. I had been embarrassed when I first came to America by not knowing who Willa Cather was. In London, Randolph Churchill had given me Stendhal's *Charterhouse of Parma*—two volumes, beautifully bound, but I had not read them. Proust. Ah, here was my familiar Proust, all seven volumes. De Maupassant. Johnny had said his stories were naughty, but not as wicked as *The Decameron* and *A Thousand and One Nights*. Johnny and I had read them at the Gargoyle Club in London. The Bible I knew. We had read a great deal of it at the orphanage. "Since Autumn 1937," Scott noted on his "Revised List of 40 Books," I had read, in addition to Proust, Henry James's *Daisy Miller* and *The Reverberator*, *A Farewell to Arms*, *The Maltese Falcon*, plays by Molnar and Wilde, with some technique (for our play), and a life of Wilde.

Reading the master plan in detail, I realized that a great portion of it would be very hard work. But I was eager to begin. With Scott's enthusiastic promise that he would help me every step of the way, I was sure I could do it.

CHAPTER SEVEN
THE CURRICULUM

SCOTT DIVIDED THE WELLS *OUTLINE OF HISTORY*
into forty sections, each one interrupted by a novel or a
play.*

READING LIST

Wells' Outline		
	158–184—Vanity Fair	Thackeray
"	185–205—Man and Superman	Shaw
"	205–226—The Red and the Black	Stendhal
"	226–252—Bleak House (1st half)	Dickens
"	252–285—Seven Men	Beerbohm
"	285–303—Bleak House (2nd half)	Dickens
"	303–322—Androcles & The Lion	Shaw
"	322–344—Henry Esmond	Thackeray
"	344–375—A Doll's House	Ibsen
"	376–387—Sister Carrie	Dreiser
"	388–412—The Red Lily	France
"	412–435—Youth's Encounter	Mackenzie
"	435–454—Sinister Street	Mackenzie
"	455–480—The Kreutzer Sonata (out)	Tolstoi

---

*The entire curriculum as conceived and written by Scott Fitzgerald will be found in the Appendix, page 228.

"	480–501—Death in Venice	Mann
"	501–523—Madame Bovary	Flaubert
"	524–546—Custom of the Country	Wharton
"	546–565—The Brothers Karamazov	Dostoievski
"	565–597—Tono-Bungay	Wells
"	599–617—Roderick Hudson	James
"	617–634—The Pretty Lady	Bennett
"	634–667—Tess of the D'Urbervilles	Hardy
"	667–698—How to Write Short Stories	Lardner
"	699–732—Chéri	"Colette"
"	733–751—My Antonía	Cather
"	751–778—The Sailor's Return	Garnett
"	778–803—The Financier	Dreiser
"	803–835—The Titan	Dreiser
"	835–866—A Lost Lady	Cather
"	867–893—The Revolt of the Angels	France
"	893–928—Ariel, or the Life of Shelley	Maurois
"	929–955—The Song of Songs	Suderman
"	956–991—The Sun Also Rises	Hemingway
"	991–1025—Flaubert & Malraux	
"	1025–1050—Byron: The Last Journey	Nicolson
"	1051–1076—South Wind	Douglas
"	1076–1101—Man's Fate	Malraux
"	1102–1128—The Woman Who Rode Away	Lawrence
"	1128–1152—The Cabala	Wilder
"	1152–1170—Tender Is the Night & Chronology	Shakespeare

Because some of the books were out of print—his own *Tender Is the Night*, which, to amuse himself, he credited to Shakespeare, was impossible to find—Scott made another list with some additions to fill in the gaps. And, to give a feeling of progress to the reading, he added time schedules. I was to read the forty books within ten months, from October to August.

He started me on the Wells *Outline* at Book Three, page 158, "The First Civilizations." He believed it would be simpler if he explained Books One and Two, "The World Before Man" and "The Making of Man." "You can absorb these prehistoric periods more easily from me than in the reading," he said, and he was right. Even with his explanations, it was hard to grasp "The Earth in Space and Time," "The Record of the Rocks," "Life and Climate," "The Age of Reptiles," "The Age of Mammals," "Apes and Sub Men." As I scan these chapters now, it is hard to believe they were ever too difficult.

After the seven sections of "The Early Empires," *Vanity Fair* (always on Scott's lists of "Books I Have Enjoyed Most") was a sweet pause, something to reach for—I was like a child taking its first step into outstretched arms. Following the twenty pages of "Sea Peoples and Trading Peoples," Shaw's *Man and Superman* with its war between the sexes and "Don Juan in Hell" was another welcome resting place. Scott admired Shaw for his courage in advocating unpopular causes such as socialism and atheism; he spoke of "Shaw's aloof clarity and brilliant consistency." I enjoyed Stendahl's *The Red and the Black*. Julian Sorel had started life as a poor boy, an opportunist who came to a bad end because of his ambition and scheming. It was something to remember. I was especially interested in Wells's "Drama and Music in the Ancient World" because of my time on the London stage, although there was nothing similar in the two periods. It was written chattily, rather like my Hollywood gossip column.

Book Four in the *Outline*, "Judaea, Greece and India," was interspersed with Max Beerbohm's *Seven Men*. The first of the seven, Enoch Soames, a third-rate writer yearning for immortality, was, Scott explained, a lampoon on the followers of Oscar Wilde. That made the story more interesting.

Thackeray's *Henry Esmond*. I enjoyed the book but found the accompanying slice of Wells's *History*, which dealt with Pericles, Socrates, Plato, and Aristotle, equally interesting. I have always been more drawn to accounts of real people than to fictionalized characters.

Four Wells sections, "Science and Religion at Alexandria," preceded my first contact with Theodore Dreiser. "*Sister Carrie*," Scott said, "was almost the first piece of American realism." It was a complicated word for something I told him I found as easy to read as I had found *Peg's Papers* in the East End of London. Except for Carrie's ruthlessness, it somewhat resembled *Peg's Papers*, a "penny dreadful" in which the poor factory girl always married the handsome son of the boss, but not until she had been almost "ruined" by the wicked foreman. In 1939 it was difficult for me to believe that when *Sister Carrie* had been published, in 1900, it had been considered scandalous. When I finally came to read Scott's *Tender Is the Night*, the turnabout in the fortunes of Dick and Nicole Diver reminded me of Hurstwood, who was prospering when he met Carrie and who, as she moved up, went down. "Dreiser is rough," Scott explained. "No social grace at all, but my

God, what a storyteller! He's the best of our generation."
They had met and, as usual when Scott was young and
close to an idol, he had to be drunk or he would have felt
awkward and tongue-tied. "I had been invited to his house
with some other people," said Scott. "Dreiser was a poor
host and it wouldn't occur to him to offer us a drink, so I
brought along a bottle of champagne." Dreiser's guests were
sitting stiffly around the wall on straight-backed kitchen
chairs, like schoolchildren, when Scott arrived. He waved
his bottle and yelled, "I consider H.L. Mencken and Theodore Dreiser the greatest men living in this country today."
Dreiser took the news calmly and put Scott's champagne in
his icebox, where it remained.

There are three embedded tomato pips, a red aster-
isk, marking the first page of Book Five in the *Outline of
History*. After the education began, I studied while eating
my lunch, and several of the books are pocked with bits
of food. The history was now as interesting as the novels.
"The Rise and Collapse of the Roman Empire," "Christianity and Islam," "The Mongol Empires of the Land Ways and
the New Empires of the Sea Ways." Book Eight, "The Age of
the Great Powers," brought us to the period after the First
World War and "The Further Outlook of Mankind," which
Wells, with his imagination, and Scott, with his insight,
could somewhat foresee.

I completed the Wells history to the end of the Chro-
nology, which I marked off as I memorized it. At any question I could accurately state that Necho of Egypt defeated
Josiah, King of Judah, at the Battle of Megiddo in 608 B.C.;
that Genghis Khan took Peking in 1218 A.D.; that Marco
Polo started on his travels in 1271 and returned to Venice in
1295; that the Anabaptist rule in Münster fell during 1535;

that the Manchus ended the Ming Dynasty in 1644; that
the suicide of Clive of India took place in the same year
that the American "revolutionary drama" began in 1774.
And that Austria annexed Bosnia and Herzegovina in 1908.
By then I had read the total of forty novels and plays prescribed by Scott.

To continue with the list, I read two books, *The Red
Lily* and *The Revolt of the Angels*, by Anatole France, whom
Scott admired greatly. When he and Zelda had first arrived
in Paris, they had waited outside Anatole France's house
for an hour, hoping he would appear. Another author represented by two novels—*Youth's Encounter* and *Sinister
Street*—was Compton Mackenzie, whom Scott had been
accused of imitating (and with some justification, Scott admitted) in his first novel, *This Side of Paradise*. Mencken, to
whom Scott had sent a copy, had written: "It derives itself
from Mackenzie, Wells, and Tarkington." Edmund Wilson,
as soon as he read the manuscript, reported back to Scott:
"It sounds like an exquisite burlesque of Compton Mackenzie with a pastiche of Wells thrown in at the end."

Flaubert's *Madame Bovary*. Flaubert, "who is eternal,"
Scott wrote, "while Zola already rocks with age ... who
consciously leaves out the stuff that Zola will come along
presently and say." Flaubert's *Three Tales*—when Scott's
secretary had found a beautifully illustrated edition in a
second-hand store in downtown Los Angeles, he gave her
the cheaper volume he had already bought. "Flaubert and
Conrad," said my professor, "sometimes took days to pol-
ish one sentence." He wanted his own style of writing as
concise as theirs.

It is interesting that, although Scott in 1939 did not regard Wilde highly, this writer was featured prominently on

his curriculum for me. When I read the "Ballad of Reading Gaol," Scott had me read A.E. Housman's poems, *A Shropshire Lad*, first published while Wilde was in prison. It didn't take any guessing on my part to know why Scott had wanted me to read the two works together; the Wilde poem was clearly an imitation of Housman. My teacher was pleased that I had spotted this. I did not like *The Picture of Dorian Gray*; the corruption and the portrait made me uncomfortable, as does everything that is not normal, but I liked the plays, especially *The Importance of Being Earnest*.

Edith Wharton's *The Custom of the Country*. In Mizener's biography he states that when Scott met Miss Wharton in Paris he had tried to shock her by telling her that when he and Zelda first came to Paris they had spent two weeks in a bordello, believing it was a hotel. She had crushed him by stating majestically, "But Mr. Fitzgerald, your story lacks data."

Dostoevski's *The Brothers Karamazov*, which had overwhelmed Scott when he had first read it in 1922. A few years later he wrote Mencken that "the influence on *Gatsby* has been the masculine one of the *Brothers Karamazov*, a thing of incomparable form."

Roderick Hudson, by Henry James, whom I find less fascinating now than when I read him in a pause from Wells. I read six of James's earlier novels during our College of One. "The others would bore you," said Scott, "like Tolstoi's later works—but in a different way. Tolstoi became too mystical, James too complex and intricate." He told me his critics believed he had been influenced by Henry James, especially in *The Great Gatsby*. "It's surprising to read of an influence you were not aware of when writing."

Arnold Bennett's very easy novel, *The Pretty Lady*; Hardy's *Tess of the D'Urbervilles*—these girls always seemed to be in trouble. Scott admired Hardy; he "had survived ... while Wells and Shaw and all those of that brave company who started out in the nineties so full of hope and joy in life and faith in science and reason" had become complete pessimists. Hardy, Scott told me, had been impressed with *This Side of Paradise*.

How to Write Short Stories by Ring Lardner, who had been a close friend of Scott when they were neighbors on Long Island. "The critics have never realized what a good writer he is," Scott said of Lardner. "He had pride and dignity even when he was drinking himself to death." Ring, said Scott, would disappear for weeks, and Scott would search for him and take him home to his wife, Alice. Ring, Abe North in *Tender Is the Night*, was enchanted with the Fitzgeralds, his "Prince Scott and Princess Zelda."

On the flyleaf of Colette's *Chéri*, Scott had pasted some printed information for me: "Cheri—one of her latest novels—is the only story of a 'gigolo' I have ever been interested to read or feel to be true. It is a brilliant work of character portrayal, a comedy in a genre new to us and full of a slightly macabre fascination."

Two novels by Willa Cather, *My Antonía* and *A Lost Lady*; *The Sailor's Return* by David Garnett, whom I envied because of the intellectual atmosphere in which he had grown up; two additional gigantic novels by Dreiser, *The Financier* and *The Titan*. I read *The Titan* in the sweet-smelling garden at the Samarkand Hotel at Santa Barbara during one weekend while I was also reading the portion of the Wells history that concerned princes and foreign policy and seventeenth- and eighteenth-century painting. André Maurois' *Ariel: La Vie de Shelley*—I was so proud to be able to read it all in French; Suderman's *Song of Songs*; my second Ernest Hemingway novel, *The Sun Also Rises*. "Ernest always has a helping hand for people who don't need it," Scott wrote at the end of my copy of Thomas Wolfe's *You Can't Go Home Again*, with another comment I cannot quite understand: "Distaste. Marcus' son had played football at Columbia and in his first year at medical school had dissected a human vagina and sent it for Xmas to his father!"

Hemingway was the shining hero of American letters during my time with Scott, who was still deeply hurt by the paragraph in "The Snows of Kilimanjaro" in which the hero remembered poor Scott Fitzgerald's romantic awe (of the rich) and how he had started a story once that began "The very rich are different from you and me" and how someone had said to Scott, "Yes, they have more money"— and when he had found they were not a special glamorous race "it wrecked him just as much as any other thing that wrecked him." "It was as though I were already dead," Scott complained to me.

The biography of Byron, *The Last Journey*, by Harold Nicolson was of the same nineteenth-century period as my Wells segment, "The Indian Precedent in Asia" to "The Rise of the Novel to Predominance in Literature." Malraux's *Man's Fate*, accompanying "The United States and The Imperial Idea" to "The Great War from the Russian Collapse to the Armistice," was marked by Scott on the flyleaf with an unfinished sentence: "The strongest scene from *Pasteur* [referring to the Paul Muni film], the inoculated sheep, was lifted from *Arrowsmith?* Might admire it and be told that ..." Norman Douglas's *South Wind*; D. H. Lawrence's *The Woman Who Rode Away*; *The Cabala* by Thornton Wilder—Scott had to explain to me the meaning of "cabala."

Glancing at my Wells *Outline of History* recently, I was amused to find inside the back cover a diagram of a football play—Scott's trademark.

It was a great deal of reading, by any standard. In a letter to Johnny late in 1939 I told him: "You would be amazed at all the books I have read this past year. It includes seven volumes of Proust, Victor Hugo, Tolstoi, Dostoievski and James Joyce. The best thing about reading is that the more you do it the more you want to do, and the easier the hard reading becomes." On January 25, 1940, I was writing Johnny:

My collection of books is growing in my living room. Bookshelves cover all one side and I just had to buy another small case to take care of the overflow ... I've just finished reading Gertrude Stein's *Three Lives*, which is in her simpler manner. She gets pretty screwy later on, devotes pages to repeating words like a stuck gramophone, something like this—"He sat in a chair, chair chair chair he sat in the chair because he always sat in the chair." That sort of thing could drive you nutty. I think Gertrude Stein is nutty as a matter of fact. But her early stuff is new, bright and fascinating reading ... I used to lunch at the studios a lot but now I have a sandwich and a glass of milk at home and read my current book ... One day when you have made your pile, I wish you'd come to California. It is quite something to see but I don't think I'd like to spend the rest of my life here. It is all too much like a painted backcloth.

I would still have another year in the College of One, but the education was beginning to take. In July 1940 I wrote Johnny: "I am reading a lot of political economy. Baby! [one of Scott's expressions] the things I didn't know and still don't know. Life in Hollywood would be dull but for the reading." And ten days before Scott died: "I am currently studying ancient Greek history. I am reading about Pericles and the Golden Age of Greece in Plutarch's *Lives*. It really is fascinating. I wish I'd had the sense to want to educate myself when I lived in London near all the big museums. I suppose when one is young, one has too good a time to think of developing the mind."

Most educators create a master plan of study at the beginning and stick to it, regardless of the needs of the pupil. But not Mr. Fitzgerald. The curriculum grew concrete as it developed. The order was changed when a book was impossible to get or because Scott believed my interest was flagging. There was nothing rigid about the education. It had an organic growth. The four sections of the plan were never considered final and were constantly retyped by Scott's secretary.

There was no time limit for the poetry, which was interspersed in the curriculum with biographies and criticisms of the poets, novels, various versions of the *Odyssey*, and Lord Charnwood's *Lincoln*. Scott headed the course: "A Short Introduction to Poetry (with Interruptions)." Rupert Brooke, Swinburne, Tennyson, and others were matched with various critical works, while Browning and Moore's *Esther Waters* were read in tandem. At the end I was able to take in aspects of Eliot's and Rimbaud's poetry along with Edmund Wilson's criticism. At one point Scott had me read consecutive chapters of the *Odyssey* from three different translations (Chapman, Pope, and Butler).

The poetry was preceded by "A Discussion of Prosody and the most familiar meters":

TYPES OF POEMS

Ballad	Short narrative
Epic	Long narrative
Dramatic	Shakespeare
Lyric	A Song
Ode	An address
Serenade	Night song
Madrigal	Morning song
Elegy or (Threnody)	A lament
Pastoral ⎤ Bucolic ⎦	Country life
Eclogue and Epode	I never knew

SOME USUAL FORMS

Couplet	Two lines rhyming
Heroic couplet	Two rhymed iambic pentameter lines like Pope's *Odyssey*
Triolet	Three lines rhyming
Quatrain	Four lines rhyming once or twice
Sonnet	Fourteen lines (8 and then 6) used in iambic pentameter with a complete rhyme scheme
Alexandrine line	Rhymed six foot couplet. Used in French Poetry (Racine & Corneille)
Hyperbole	Exaggeration

SOME TERMS

A stressed or "long" syllable
A slighted or "short" syllable

as   alone   or   monkey   or   teepee

The French language has no exact equivalent for this. In English either *stress* or *slight* every syllable.

We break verse into "Feet." According to the stress, we give these "feet" different names. The most important is the *iambus*. Alone is called an iambus. Also Oh Yeah! Five iambuses form a line of iambic *pentameter* (which means five feet in Greek).

But still the house affairs would call her hence

(Othello)

Shakespeare is all written in unrhymed iambic pentameter (except his songs). He takes liberties with it of course, adding an extra syllable sometimes or dropping one or inverting a foot. At the end of a scene he sometimes rhymes a couplet (2 lines).

OTHER TYPES OF "FEET"

a dactyl	Ex: Perlmutter
a trochee	Ex: Feeble
an anapest	Ex: on a bat
spondee	Ex: Oh God (which can also be an iambus or a trochee, as pronounced).

A trochaic line:

Come and kiss me sweet and twenty

Song of Shakespeare's

A dactylic meter:

> This is the forest primeval

Longfellow

(The song "Little Wooden Shoes" is dactylic—so are many waltzes.)

TYPES OF POETIC WRITING

Rhymed Verse	has metrical pattern (feet) and rhyme
Blank Verse	has metrical pattern but no rhyme (Ex: Elizabethan blank verse)
Free Verse	has a very *loose* metrical pattern which it neglects at will. No rhyme. Like Whitman or Masters' "Ann Rutledge"
Ogden Nash Verse	Free verse that rhymes
Prose Poetry Polyphonic Prose	Loose terms to denote anything from Butcher's & Lang's *Odyssey* to mere flowery language

Didn't I tell you not to shut the door
I told you not to shut the door

Once we started, the poetry flowed and overflowed through all the hours and days. Again it was not *how* it was done. Despite Scott's painstaking explanations, I was less interested in how the poetry was put together than in the actual poems. His examples for the various meters were revealing. Perlmutter—the long wait on the Perl, the two short u's in mutter; in Hollywood you cannot fail to know a Perlmutter. The example of "feeble," with the long sound on "feeb"—Scott called some of the producers and writers he met in the studios "Feebs," also any friends of Scottie's of whom he disapproved. His anapest, "on a bat," is not hard to understand. When a man called without leaving his name, Scott said with a straight face, "Oh, that was my old friend Onabat." His example for a spondee, "Oh God,"—it was his constant expletive. I had never known there were so many types of poetry.

I was interested in the sonnet. Eddie Mayer had written one to Hedy Lamarr, which had pleased her, and she had consented to dine with him. The evening had fallen rather flat, Eddie told me later, because his producer had called him just before he had left for her home to order him to a conference at ten p.m. I thought of his sonnet when Eddie died in poverty and forgotten by Hollywood a few years ago. I had not realized when Eddie read me his poem that it was a sonnet because it had fourteen lines—eight and six—in iambic pentameter.

When Scott believed that I understood the meters and the types of poems, we plunged into Keats and, between the poems, read about him in Sidney Colvin's biography. "If poetry had not gone out of fashion, I would have been a poet," Scott assured me, adding, "Poets don't make any money today. I couldn't afford to be one." At Princeton he had decided he would write prose on the same fine lines as Keats's poetry. In the letter on Keats to his daughter, Scott wrote of the "Grecian Urn": "Every syllable is as inevitable as the notes in Beethoven's Ninth Symphony ... It is what it is because an extraordinary genius paused at that point in history and touched it. I suppose I have read it a hundred times ... likewise with the 'Nightingale,' which I can never read through without tears in my eyes ... the 'Eve of St. Agnes' has the richest most sensual imagery in English, not excepting Shakespeare. For a while after you quit Keats, all other poetry seems to be only whistling or humming." The letter is dated August 1940. I had read and memorized the "Grecian Urn" and the "Nightingale" months before, but we were still discussing them in practically the same language as that of Scott's letter to his daughter.

So many of the poets had died young, Scott told me, although Shakespeare had lived to the comparatively ripe age of fifty-two. "He was a good businessman," said Scott, who was not. "He knew the value of his work to the penny." Shakespeare, said Scott—who believed that I should never be psychoanalyzed because "all your impulses are so near the surface"—had antedated Freud with the scenes between Hamlet and his mother and the relationship of Ophelia with her father.

I was surprised when Scott referred to Byron as a minor poet. At the orphanage he had been rated highly. Apparently there were not enough major poets to round out a college curriculum, so some of the minor poets were perforce included. "Byron's best work," said Scott, "was his unfinished novel in verse, *Don Juan*. Goethe described it as a work of boundless genius." Scott did not agree.

Never too long with any poem or portion of a book or biography; this was part of Scott's system—"the little courses," to keep me interested. Nothing must drag. I must never be bored. In the days of strain with his friends, he had advised me, "Look bored; then they will think you know all about the subject." Now the faking was over. I really would know—not a great deal, perhaps, but enough to feel confident.

There are only five poems by Keats listed on the curriculum. In actual fact, we studied thirteen of the works

"for Shielah
        — ole misery !
To tata my Basil pot
        away from me."

in memory of iambic hours
                Scott, 1940

of Scott's favorite poet: in addition to "The Eve of St. Agnes," "Isabella or The Pot of Basil"—"Oh misery to take my basil pot away from me; in memory of iambic hours, Scott, 1940," he wrote on the Keats flyleaf—"Bright Star," "When I Have Fears," "On First Looking into Chapman's Homer," "Ode to a Nightingale," "Ode on a Grecian Urn," "Ode to the Poets," "Ode on Melancholy," "Fragment of an Ode to Maia," "In a Drear-Nighted December," "The Eve of St. Mark," "La Belle Dame Sans Merci," on the margin of which Scott explained: "This is the bad form as edited by Leigh Hunt. See below."

"On First Looking into Chapman's Homer" was followed by the page of Chapman's *Iliad* to reinforce the poem. Scott pointed out the mistake of Cortez for Balboa—"Silent upon a peak in Darien." When an immortal like Keats makes a mistake," he said, "that too is immortal." I realized that the more famous you become, the more careful you have to be, not only in your work but in your private life. Scott might have given me an argument on this, as he gave Edmund Wilson in a letter in the early twenties: "Wasn't it Bernard Shaw who said that you've either got to be conventional in your work or in your private life or get into trouble?" He wanted me to compare several translations of Homer—Butcher and Lang, Chapman, Pope, and Butler. The authors used different names for the various gods and places, and to avoid confusion in my mind as I skipped from one to the other, Scott wrote for my guidance:

NAMES IN POPE AND BUTLER
Butler uses the Roman instead of the Greek names for the characters. Thus:

Greek		Roman
Odysseus	=	Ulysses
Pallas Athene	=	Minerva
Artemis	=	Diana
Zeus	=	Jove (Jupiter)
Apollo	the same	Apollo
Hephaestus	=	Vulcan
Lacadaemon	=	Sparta
Poseidon	=	Neptune
Hermes	=	Mercury

POPE uses the Greek name for one character, the Roman for another. Athene is Pallas—Odysseus is Ulysses, etc.

Scott had met Gertrude Stein in Paris in 1925. He showed me the letter she had written him after the publication of *The Great Gatsby*, complimenting him for creating the world of the twenties as Thackeray had created his contemporary times in *Vanity Fair*. He had liked her. Zelda had not. Miss Stein never bothered much, Scott told me, with the wives of the authors who came to her home. Her companion, Alice B. Toklas, took care of the unfamous women. Zelda, with her compulsion to compete with Scott and her jealousy of his fame, had sulked on the way home after the first meeting and vowed she would not return to the house on the Rue de Fleurus, although she did. Miss Stein spent the Christmas of 1934 with the Fitzgeralds in America and offered to buy two of Zelda's paintings.

Swinburne, my teacher informed me, was considered shocking by the Victorians. Some of his poems shocked me in 1939. Of the four Swineburne poems on the list, Scott penciled at the top of "Atalanta in Calydon": "The fullest and most talented use of *beat* in the English language. The *dancingest* poem." And with "Laus Veneris": "Notice how this influenced Ernest Dowson. In this, read only as far as you like. When it was published (1868?), it was a great mid-Victorian shocker."

My mind, so long sleeping, grasped the musical-sounding words and, after reading them several times, I could not forget them. A letter to Johnny early in the Second World War—he was serving again in the army: ". . . You would be amazed at how much poetry I know by heart. Keats, Shelley, Shakespeare, Browning, E.B. and R., Wordsworth, Coleridge. I know long verses from these poets. I recite them to myself on the way to the studios—and presto! I'm there."

Scott admired Matthew Arnold and believed I would benefit from his critical essays on Keats and Wordsworth. He disagreed with the author's opinion that Milton would be remembered for the "simple sensuous impassioned poetry" (Milton's own phrase), and that Keats would be remembered because his poetry was "enchantingly sensuous." On the margin against this, Scott wrote: "Later ages have entirely disagreed with this. It shows Victorian stiffness and primness in its most unattractive pose." On the flyleaf of *Arnold's Essays in Criticism, Second Series*, "For Sheilah, with love (and annotations)," there were several of the latter. Scott put quotation marks around Arnold's "Yet I firmly believe that the poetical performance of Wordsworth is, after that of Shakespeare and Milton, of which all the world now recognizes the worth, undoubtedly the most considerable in our language from the Elizabethan age to the

This, with its
following
artillery, is a
famous
Critical
sentence.
Why it is
accepted
with such
authority
is a
mid-Victorian
mystery,
yet - it
has effected
everyone.
Places Keats
above him
but I am
such a
personal
critic &
may be
wrong,
because of
the sincerity
of this god damned scholar ①.
F.S.F.

132   ESSAYS IN CRITICISM   v

steady light of glory as yet shines over him.   He
is not fully recognised at home ; he is not recognised at all abroad. " Yet I firmly believe that the
poetical performance of Wordsworth is, after that
of Shakespeare and Milton, of which all the world
now recognises the worth, undoubtedly the most
considerable in our language from the Elizabethan
age to the present time. " Chaucer is anterior ;   previous
and on other grounds, too, he cannot well be
brought into the comparison.   But taking the roll
of our chief poetical names, besides Shakespeare
and Milton, from the age of Elizabeth downwards,
and going through it,—Spenser, Dryden, Pope,
Gray, Goldsmith, Cowper, Burns, Coleridge, Scott,
Campbell, Moore, Byron, Shelley, Keats (I mention those only who are dead),—I think it certain
that Wordsworth's name deserves to stand, and
will finally stand, above them all.   Several of the
poets named have gifts and excellences which
Wordsworth has not.   But taking the performance
of each as a whole, I say that Wordsworth seems
to me to have left a body of poetical work superior

present time." Scott's comment covered all the left side of
the page:

> This, with its following artillery is now a famous criti-
> cal sentence. Why it is accepted with such authority is a
> mid-Victorian mystery. Yet—it has affected everyone. I
> place Keats above him, but I am such a personal critic
> and may be wrong because of the sincerity of this God
> damned sentence. F.S.F.

On the next page, with Arnold still giving the top palm of
poetry to Wordsworth, Scott harrumphed on the right-
hand margin:

> Mister Arnold had not read Pushkin—nor seen evi-
> dently that Dostoievski (if he knew him) was a great
> poet. Later you must compare this essay with Wilson's
> in *The Triple Thinkers*.

Arnold, still praising Wordsworth on page 142 of my copy,
says in regard to the poet's morality: "The question how to
live is in itself a moral idea." This was underlined for my
special attention by Scott. He penciled on the left margin:

> This is Arnold at his best, absolutely without
> preachment.

On page 145, concerning Epictetus, Scott made another
note.

> Now he [Arnold] becomes "moral"—nevertheless fol-
> low him because this is real thinking through.

At the bottom of the same page:

> I'll bet Arnold got his idea for his poem about his fa-
> ther ["Rugby Chapel"] from this idea of Epictetus.

Scott admired Wordsworth, but not quite as much as Arnold had. Browning's poem "The Lost Leader," he told me, concerned Wordsworth's sell-out to what we now call The Establishment. I can still recite the verse beginning, "Just for a handful of silver he left us, Just for a riband to stick in his coat ... They, with the gold to give, doled him out silver ..." Wordsworth seemed to have sold himself cheaply—but didn't everyone, even Scott? Some of his early potboilers to make fast money for Zelda and the Pat Hobby stories that he wrote for *Esquire* for $200 each were not worthy of his talent. We all have our pieces of silver, I thought, remembering Johnny and me.

On the poetry list there were three poems by Wordsworth, but I asked him to add "I Wandered Lonely as a Cloud," the first verse of which I had read at the orphanage. Now for the first time, I could feel the tremendous loneliness of the line "I wandered lonely as a cloud."

Scott's title *This Side of Paradise* had been taken from the last two lines of Rupert Brooke's "Tiara Tahiti"—"Well, this side of Paradise, there's little comfort in the wise." As a child, I had grieved with Brooke's premonition of his death: "If I should die, think only this of me; That there's some corner of a foreign field, That is for ever England." "The Great Lover," on page 124 of *The Collected Poems* of Rupert Brooke bought me by Scott, still has the corner turned down for easy reference, a habit Scott tried to cure me of; to hear him remonstrate, you would think books were human. I loved the boast of the handsome Mr. Brooke: "I have been so great a lover: filled my days So proudly with the splendor of Love's praise." The sonnet "Oh, Death Will Find Me" was marked for me by Scott and I learned it although it was not on the poetry list. Neither was "The Old Vicarage, Grantchester." I read and reread the poem until I too was sitting at the Café des Westens, Berlin, in May of 1913, yearning for England, where "the lilac is in bloom ... the poppy and the pansy blow ..." The last line, "And is there honey still for tea?" is repeated in one of Zelda's poignant letters to Scott. Why is this line so sad?

Elizabeth and Robert Browning's juxtaposition with George Moore's novel *Esther Waters*, about the servant girl who struggled to raise her illegitimate son, puzzles me today. George Moore had a special attraction for Scott, and it could be explained by Max Beerbohm's description of him: "Of learning ... he had no equipment at all; for him everything was discovery; and it was natural that Oscar Wilde should complain ... George Moore is always conducting his education in public"—which, in a way, Scott did with his vociferous enthusiasms. "Also he had no sense of proportion, but this defect was, in truth, a quality. Whenever he discovered some new master, that master seemed to him greater than any other: he would hear of no other. And it was just this frantic exclusiveness that made his adorations so fruitful ... The critic who justly admires all kinds of things simultaneously cannot love any one of them ... that kind of writer is often ... very admirable. But it is the Moores who matter." This could have been written about Scott Fitzgerald, who died only seven years after the author of *Esther Waters*. "Sheilo, this is the only decent edition in

English and impossible to get so don't lend it. Love, Scott," my professor wrote on the flyleaf of my now battered copy. It is like hearing him speak.

I enjoyed the poems by Robert Browning, "My Last Duchess" and "The Lost Leader," but, because I am inclined to be sentimental, I preferred Mrs. Browning's *Sonnets from the Portuguese*, especially the sonnet "How do I love thee, let me count the ways"; I loved Scott like that. Whenever I learned a sonnet I carefully counted the lines to be sure they totaled fourteen. They always did.

On looking over the curriculum, I was surprised to find only one poem by Shelley, "Ode to the West Wind." How could this be? I wondered—until I realized that the rest of the selected Shelley poems, to be read with Maurois' *Ariel: La Vie de Shelley*, were on the bookmark Scott headed "How to Learn from a Frenchman about an exiled Englishman by an American." The poems: "Ariel to Miranda"; "To the Moon"; "Best and brightest, come away"; "To a Skylark"; "The Indian Serenade"; "I dreamed that as I wandered by the way"; "Ozymandias"; "Many a green isle needs must be"; "Music, when soft voices die"; "Now the last of many days"; "A Lament"; "One word is too often profaned"; "To Night"; "Love's Philosophy"; "The sun is warm, the sky is clear"; "When the lamp is shattered"; "Come into the garden, Maud" (actually by Tennyson). And should I lose the bookmark, they were marked by Scott in the indexes of the *Oxford Book of English Verse* and Palgrave's *Golden Treasury*.

On the inside back cover of the Palgrave, Scott wrote for my amusement a tough-guy account of *Ode on a Grecian Urn*:

A Greek Cup They Dug Up. S'as good as new! And
think how long it was buried. We could learn a lot of
history from it—about the rubes in ancient history,
more than from any poetry about them. Those pictures on it must tell a story about their Gods, maybe,
or just ordinary people—something about life in the
sticks at a place called Tempe. Or maybe it was in the
Arcady Valley. These guys chasing the dames are either Gods or just ordinary people—it doesn't give the
names on the cup. They sure are tearing after them and
the dames are trying to get away. Look—this guy's got
a flute, or maybe it's an obo and they're going to town,
etc. etc.

This was a father teasing his favorite child.

I was not as excited by Shelley's "Skylark"—"Shelley was
a god to me once," Scott had written Max Perkins—as I
was by Keats's "Nightingale," which Scott recorded for me
one evening. We were walking on Hollywood Boulevard,
reciting the poem softly, and happened across a recording
place. The original record, declaimed by Scott in deep professorial tones, is at Princeton.

Another Fitzgerald bookmark was headed "Suggestions
About Byron." "The excerpts from long poems are short
because of the fine print," he wrote. "I have never been able
to admire but five or six of his short lyrics in comparison to
his contemporaries." With the Harold Nicolson biography
I read *Childe Harold*, "Maid of Athens," "So We'll Go No
More a-Roving," "She Walks in Beauty," and *Don Juan*.

I was glad to read about Lincoln again in Lord Charnwood's book, sliced in three, threaded through the *Odyssey*,
Shelley, Walt Whitman, and Rupert Brooke's "Menelaus

and Helen." There was a book about Lincoln at the orphanage, *From Log Cabin to White House*. One of Scott's
great-aunts, Mrs. Suratt, had been hanged for her part in
the assassination. He was not proud of the relationship,
and I was surprised that he told me. Where I came from in
England, if any member of your family had been hanged,
you simply did not talk about it, although I was aware that
many of the great families in England and France had ancestors who had gone to the chopping block or the guil-
lotine. If you happened to have an illegitimate child by a
king—an unmarried mother in the East End was treated
like a leper in my day—well, you became a countess and
the child was made a duke or duchess. Reading of the great
mistresses in College of One, I was fascinated to learn that
an illiterate girl like Nell Gwynn could have two sons with
Charles II and one would be the Duke of St. Albans. This
was a delightful aspect of learning, that you discovered it
was possible to misbehave and be rewarded—but only if
you associated with aristocrats. No wonder they were so
relaxed. They were rarely punished.

My *Lincoln* was peppered with comments from Scott.
When Charnwood compared Jefferson disadvantageously
to Hamilton, Scott penciled between brackets: "This is the
Tory Charnwood speaking." There was a message to me at
the bottom of the next page, again in reference to Charnwood's disparagement of Jefferson:

He means that from 1770–1820, our legislation was
more progressive than yours, but that later it bogged
down—i.e. when Dickens paid his visit.

A Greek Cup They Dug Up

S'as good as new! And think
how long it was buried. We
could learn a lot of history
from it — about the rubes in
ancient history, more than from
any poetry about them. Those
pictures on it must tell a story —
about their Gods, maybe, or just
ordinary people — something
about life in the sticks at
a place called Tempe. Or maybe.
it was in the Arcady Valley.
These guys chasing the
dames are either Gods or
just ordinary people — it
doesn't give the names on the cup. They sure
are tearing after them and the

dames, trying to get away,
took — This
~~the~~ guys got a flute, or
maybe its an obo and
they're going to town.
etc, etc.

After another attack:

> The above is unfair to Jefferson. The great American
> line: Washington-Jefferson-Jackson-Lincoln would
> have been impossible without Jefferson, the French ra-
> tionalist link.

Scott underlined a reference to Eli Whitney, who had contributed to unemployment by inventing the first cotton gin
during a vacation from Yale. "You see," Scott commented,
"it's always Taft or Don Stewart or Archie MacLeish (Yale
men all) who cause trouble!" Scott, underlining *compromise* (in reference to Henry Clay), brought it into current
politics. "Compromise is the word Willkie associated with
him on the Information program." And, on the following
page:

> This attack on Calhoun is excellent—I fully agree with
> him and concur with the more generalized statements
> about the American Period temperament at this point.

Commenting on Charnwood, page 57:

> Here we have irony and condescension—and a certain
> simple misunderstanding thru distance.

Scott sometimes used the films we saw to reinforce
a historical lesson. In my *Lincoln*, underlining "*almost
boundless* western theater" concerning the Civil War, Scott
wrote: "Do you remember Quantrell's Irregular Cavalry
we saw in the picture, who operated as far west as New

Mexico?" Whenever he could get in a bit about his family he did. On page 280, underlining that General Grant had worked in his father's leather store "in *Illinois* and *in gloomy pursuit of intoxication*," he noted at the bottom: "In Galena, Illinois, then thought the coming city. My grandfather, a young Irishman, lived there in 1850 before going to St. Paul." And on page 394: "My father marched with the rebels to Washington and back." The penciled comments were Scott's method of making history alive for me, and also to give himself a sense of belonging, through his reading and through his family, to the "dark fields of the republic . . . borne ceaselessly back into the past."

Milton's "L'Allegro" was moved up to give a change of pace from Lincoln and Walt Whitman. I found Milton oppressive; *Paradise Lost*, a huge battered book with heavily embossed brown covers—where had Frances found it?—and inside, terrifying angels of Hell illustrated by Gustave Doré. Whitman's role was to reinforce my knowledge of and love for Lincoln. Glancing through the huge *Leaves of Grass*, I was relieved that only two poems were marked: "O Captain! My Captain!" and "When Lilacs Last." I liked them well enough, but preferred Edgar Lee Masters' poignant poem on Ann Rutledge, the young girl who had died before she could marry Lincoln: "Bloom forever, O Republic, from the dust of my bosom."

Shakespeare as a poet was difficult. With Scott's help and with deep concentration on the four prescribed sonnets, I understood and loved them and was able to agree with him that this was the best poetry of all, sometimes,

not always, even better than Keats. Encouraged by my enthusiasm, Scott revised the curriculum to include passages
from *Julius Caesar* and *Henry IV* (*I*).

The poems and plays on the list were a growing delight:
Blake's "The Tiger"; I can never forget John Donne's "The
Ecstasy"—"Where, like a pillow on a bed, a pregnant bank
swelled up"—and his "Song" "∴ teach me to hear mermaids singing." I was delighted to recognize so many lines
from Donne in T.S. Eliot—"I have heard the mermaids
singing, each to each." Eliot was, in Scott's boundless praise
for what he considered good, "the greatest living poet in any
language." He had read *The Great Gatsby* three times, Eliot
had informed Scott, adding that the book was the first step
forward American fiction had taken since Henry James. To
have Eliot praise his work so highly sent Scott bounding to
the top rung of happiness. Fitzgerald was not like his literary conscience, Edmund Wilson, who has never, it seems
to me, judged his own work by the praise or lack of it from
others. Scott needed to be told he was a good writer. "They
ganged up on me after *This Side of Paradise*," he explained,
"but the same critics not only praised *Gatsby*, but some,
in retrospect, the first book as well." Scott was still talking in 1940 of his meeting with Eliot in the mid-thirties at
the home of the Turnbulls in Maryland. He had wanted to
impress the poet with his knowledge and appreciation of
his work. As always, he was intimidated by the proximity
to an idol, but he insisted on reading a section of *The Waste
Land*—very movingly, according to Andrew Turnbull. This
new kind of conversational verse was as interesting to me
as it had been for Scott.

To my astonishment, because I assumed they would be
too intellectual for me, I enjoyed Edmund Wilson's essays

in *The Triple Thinkers* and *Axel's Castle* and Mary Colum's *From These Roots*. In this Scott, underlining Longfellow's "A boy's will is the wind's will, and the thoughts of youth are long, long thoughts," commented, "My god! His best line." It was exciting for me to read examples of Verlaine and Rimbaud in French, in the Colum and Wilson books, with the English translations underneath. Scott had his own translation for me of Rimbaud's "Voyelles" in my copy of *Poésies*:

> A black, E white, I red, U green, O blue vowels
> Some day I'll tell where your genesis lies
> A—black velvet swarms of flies
> Buzzing above the stench of voided bowels,
>
> A gulf of shadow; E—where the iceberg rushes
> White mists, tents, kings, shady strips
> I—purple, spilt blood, laughter of sweet lips
> In anger—or the penitence of lushes
>
> U—cycle of time, rhythm of seas
> Peace of the paws of animals and wrinkles
> On scholars' brows, strident tinkles
> On the Supreme trumpet note, peace
> of the spheres, of the angels. O equals
> X ray of her eyes; it equals Sex.

I memorized them all, some in English, some in French, for sheer intellectual joy. Verlaine's "Il pleure dans mon coeur comme il pleut sur la ville," and the four stanzas from Rimbaud's "Bâteau Ivre" ending with "O, que ma quille éclate! O, que j'aille àla mer!" I walked around declaiming the lines as fervently as I had recited poetry and songs at the orphanage. And Eliot's "I grow old ... I grow old ... I shall wear the bottoms of my trousers rolled," and "We have lingered in the chambers of the sea ... Till human voices wake us and we drown." And "Of lonely men in shirt-sleeves, leaning out of windows." The imagery affected me as though I had been blind and was seeing for the first time.

At the back of *From These Roots*, Scott penciled:

Poe influenced Baudelaire (184)
    influenced Rimbaud
    influenced Lafargue (339)
    influenced Eliot.

Verlaine and Rimbaud had led disreputable lives, Scott told me. Verlaine had quarreled with Rimbaud, his disciple, and shot him. He was imprisoned for a year and a half. "Rimbaud deliberately experienced the worst kind of dissipation. He took opium, hoping to break the barriers of human limitation," Scott said. To write a completely uninhibited type of poetry, Rimbaud wallowed in the depths of degradation. "But only as a young man. Quite early in life he abandoned poetry completely and led a respectable life as a white-slave trader in Africa." I was never quite sure when Scott was teasing me. It seemed that so many geniuses drank or took drugs. Edgar Allan Poe had died a dreadful death in Baltimore at the age of forty, "after," Scott informed me, "he was picked up by the police in a drunken delirium." I did not dare say it, but I hoped this would never happen to Scott. I was curious about what drunks actually saw when they were having DTs. Scott assured me solemnly he had seen pink rats that were as big as elephants. I did not care for the poetry of Poe; it was too full of gloom and death and ghosts and decaying houses and I did not memorize any of the poems. Scott's father had introduced him to Poe's poetry when he was a small boy, with "The Raven" and "The Bells." In *This Side of Paradise*, when Amory meets Eleanor he is reciting Poe's "Ulalume" while she is singing a song based on a Verlaine poem. Scott, who disliked poverty, agreed with Poe's statement that he would not have the hero of "The Raven" in squalid circumstances because "poverty is commonplace and contrary to the idea of Beauty." It wasn't the actual money of the rich that appealed to Scott, although he was always in need of it, but the way people like the Gerald Murphys used it, to give grace to their surroundings.

In *Axel's Castle*, in Wilson's chapter on symbolism, I memorized the line Scott had underlined, that one of the principal aims of symbolism was to approximate the indefiniteness of music. You find yourself swaying to such a line. I did not care that these poets were symbolists or romantics, although I memorized this fact against the day of the examinations. What poetry was *called* didn't matter to me. I was interested in what it *was*, and in the lives of Scott's great poets, who, I was sure, could never be dislodged by passing fashion.

We discussed W.H. Auden and some of the modern poets, although Auden was not in *The New Poetry*, which Scott gave me in 1940. "Remember," he wrote on the flyleaf, "this poetry dates from a quarter of a century ago—some of it as far back as 1900. The 'New Poetry Movement' started before the rise of prose fiction here and really faded in the 20's—it had done its work well though as this book proves." Rupert Brooke and Willa Cather were represented;

also T. S. Eliot, Robert Frost, Thomas Hardy, Joyce Kilmer ("Trees"), Vachel Lindsay, Amy Lowell; John Masefield, England's durable Poet Laureate; a large slice of Edgar Lee Masters; Edna St. Vincent Millay, whom I had met with Deems Taylor in Connecticut; Ezra Pound, Carl Sandburg, Louis Untermeyer, and a host of less familiar names. Except for Eliot, I could never be as drawn to them, or even to Yeats or Dylan Thomas, as to Keats and Shakespeare and Shelley and Wordsworth, who were so much longer ago.

CHAPTER EIGHT
THE CURRICULUM CONTINUED

THE THIRD COURSE, "RELIGION AND FICTION," was the easiest and the shortest. Each section had three parts: religion, a novel, and a section of Thomas Craven's *Masterpieces of Art*. The art book is inscribed: "Sheilah from Scott, Christmas, 1939." It was his last Christmas present to me. Among the important novels on the third list were *Portrait of a Lady*, *Anna Karenina*, and *Sanctuary*. "This is a powerful novel," Scott remarked of *Sanctuary*. I was fascinated with the violence and the terrifying rape of Temple Drake by the impotent Popeye and the half-wit Red. Faulkner was born a year after Scott, and they were in Hollywood at the same time, but to the best of my knowledge they never met.

I had read *Look Homeward, Angel* before I met Scott; a friend had praised it highly, and, as usual, looking for a magical formula, I had rushed to buy Wolfe's fictionalized autobiography, hoping I would be transformed immediately into a well-read woman. But the author, going on and on and on, had bored me and I had not finished the book. Scott had me attempt *Of Time and the River* and *The Web and the Rock* with the same result. Scott believed that Wolfe's novels were too long and too verbose. When he had said this in a letter to Wolfe, he received a long answer reminding him that it was just as important to be a putter-inner as a taker-outer. But Scott could not dismiss the burly longwinded Mr. Wolfe. He considered him an important American writer.

"Not Ecclesiast*icus*," Scott wrote above Ecclesiastes on page 775 of my Bible, the Old and New Testaments in the King James version, designed in 1936 by Ernest Sutherland Bates to be Read as Living Literature. After "Vanity of vanities, all is vanity," Scott underlined in the introduction that Hemingway had taken his title *The Sun Also Rises* from the Preacher's line "the sun also ariseth." In paragraph five he underlined the sentence "*See, this is new*," commenting in the margin: "Before the age of science and invention." I memorized all the "times"—a time to weep, to laugh, to mourn, to dance, to love, to hate, for war, for peace. It was as beautiful as Scott had thought when he wrote his daughter in 1938: "Remember when you are reading it that it is one of the top pieces of writing in the world." At one time he considered titling *Tender Is the Night* "The World's Fair," after Thackeray's *Vanity Fair*, which was after Ecclesiastes' "vanity of vanities."

The Book of Job appealed to me less, although Scott, to make it somewhat easier for me, had carefully underlined the names of all the Speakers in part four, with the Voice out of the Whirlwind. Job was depressing, with its interminably long pages, part prose, part verse. I had been punished, sometimes unjustly, at the orphanage and I did not enjoy reading of the same treatment for Job, who was a good man. It seemed to me that God was trying Job's patience much too far. What was He trying to prove?

The Gospel of Saint Mark, Scott informed me, had been

used as a source for the Gospels of Matthew and Luke. Mark seemed mostly interested in miracles, which I have never believed in, although it was a miracle that I was getting the education for which I had prayed. In succeeding years I have reread the Gospels of Mark, Matthew, and Luke and thought both the other books were better than Mark. The Song of Solomon was on the master plan, but not on the course for religion. Neither was the Book of Ruth. We read them for the poetry and the prose, not because of any religious fervor on Scott's part. He had long ago given up his Catholicism. In a letter to Max Perkins about a passage from the Bible in *The Beautiful and Damned* he said: "I do not suppose any but the most religious-minded people in the world believe that such interludes as the Song of Solomon or the Story of Ruth have, or ever had, even in the minds of the original chroniclers, the faintest religious significance."

Renan's *Life of Jesus* was, as I wrote Johnny, realistic, with its rejection of miracles and the supernatural. It had caused a sensation, Scott told me, when it was published in 1863. "Ernest Renan was originally trained for the priesthood." He had repudiated his faith, as Scott had, preferring science and facts. In *This Side of Paradise*: "There were ... sword-like pioneering personalities, Samuel Butler, Renan, Voltaire." His sister Annabel believed these authors had caused Scott to lose his religious faith.

Shaw's Preface to *Androcles and the Lion* was a comical addendum to Renan, which was followed by Lewis Browne's *Stranger Than Fiction: A Short History of the Jews*, published in 1938. There was only one comment by Scott in this book, which has his name on the flyleaf, dated "Encino 1940—January." On page 122, underlining the word *sports*,

Scott wrote: "misuse of word—he means sports-conscious."
I also read *The Story of Budda and Buddhism* by Brian
Brown. An ironic underlining by Scott in the book about
Buddha: "*It is iron's own rust that destroys it. It is the sinner's
own acts that bring him to Hell.*"

The fourth list (part I), "Philosophy and History," was
interwoven with fiction and drama to compensate for the
heaviness of the main subjects. The education was getting
harder. There was some Wells at the beginning to coin-
cide with Jowett's *Life of Plato*, pages 7–20. It was crucial at
this point for me to continue. If I survived the philosophy,
history, and economics, I would finish the courses. After
Chekhov's short story "The Darling," I was ready to tackle
Plato himself, but only thirty-three pages, in the *Apologia*. For reasons I have forgotten, Balzac's *La Peau de Chagrin* was switched with Pierre Louys' *Aphrodite*, which was
ahead of Swinnerton's *Nocturne*, which then had its turn
after Lafargue's *Evolution of Property* in place of *La Peau
de Chagrin*. Scott, at some time in the future, he told me,
would write a modern version of Balzac's *The Wild Ass's
Skin*. There were several projects for "the future," but his
future would be his past before the year was out. *La Peau de
Chagrin*, Scott told me, had been imitated by Oscar Wilde
in *Dorian Gray*, a book he despised, with its author.

Maupassant was used as a brain-soother after the difficult four chapters on church architecture marked in Sartell
Prentice's *Heritage of the Cathedral*. As the subjects became
more difficult, the novels, short stories, and plays were easier: Conan Doyle's medieval novel *The White Company*; ten
short stories from *The Decameron*; Wycherley's sweetmeat,
The Country Wife; the fascinatingly wicked *Liaisons Dan-
gereuses*. Soon after Scott's death I was to win a bet from

a Professor of Logic at Oxford University because I knew that *Liaisons* was by Laclos and he did not. Against a long involved sentence about widows in Balzac's *Succube*, Scott wrote, "My god! What a sentence!" After a comment on Pantagruel, Scott margined: "Panurge and Pantagruel are also heroes of Rabelais." There were Francis Steegmuller's *O Rare Ben Jonson*, Kipling's *Puck of Pook's Hill* with Max Beerbohm's burlesque of Kipling in *The Woolcott Reader*— "Read all you can"—in conjunction with the same period of history. There were dozens of explanations in Kipling's *Puck*, mostly translations of Latin and Roman terms. A centurion was "one who commanded a company of a hundred." Simple, but I hadn't known it. A "cohort" was a battalion (a thousand men). The Roman Eagles "correspond to modern flags"; Caesar had "become the name for all those who aspired to be Emperor." Kipling belonged to Scott's Princeton days and *This Side of Paradise*. In *The Crack-up*, Scott had written: "I have asked a lot of my emotions— one hundred and twenty stories. The price was high, right up with Kipling." During my time with *Puck of Pook's Hill*, Scott wrote his Princeton roommate, Judge Biggs: "Who'd want to live on like Kipling with a name one no longer owned—the empty shell of a gift long since accepted and consumed?"

Scott divided A.L. Morton's *A People's History of England* into sixteen parts, reinforced with the dates in Wells's *Outline*. Morton's *History* revolutionized my political thinking. In my schoolbooks the kings had been good and bad but they had ruled by divine right. Their word, until they were deposed or murdered, and even after Magna Carta, was law. I considered Wat Tyler a traitor and justly killed by the nobles of Richard II even though carrying a flag of truce. Morton removed the blinders. The people had been betrayed. It was amazing that they still wanted a monarchy. I had been right at the orphanage in advocating a republic.

It was part of Scott's method to read the book first, usually making notations or amusing comments, especially in the heavier subjects, to make a break while I plodded through the chapter. Despising the Henri Barbusse version in *The New Republic Anthology* of the collapse of the Roman Empire, he commented: "The man is made as a hatter—after first being obvious." And on the next page, Scott pooh-poohed "A single night of Christianity led to the collapse of the magnificent edifice of antiquity," with "What history!" A non-sequitur message penciled at the back of the *Anthology:* "Let Richard Whitney out. Let Leopold retell the saddest story ever told. How Darrow wept for him. We'll organize ten regiments of pansies, parlor-size."

This was mild compared to his comments on Cowper's "Loss of the Royal George": "If this is not horse dung, then Shakespeare never wrote! F.S.F." And at the end: "It sounds like an insurance report. They may still be able to use the keel!" At the beginning of the appendix to Palgrave's *Treasury*, Scott stated: "Compiled by a Protestant Pansy."

At the end of my Plutarch's *Lives* he pasted a color drawing of a tall Grecian girl with a small man at her feet twanging a lyre, underneath which my professor wrote:

Scott and Sheilah thru the ages. She has taken away his Samian wine. He has just finished painting a pediment and is trying to sooth her with a Lydian air (matchless tone, authentic period design, nearly an hour's continuous entertainment. ADVT.). Her martyred

Scott and Sheilah thru the ages. She has taken away his Samian wine. He has just finished painting a pediment and is trying to sooth her with a Lydian air (matchless tone, authentic period design, nearly an hour continuous entertainment. ADVT.) Her angelic expression is deceitful. She is thinking of the cocktail party for Greece at the Browns's.

expression is decietful. She is thinking of the cocktail party for Greece at the Skouras's.

Scott's inscription inside *Greek History* by C. B. Newton and E. B. Treat reads: "For S.G. For her proficiency in pre-Socratic Philosophy, Hellenistic Anthropology and Trojan Archeology, from her loving Prof, T. Themistocles Smith, Olym[p]ic Games, 1910."

Underlining *lawyers* in Morton's account of the time of William the Conqueror, Scott wrote: "These were mostly churchmen, mostly unmarried, a rather intense lot!" It was easy to understand Morton's opinion of the greedy kings and noblemen of the Middle Ages, with Scott's translation of a popular Latin verse of the time: "The truth is that all the money flies into the hands of the greedy ones." On the margin next to the revolt of the Lords of the North, "Northumberland, Mortimer and March," Scott penciled. "The material for Shakespeare's *Henry IV* and *V.*" The Marian persecutions cited by Morton from Foxe's *Book of Martyrs*, published in 1563, were explained by my painstaking teacher: "i.e. Bloody Queen Mary." And when Queen Elizabeth withdrew the monopoly of selling sweet wines from her favorite, the Earl of Essex, an act that led to his rebellion, Scott noted: "The truth behind Errol Flynn." Against the date of 1629, when King Charles was fighting Parliament, Scott mentioned: "Harvard College founded. No Donegals [to whom I had been engaged] in the first class, but a few Cabotts and Lowells." He had the Harvard date wrong by a year, and of course he had misspelled Cabot and Lord Donegall. Sir Robert Walpole had fallen from office in 1742 and Scott did not overlook this important date: "Princeton founded."

For SG.

Further proficiency in
pre-socratic philosophy,
Hellenistic anthropology
and Trojan archeology
from

Her Loving Prof

T. Themistocles Smith
Olympic Games, 1910

There was an amusing comment by Scott about the
trading situation of England immediately after Waterloo.
Commerce with North America and Europe had declined
because of war, but one good new market had developed—
South America, which was promptly flooded by the British
with all sorts of inappropriate goods. I could see Scott smiling as I read the comment penciled at the foot of the page:
"English teacups were one thing shipped. Some of the Indi-
ans chipped off the handles and strung them on necklaces
to wear around their necks!" Another note in Morton, at
the time of the first Charles of England: "My first American
ancestors, William Godwyn and Phillip Key, emigrated to
Maryland about this time."

Morton—and Scott—went into great detail about the
transformation of the working class from the "beef, bread
and ale standard of living" to a "potato and tea standard"—
"the origin," said Scott, "of fish and chips." Morton quoted
the politician Cobbett's denunciation of tea as "a destroyer
of health, an enfeebler of the frame, an engenderer of ef-
feminacy and laziness, a debaucher of youth and a maker
of misery for old age." Tea?

At the back of my Morton, with Scott dictating, I wrote
down the Kings of England from the Normans, the Planta-
genets, the Houses of Lancaster and York, the Tudors, the
Stuarts, to the House of Hanover and Windsor, Georges I
to V, to Edward VIII and the reigning George VI—some of
which I had of course already memorized as a schoolgirl.

Ploetz's Manual of Universal History, a large dictionary
of historical names, is not on the curriculum, but Scott had
me go through it to reinforce what I was learning. Some of
his comments in the Ploetz: Against Arnulf of Carinthia—
"Finds perhaps midway in career he's not the real heir but

son of serf. Mother had been neurotic promoting herself."
Next to Karlmann in Aquitaine—"Success after lowpoint."
And penciled against Charles the Fat—"Kills buddy trou-
badour who insists on chanting."

The fourth list, part II, included economics. The interrupting novels and drama were mostly about social up-
heaval—Conrad's *Heart of Darkness* (*The Nigger of the
"Narcissus"* and *Lord Jim* were in other sections). Scott envied Conrad his years at sea before he became a writer. "I
have not worked at anything except writing, so I've had to
create my own experiences." When people told him of an
interesting experience, he often paid them to let him use it
in his writing. One of Conrad's lines repeated by Scott: the
battleship "firing into a continent." In his own writing, Scott
told me, he was trying to follow Conrad's precept, to make
the reader see and hear. On Scott's solid gold bar there was
"Ernest's courage and Joseph Conrad's art." As a model to
study he ranked Conrad with Keats. Conrad's *Nostromo*
was on Scott's list of the ten most important novels. When
Conrad was visiting the Doubleday estate on Long Island
in the early twenties, Scott tried to show his admiration for
him in typical Fitzgerald fashion. He roped in his friend
Ring Lardner and they danced with vocal accompaniment
on the lawn in front of Conrad's window. The author, a
year from his death, was ill and angry. His terpsichorean
admirers were arrested for creating a disturbance. Scott's
regard for Conrad had not diminished in 1939 and 1940,
but he had long been cured of Compton Mackenzie, who,
he complained, "wrote 2½ good books (but not wonderful
novels) and then died"—that is, as far as Scott's interest in
him was concerned.

On the flyleaf of *The Octopus* Scott wrote: "Frank Norris

after writing three great books died in 1902 at the age of just thirty. He was our most promising man and might have gone further than Dreiser or the others. He claimed to be a disciple of Zola, the naturalist. But in many ways, he was better than Zola. The time of the events is 1880." After reading Norris, Scott wrote Max Perkins that he had fallen under the influence of a writer who had completely changed his point of view. ". . . I think *McTeague* and *Vandover and the Brute* are both excellent." Scott had become enthusiastic about books on social realism in 1922, when he read *Salt* by Charles Norris, Frank's brother. He was impressed with John Reed's story of the Russian Revolution, *Ten Days That Shook the World*, and recommended it to Scottie in 1940, during the time we were discussing it in the College of One. E. E. Cummings' book, *The Enormous Room*, and Upton Sinclair's *The Jungle*—dedicated to the working men of America—were in his early twenties part of Scott's social-consciousness pattern and were passed on to me in the hope that my strong conservatism would shift to liberalism. It did, with the help of Morton's *History, The Book of Daniel Drew* (the robber baron) by Bouck White; E. M. Forster's *A Passage to India*, Edmund Wilson's chapter on Lenin and literature in *The Triple Thinkers*, and M. Ilin's *New Russia's Primer*, on the flyleaf of which Scott wrote: "A beautiful, pathetic, trusting book—old and young, rather haunting and inspiring like the things read and believed in youth. A sort of dawn comes up over the book all through—too often it illuminates old shapes that our cynicism has corrupted into nonsense. But if our totem-poles can become their girders, so be it." And, at the end of the book: "The N.Y. Times carries a story that the author is in Siberia. I hope it's a canard."

Russian writers figured prominently in every section of the curriculum. Turgenev, Scott told me, was objective—"as I try to be." He considered Tolstoi's *War and Peace* a man's book, although I enjoyed it tremendously, even the dissertations on the Napoleonic battles between the chapters about the aristocrats and the serfs of Russia. Dostoevski was my favorite Russian, *War and Peace* my favorite novel. Chekhov I have always found too vague. I prefer the reality of Ibsen. "You are accepted in a man's world and able to work in it," Scott assured me, "because of *A Doll's House.*"

Scott was extremely interested in my reaction to *The Communist Manifesto.* He might have become a Communist; many intellectuals of the late nineteen thirties veered in that direction and some went all the way. At a small dinner party in Budd Schulberg's house, Scott had taken his host and Ring Lardner, Jr., into another room and discussed Communism with them for an hour. He was disappointed, he told me later. "Nothing original. They are content to follow the party line." I was surprised when I read of Scott's adoration of the rich because during our College of One he was always so vehemently on the side of the poor and oppressed. He detested people like Barbara Hutton, Woolworth Donahue, and especially business tycoons. "I don't know any businessman I'd want to meet in the next world—if there is a next world," said Scott. Members of the Communist Party in Baltimore had had several long discussions with Scott, he told me, hoping he would join the Party. Scott writes of Stahr having a fight with the Communist Brimmer in *The Last Tycoon.* It was probably Scott who had fought the real man with his fists, as ineffectively as Stahr had done. "I could never be a Communist,"

Scott assured me. "I could never be regimented. I could never be told what to write." But the subject was important, and I must be aware of the pros and cons.

Scott's library contained two large volumes of *Das Kapital*, from which I read Section 4 in Chapter 10 of the first volume, on "The Working Day." Because it was so difficult, Scott interspersed it with Henry James's *Aspern Papers* and Beerbohm's short parody, "A Burlesque of Henry James." The Beerbohm "Burlesques" were in my [*Alexander*] *Woolcott Reader*.

My understanding of "The Working Day" in *Das Kapital* was helped by Scott's translations of Latin, French, and even Russian words. He eliminated the entire first page and a half as completely beyond my comprehension, with the bracketed injunction: "Skip. Begin on following page." Where Marx writes of the "small thefts of the capitalists from the laborers' meals and recreation time" and the "petty pilfering of minutes," Scott commented in the margin: "They do this at M.G.M. in a big way; so the secretaries say."

Marx's "The unity of the ruling classes, landlords and capitalists, stock-exchange wolves and shopkeepers, protectionists and free traders, government and opposition, priest and free thinkers, young whores and old nuns, under the common cry, For the Salvation of Property, Religion, the Family and Society," elicited from Scott: "Grand prose." My professor had read all of *Das Kapital*. "The Working Day" was all I could manage then—and probably now. It was culled from the body of the book because Scott knew I would be interested in the early industrial working conditions of my native England.

Mein Kampf—Hitler's alarming bible was not on the

NEW RUSSIA'S PRIMER

A beautiful, pathetic trusting book —
old and young, rather haunting,
and inspiring like the things
read and believed in youth. A
sort of dawn comes up over the
book all through — too often it
illuminates old shapes that our
cynicism has corrupted into nonsense
but if our totem-poles can become
their girders, so be it.

curriculum, but Scott gave it to me to read while it was all coming true before our paralyzed eyes and voices.

An easy course to follow the difficult one: Hendrik Willem Van Loon's sixty chapters of *The Arts*, divided by, as Scott noted at the bottom of the "Art Book and Fiction List," "13 novels, 4 French, 3 Russian, 2 Irish, 2 American, 1 Norwegian, 1 English." The two Joyces—*A Portrait of the Artist as a Young Man* and *Dubliners*—were fascinatingly simple, so different from *Ulysses*, which I tried much later. (*Finnegans Wake* was impossible.) Scott identified with Joyce, who was to outlive him by one year. They had met at the home of Sylvia Beach during the twenties in Paris, and, as usual when his admiration was enormous, Scott was impelled to create a disturbance. To prove his respect, he threatened to jump out of the window. Joyce, by most accounts cold, arrogant, and in spite of his writings somewhat prudish—as I found Henry Miller to be when I met him in Hollywood—remarked to Miss Beach, "That young man must be mad. I'm afraid he will do himself injury." It wasn't always liquor. It was enthusiasm so great that it could not be expressed by words. Scott often bracketed himself with Joyce, asserting they had both aspired to the same heights of craftsmanship. When Mary McCarthy advised Scott to read Kafka during the evening we spent with her and Edmund Wilson, to whom she was then married, he read *The Trial* and described it "as an influence among the young comparable only to Joyce in 1920–25."

There are dozens of notations by Scott in my Joyce novels, mostly his translations from the Latin, and this sometimes discouraged him. In *Portrait of the Artist*, after translating "Pax super totum sanguinarium globum" to "Peace over all the bloody globe," Scott commented in brackets: "All this of course is lowsy Latin." I would not have known. On the flyleaf of *Dubliners*: "Note especially the story 'Counterparts'—and the last part of the story, 'The Dead,' that ends the collection. Scott."

In the Van Loon book, which concerned all forms of art from works of prehistoric man to the impressionism of Debussy, there were two penciled comments. Mine at the beginning: "I am standing on a deserted range at twilight with an empty rifle in my hand and all the targets down. From F. Scott Fitzgerald's Blue Period." I was teasing Scott, who had recently shown me his *Crack-up* stories: he had been worried about my reaction to them. I had thought they were fascinating and beautifully written. Scott's message to me at the back of the book was a guide for the different phases of art. He was pleased when I told him that I thought Van Loon was condescending to his readers, treating them as children. I was just as pleased when he agreed with me.

Now Scott divided a course in music appreciation with ten novels and Graeco-Roman history. As we proceeded from Bach and Handel to Chopin and Debussy and from Schubert to Stravinsky, we also read Plutarch, Gibbon, Froude, Suetonius, and Bolitho, as well as the matching sections in Wells. Frank Norris's *McTeague* accompanied Mendelssohn's violin concerto and James's *The Bostonians* the Brahms Concerto Number 2 in B flat. With so much more recorded music available today at so little cost, the choice might well have been broader, but in 1940 I was lucky in my College of One to be able to range from the *Well-Tempered Clavichord* to *Der Rosenkavalier* and from the *Water Music* to the *Death and the Maiden* quartet.

With the records, I read *From Bach to Stravinsky*; *The*

History of Music by Its Foremost Critics, edited by David Ewen, and a *Music Lovers' Encyclopedia* edited by Deems Taylor and Russell Kerr and compiled by Rupert Hughes. The *Encyclopedia* contained brief facts about all the composers and all the known musical instruments. In addition, I was instructed by Scott to look up the composers in the large one-volume *Columbia Encyclopedia* he had bought me.

It was now necessary to have a record-player. A machine in blond wood arrived from Scott, to match the bookcases, which were also from him. At this time each 78-rpm record cost one or two dollars, depending on the artist, and some of the albums were correspondingly expensive. In those last months of his life Scott had very little money, and the prices of the records often determined the order of buying them. My Chopin records—"Mazurka" and "Études," recorded by Vladimir Horowitz and Artur Rubinstein's "Polonaise"—cost two dollars each. Before playing them I read ten pages on Chopin in Ewen, which of course Scott misspelled as Ewan. His spelling for some of the composers in his "Preliminary List": Bethoven, Menddilshun, Litz. How could he write so well and spell so badly?

The Debussy records—Stokowski's "Prélude à l'Après-Midi d'un Faune" and the Heifetz recording of "Le Plus que Lent"—were each $1.50; the *Iberia*, $5.00. While the *Iberia* was first on the list, I played it last, because Scott did not immediately have the $5.00 to spare. For Tchaikovsky's *Nutcracker Suite*, with Stokowski conducting the Philadelphia Orchestra, and the Concerto in D major with Heifetz, "$14.50 alone" noted my hard-up professor. Von Weber was cheaper: "Invitation to a Dance," $2.00; the overture to Der Freischutz, $1.50. Rimski-Korsakov's "The Flight of the

To Paris   (15.00 & 20.50)
                                                              and 15 (1.00
1. Bach, Handel, Gluck $17.50

4. Haydn, Mozart $20.50

7. Beethoven, Weber, Rossini   17.00

10. Schubert, Mendelssohn $15.50   Meyerbeer?

13. Schumann, Chopin $20.50   ⌈ Chopin, Debussy
                                                                    Ravel

                                                                    Weber, Schubert
16. Liszt, Wagner $17.55   ⌊ Mendelssohn

19. Brahms, Verdi $17.25   (Puccini?)

22. (Strauss) 4.50 (plus Gounod, Borodin [Stravinsky Suites] and
                                    Grieg [Kreisler's dance]

25. Tchaikowski   14.50 (plus Rimski-Korsakoff Borodin Bizet + Moussorgsky)

                                                                   (Franck)
28. Debussy $8.00, Sibelius $9.00

31. Ravel Bolero, Stravinski 15.50   Prokofiev

Bumblebee" ($1.50) was a favorite of Scott's. We smiled at the buzzing, as I still do when it is played, usually as a fast encore by the violinist.

The Haydn Symphony Number 94 ("Surprise," $5.00), Symphony Number 101 ("Clock," $8.00), and the String Quartet in D major ($1.00) were accompanied by this note from Scott.

HAYDN

   I. The big chord in 2nd movement after the pastoral goes off like 21 guns.

  II. The sonata to prove that a young lady couldn't sit through a concert. It ended 9 times and each time she got up.

 III. The Farewell Symphony—each one lights a candle and goes out until only one is left.

Scott's list went on to note prices from Handel's *Water Music*—$3.50—to $13.50 for Beethoven's *Kreutzer Sonata*. Schnabel's *Quintet in E Flat Major* cost $8.00.

On Scott's carefully planned list of prices, the records for my music course would cost him about $200. It was a great deal for a man who sometimes had less than $50 in his bank account. If only I had known.

Music, history, a novel. I had read Evelyn Waugh's *Decline and Fall* when it was published in England. But seeing it now, intermingled with Greek and Roman History, I understood the title for the first time, that the wild twenties of Waugh's England had been a herald of the decline and fall of the British Empire, similar to the orgiastic dissipation of the Romans.

On page 1 of Gibbon's *The Decline and Fall of the Roman Empire*, Scott noted: "It is important to remember that Gibbon wrote this history late in the 18th century (1765—1785) *before* the French Revolution and the Industrial Revolution—when men believed that 'The Age of Reason' had indeed arrived. Yet the stuff is full of irony—especially when he speaks of the Church and compares the rich men of antiquity to those of his time—to the *pretended* advantage of the latter."

I enjoyed Froude's *Julius Caesar*. Previously I had confused Froude with Freud and pronounced the latter "Frood."

The extra pages attached to the curriculum—adapted from Spengler, to be studied in connection with readings on the sixth list—were copied exactly from Spengler's charts at the end of my heavy volume, which I did not read. Like Kathleen's ex-king in *The Last Tycoon*, Scott had departed before we got to Spengler. The last page of the curriculum was Spengler's "Political Development of the Anglo-European World," with its accompanying mixture of epic poems, Shakespeare, Descartes, Michelangelo, Bach, Voltaire, Kant, Marx, Darwin. And the last segment:

CIVILIZATION

(a) 19th Century. From Napoleon to the World War. "System of the Great Powers," standing armies, constitutions.

(b) 20th Century. Transition from constitutional to informal sway of individuals. Annihilation wars. Imperialism.

(c) ???

The question marks were as though Scott were questioning "I wonder what comes next?" The music course was almost completed when Scott died a few days before Christmas 1940. He had told me at the beginning of the music study that he was saving Beethoven for his old age. It was a strange coincidence that he asked me to play the Eroica Symphony while he was making some notes about football on the *Princeton Alumni Weekly*. Soon after it ended, Scott suffered his fatal heart attack. There was still an echo of the music in the room with the afternoon sun through the venetian blinds making patterns on his pale face on the dark green carpet.

I finished the music course, with the history and novels, on my own. But Spengler without Scott was too difficult for me. Everything else in the curriculum was followed faithfully, and a great deal of it has stayed with me—perhaps because of the unusual methods adopted by Scott to insure that I would remember what he taught.

CHAPTER NINE
THE METHOD

IN A DISCARDED VERSION OF *THE GREAT GATSBY*, the hero confesses, "I don't care how much people talk about me, hate me. Just so I could make them admire me, make everybody admire me." This was the Scott of 1924. He had matured greatly in the following fifteen years, but he still enjoyed being the focal point of the few parties we attended. I remember at the home of Frances and Albert Hackett he simply took over the party, sliding down the staircase, inventing games, involving everyone there. He still sometimes felt the need to impress, to extend himself, to be different.

When he decided to give me an education—as the Irish and Scotch pioneers who had struck it rich in the West had done, importing peasant girls to marry, he told me—I soon realized that we would not try to cover the usual courses listed in college catalogues. This education would bear the unmistakable stamp of Scott Fitzgerald. It was not enough to have a good curriculum. There must be a fascinating new system.

There was a question of time. We were both busy people. How many hours a day could we spend on this extracurricular project? There was the great necessity for us both to earn money, especially Scott. He was always short of cash and always trying to make it in a hurry, to pay his bills, so many of them; to send checks to Zelda's sanitarium, to her mother in Montgomery, Alabama, when Zelda was well enough to stay with her; to pay for Scottie's school and clothes, for the cost of her visits to her mother and her friends; then his own living expenses. He paid $60 a month, the top price at the time, to the majestic Negro housekeeper at Encino who created the exotic meals he enjoyed—crab soup, lobster soup, strange salads, frothy desserts, delicious iced tea topped with a sprig of mint. He paid $130 a month to his secretary, which was good pay for a girl in her first job (I was giving mine $25 a week). There were the telephone bills; when he was drinking he would call all over America. The rent: $280 a month at Malibu, $250 at Encino, where we started our College of One. It was a large house with a paneled living room, dining room, and study on the ground floor, as well as a huge kitchen and pantry and a maid's room and bath. Upstairs was his spacious bedroom with a dressing room, bathroom, and balcony, on which he paced while dictating. On weekends I occupied the spare bedroom, its bathroom papered with ancient maps of the Pacific Islands. Whenever I awakened at night, I could hear him walking up and down, up and down. Sometimes he did not sleep until six in the morning, after all the sleeping pills had finally taken effect. Doctors were always coming for one thing or another. One of the early ones—not Dr. Clarence Nelson, who helped him so much in the last eighteen months of his life—charged him $100 a visit when he came late in the evening. This doctor actually encouraged Scott to drink, and one desperate evening I wrote him a letter.

The only way to save Scott is to get him to a hospital where he cannot get liquor. Otherwise you know better than I do what will happen to this very fine person. Everything else is utterly futile and you know it. At present, the situation is ridiculous. He has two nurses and one doctor and he is drinking at least a pint of gin a day! It is also stupid for you to regard me as the villainess in the piece because I cannot bear to see him drinking. I shall definitely not see him again. My absolutely last word on the entire unhappy matter is that if you cannot do anything to save him, in the name of God, find someone who can. Please don't communicate with me in any way.

Scott was paid well when he worked at the studios, sometimes as much as $1,500 a week. But after the first eighteen months (during which he had been under contract at Metro), and especially following the disastrous episode at Dartmouth, when he was unable to continue with Walter Wanger's film *Winter Carnival*, the studio jobs were of brief duration. Usually after a few weeks there would be a problem, a clash with a "feeb"—the producer or director—or the sudden illness that fooled no one. Or he would be fired by executives too content with what Scott described as the "practiced excellence" of hack writers. They were really puzzled by his scripts. When he was hired by 20th Century-Fox to write the film version of Emlyn Williams' play *The Light of Heart*, in which John Barrymore was to play a drunken Santa Claus with a lame daughter (he had dropped her when she was a baby), he thought of a better plan than the one he had originally outlined to Darryl Zanuck. One scene I remember was to have the camera pan to the queue waiting to see Santa, and there at the end of the line, Barrymore in his red suit and cap, blind drunk. As with so many of Scott's film projects, it was never made. When he had presented his new outline to the producer, he was reprimanded: "This is different from what we discussed." Nunnally Johnson, who was brought in to rewrite the story, remonstrated, "It's the best script I have ever read." Joe Mankiewicz, the producer of *Three Comrades*, Scott's sole "credit" in Hollywood, had used the same words, zooming Scott to the heights, but had brought him sharply to earth when he rewrote two-thirds of the script. Scott had been on this project several months and preserved a scrap of his dialogue on the inside back cover of my copy of the Remarque novel:

PAT: There never was much.

KOSTER: Yes, there was. I am very sure when he speaks of you and I look into his eyes that there has been everything.

PAT (*faraway*): For me too—everything. (*Shakes her head in sudden fear.*) Oh, God!

KOSTER: It's been absolutely right, Pat. Even if things were as bad as you say, I'm glad you and Bob have had this happiness together. Bob's my son, Pat. It wasn't in the cards for me to marry and have a home, and one imagined, sometimes, he was my son growing and developing, but it was a pretty bleak world I brought him up in—until you came. Yes, I know you feel that (*breathlessly*) it hasn't been hard to give everything, but you're what the doctor ordered . . .

Between studio jobs Scott would write another Pat

Hobby story for *Esquire*; some of these gave him great amusement. I remember his discussing "Boil Some Water, Lots of It." "This line is said in nearly every movie," Scott said, laughing. Some of the Pat Hobbies he wished he had never written. "There were two in your last editions," I wrote Arnold Gingrich of *Esquire* magazine on December 24, 1940, three days after Scott's death, "he wouldn't let me see them and was quite embarrassed when I asked him to show them to me. He said they were terrible. All of the previously published Pat Hobbies he had wanted me to read." Then, before making a request, I told him about *The Last Tycoon*.

> Did you know he was writing a novel? He was three-fourths of the way through the first draft. It had brilliant passages, but of course he had intended to rewrite. I know the finished result would have been as brilliant as anything he ever published. We'll never know. I tell you this because I hope you will do something that I know Scott would want.
>
> I think you have four Pat Hobbies left. Against two of them—"Two Old Timers" and "Mightier than the Sword"—on the copies of these he had written "Poor." As for "College Days"—this was written during a drinking period, and he did not read it to me so I don't know whether it was as good as the best Pat Hobby or as bad as the worst. I think you still have "Fun in an Artist's Studio" to publish. This one he liked very much. Would it be asking an awful lot of you to refrain from publishing the two Pat Hobbies he had marked "Poor"? And, if you think "College Days" not good, to refrain from publishing that one as well? It breaks my

heart to have people, young people who didn't know how good a writer Scott could be, read those bad ones and say, "Oh, so that was the sort of thing he wrote. I wonder why they made all that fuss about him?"

About a week ago I read the "Great Gatsby" again, and he was a great, great writer. I told him at the time that if he never wrote another line again, his place in literature was fixed for all time on "Gatsby." And, of course, there were passages in "Tender Is the Night" that are the best I've ever read, and I've done a lot of reading.

I'll tell you the story he liked best of all the recent stories he sent you—"Between Planes," which I believe you were going to publish under another name. Of course, there's no need to hide the identity now. I know he would appreciate it if you could publish that one next, because the next story by him that appears will naturally have a wider interest, and I think this one is the best of those you have. I think he quite liked "A Woman from 21," and I've forgotten how he felt about "On an Ocean Wave."

Yours sincerely,
Sheilah Graham

P.S. He had not had anything stronger than Coca-Cola for a year and three weeks.

When I mentioned this to Edmund Wilson recently, he disagreed with me. He believed that everything written by Scott should be published. I now realize that Gingrich was right in publishing all the Pat Hobby stories.

The time Scott gave to our College of One meant that

he earned less money. He never did anything halfheartedly, and the education consumed an enormous amount of his remaining hours, days, and months. When his money situation was critical, late in 1939; when he had been drinking heavily and his agent, Harold Ober, had regretfully refused further advances for the book no one believed he was capable of completing, Scott became his own agent and sold his fine short story, "Babylon Revisited," to an independent producer, Lester Cowan, for the shockingly low price of $1,000. Cowan hired Scott to write the screen play and paid him another $300 a week for ten weeks. The $4,000 gave the producer eternal film rights to the story, whatever kind of films were made from it—no matter where they were shown, to one person or a million. It was the most ruthless contract I have ever read. Cowan later sold the story to Metro with a different script for $100,000, and they produced it with Elizabeth Taylor and Van Johnson, under another title, *The Last Time I Saw Paris*, from the book by Elliot Paul. Cowan still has Scott's original scenario, which was to have starred Shirley Temple (she was eleven at the time) and Cary Grant. On the Fitzgerald market today, it could bring a price in six figures. Mr. Cowan, I was happy to learn, had to pay Scottie $75,000 for *The Last Tycoon*, and another $150,000 to Irwin Shaw to complete the story for the film he plans to produce at MGM. But the $4,000 was a lifesaver. It kept Scott going. It gave him time for his book and for my education.

I was busy with my seven columns a week. This meant going to the studios almost every day, telephoning stars, producers, and agents, chasing news leads, undertaking a lecture tour arranged by my syndicate as a means of keeping in contact with my editors, entertaining the editors when they came to Hollywood with their wives and children, an occasional press junket out of town for the premiere of an important picture—only once in the last year; I didn't want to leave Scott or the education for the various industry functions. Scott came with me to the Academy Awards of 1938. In those days the Oscars were presented at a dinner in the Cocoanut Grove, accompanied by interminable speeches. Completely bored with the proceedings, Scott took out his pencil and notebook and wrote a poem:

THE BIG ACADEMY DINNER

The men were wearier and wearier,
    The women were thinner and thinner,
The speeches drearier and drearier
    At the Big Academy Dinner.

Writers were more and more pensive
    Except for an occasional beginner,
Women were horribly expensive
    At the Big Academy Dinner.

At the Metro-Goldwyn table
    Winner sat next to winner
And cheered as much as they were able
    At the Big Academy Dinner.

Garbo, the lovely barber,
    Cooper, the tall mule skinner,
Had all sailed into harbor
    At the Big Academy Dinner.

But also the pimp and crook,
　　Also the pious sinner,
And none of them got the hook
　　At the Big Academy Dinner.

May the peritone cause me pain,
　　May ulcers puncture my inner
Tubes if I go again
　　To the Big Academy Dinner.

Once we had embarked on College of One, I gave it all the time I could. I employed Jonah Ruddy to cover the banquets, the junkets, and the studios, although I did the writing and the important interviews. Scott and I both enjoyed films—he was avidly studying techniques—and we attended most of the previews. Also we went to the plays that originated in Los Angeles or came from Broadway; that was part of the education. When Maurice Evans came with his complete five-hour *Hamlet*, we studied the play as a preliminary and I was so excited with my new appreciation of the marvelous poetry that for once I too was awake most of the night, reliving the play. We went to the opening nights of *Pins and Needles* and *Meet the People*. What I remember most from them are the songs, "It's Not Cricket to Picket" from the first and "Let's Steal a Tune from Offenbach" from the other. We sang them until we were sick of them.

At the beginning of the education, we continued to dine once or twice a week with Scott's friends. I remember a dinner at Dorothy Parker's home in Beverly Hills. It was raining heavily; her dogs were in the yard outside. Dorothy kept going to the window and exclaiming, "Oh, those

poor dogs!" Driving home, Scott laughed. "It didn't occur
to Dotty to bring the dogs inside." It had been a farewell
party. Miss Parker and her husband were to leave for New
York the next day, but something came up and they did not
go. We heard afterward they were embarrassed because
they had said good-by to their friends. They remained in-
doors all day and went out only at night to walk. Dorothy
was more emotional than intellectual, Scott noted, and did
not forget that she carried "a sting in her tail."

There was a dinner at Herman Mankiewicz's with Margaret Sullavan and Leland Hayward; a visit to another
home—whose I have forgotten—where the guest of honor
was André Malraux; and a party at the Ira Gershwins'—I
had met his late brother on a weekend in Connecticut in
the summer of 1934. We had played tennis in the afternoon,
and after dinner George had sat at the piano and played
all of his music. Now the Ira Gershwins had charades after
dinner—this was during my course on art—and when it
was my turn I acted out Picasso's Blue Period. How pleased
I was when Ogden Nash finally guessed it! Scott had briefed
me on the pronoun, because, he told me, "at charades, they
always ask 'Is it a pronoun?' " He knew I was not sure what
a pronoun was.

Acting things out became very important in the education. We had started with Madame Verdurin in Proust and
we took on some of the characters in the others novels.
During *The Brothers Karamazov*, I was the passionate, tu-
multuous Grushenka, shortened by Scott to "Grue." He was
Alyosha or Yosh. We addressed each other in these terms
without any selfconsciousness. With *War and Peace*, I was
Helene—haughty, cruel; delivery boys and press agents
were intimidated. Scott was the stumbling, bumbling

Pierre. I still have the note he sent me with some flowers: "Helene, je t'aime. Pierre." Later, as Natasha became more mature and Helene more obnoxious, my professor relented and I was Natasha. While reading *Bleak House*, I was Esther Summerson, sweet and loving. At the beginning, he was Mr. Jarndyce; then we both became the Smallweeds. We slumped in a heap, facing each other in our chairs, and alternately shook each other upright as they did. This was a different kind of education. You could never forget the Smallweeds, who prayed against each other. I was Becky Sharp in *Vanity Fair*. He was Rawdon Crawley. For a change of pace, he switched to fat Joseph Sedley, using the same language and making idiotic grimaces.

The acting was not always for my benefit; sometimes it was to help him. When dialogue was difficult, he asked me to act it out for him. When he was writing the staircase scene in *Gone With the Wind* for David Selznick, I was Scarlett O'Hara and he was Rhett Butler. He was fired after two painful weeks because he refused to use all of the Margaret Mitchell dialogue. He had been commanded not to change a word. "They regard her as Shakespeare," he grumbled to me. When he wrote the script of *Babylon Revisited*, he was Cary Grant and I was Shirley Temple; it was sometimes hysterically funny. We were Monsieur and Madame Curie when he was writing the script for Greer Garson and Walter Pidgeon. It didn't help; after a few months, he was replaced.

Scott used a Cockney accent with some of the Dickens. It was atrocious, nothing like Cockney, and made me wince, but as I was more and more in love with him, I found amusing anything he said that was meant to be funny, even the baby talk. Of course, this was unusual baby talk. The war was on in Europe and, walking down Hollywood Boulevard, we stopped to look at the miniature war weapons in the window of a toy shop. Scott squeaked, "Mama, I wanna a bomma." Driving down La Cienega Boulevard one time, he lisped, "On La Cienega, there is a five and ten-ager." Another time he cackled, "Mama, I wanna walk on a floor covered with babies." And, crossing his eyes: "I wanna hear them squish."

We danced to some of the poems. Scott Fitzgerald was not one to make a statement without proving it, and when he wrote that the "Chorus" from *Atalanta in Calydon* was "the dancingest poem," he invented a wooden-soldier dance to go with it. I would follow him around the room, flapping my arms as stiffly as he did. There was a tap dance to "Jenny Kissed Me," and it was not unusual for us to shuffle off to Buffalo to T.S. Eliot's "The Boston Evening *Transcript.*"

The education started slowly: only one novel or play with each portion of history, poetry, philosophy, or music—on the theory that a heaped-up plate destroys the appetite—and never too long with any segment. I was not used to sitting still for long periods, and at the beginning I managed only one or two hours of reading a day. "Read when your mind is the freshest," he advised me. I am a day person, soaring with the sun, drooping as the day wanes. I read at breakfast with my coffee and toast, and during lunch with a sandwich and milk. In the evening, when Scott came to my home, we discussed what I had read for an hour or two before dinner. In the last months, dinner was always a T-bone steak (at thirty-five cents a pound) or lamb chops, a baked potato, and string beans. When his life was calmer, he was less exotic about his food. And he also liked me better. On one tipsy occasion he told his secretary that he preferred the Loretta Young type of good looks to mine. She had a more fragile beauty, he insisted. Another time he compared me with Zelda, to my disadvantage. When he was sober, he felt only pity for Zelda. "If only you and I had met earlier," he used to say. "Zelda and I were wrong for each other from the start." But I might not have liked him at all in those early years of his success. I have never cared for the kind of man he was then, although, if we had met, he might not have been that kind of man. The question is, would he have been as good a writer? He might not have started as a novelist without the compulsion to make money to marry Zelda. While I have always wanted money, it has never meant very much to me. I eloped with Johnny, knowing he was going bankrupt, because I loved him, although it meant ditching a millionaire to whom I was engaged at the time.

The time for reading and discussion was increased as I understood more of what I read and became more interested. We no longer gossiped with our friends about what was happening at the studios. We were almost hermits, completely committed to my education and his book, portions of which he would read to me in the evenings. I was delighted to find that Stahr was falling more and more in love with Kathleen. Before long, my reading consumed three or four hours a day and the discussions were without limit. We talked of the book or the poem I was reading at his home and mine, or when we walked on Sunset or Hollywood Boulevard after dinner. We walked and talked in the lanes at Encino with the overpowering scent of honeysuckle and jasmine in the vast night air. We discussed the books while we ate, while we drove, on the telephone. We often went for weekends to Santa Barbara, which took three hours the way Scott drove his Ford, and we talked of what I was studying most of the way. We had a five-hour conversation on Communism and Fascism when we drove to Bakersfield. We had intended driving to San Francisco for the World's Fair; we were mostly interested in the paintings in the exhibition, the Cranachs and El Grecos. It was hot and Scott was tired, and at Bakersfield we took the train. Someone had a radio, and we heard Anthony Eden announce the evacuation of the British Army at Dunkirk. Scott chose this occasion to give me a history lesson. "Without your army, England would have to capitulate. Now you can fight again," he said respectfully, addressing me as though I were the Queen of England.

With so much reading, it was essential for me to have exercise and relaxation. I have always been an energetic person. In the fall and winter we went to all the football games at the Los Angeles Coliseum. Scott explained the tactics while the people around us smiled and I too became an expert.

For exercise, Scott was content with walking, some shadow boxing, dancing to the poems, and ping-pong. He bought a table and installed lights outside at Malibu and later at Encino, for us to play in the evenings, where he wrote down my remark that the white ping-pong balls on the dark grass looked like stars. We played for money—fifty cents a game—and Scott always made sure I would win, running suddenly to my side of the table after hitting the ball or doing a comical pirouette or crossing his eyes, which made me laugh so much that he would sometimes win a point.

He had played tennis and had been a good swimmer in the years with Zelda, who was indolent in some areas but liked sports. Scott told me she played tennis at the sanitarium with the doctors and that once when she was badly beaten she had sailed across the net and broken her racket on the doctor's head. "After that, they let her win." We weren't sure whether we were laughing or crying.

Scott had cracked his shoulder in 1936, diving from a fifteen-foot board into a pool. It seemed that most of his bones at one time or another had been broken. In our years together he was too tired and ill for tennis or swimming. I belonged to the West Side and the Beverly Hills Tennis Clubs; I played there at least three times a week and always on the estate of Edward Everett Horton (his landlord at Encino) on weekends. Scott sometimes stopped working to stroll over and watch, but he never wanted to play. I was a bad swimmer, and while the only time I saw Scott in the water was at Malibu when he was wildly drunk and he jumped into the ocean fully dressed, he thought it essential to teach me to swim. He paid Mr. Horton thirty dollars a month to keep his pool clean and filled with water. Scott would stand on the shady side of the concrete border of the pool; he was convinced the sun was bad for his TB. (In spite of his hypochondria, he *did* have TB flare-ups, his doctor told me.) I tried to copy his movements, but it was difficult with him on land and me in the water. Scottie was delighted with the pool when she stayed with her father in the summer of 1939. It was her last visit to California and the last time they saw each other. Scottie has always been popular, and there were crowds of nineteen- and twenty-year-old boys and girls from Eastern colleges swimming and diving in the pool day and night to escape the intense heat of the Encino summer.

There is a note in Scott's outline for *The Last Tycoon* about a hot day in Encino: "Last fling with Kathleen. Old stars in heat wave in Encino." It was boiling in the valley, with the heat rising in steamy gray layers. All the shades of the house were drawn and everyone in it was in a state of semi-undress: Scott in the living room, naked to the waist in shorts; Frances in a swim suit typing stickily in the dining room; the maid in her room with, said Scott, "just a towel." There was a sigh of exhaustion all over the house, a desperate gasp for air. After Scott died and I read the note, I thought: No one will ever know what a hot day is like in Encino, because Scott Fitzgerald died before he reached that part of his book. During August and September after Scottie had gone back to Vassar (it was too hot for tennis), I went to the pool every afternoon and stayed until the breeze came up at five o'clock as punctually as the grunion spawned on the beach at Malibu, as Scott described them in *The Last Tycoon*.

Except for my poor swimming, I was sure of an A in physical education. I hoped the grades would be as good in philosophy, economics, and history. To help my understanding of these subjects, Scott underlined words and sentences and explained them. Every Latin sentence was translated, from *Puck of Pook's Hill* to Gibbon's *Decline and Fall*. He frequently underlined difficult and sometimes fairly simple words: interpolations were "inserts"; allegory was "mad," which I don't quite understand. He explained subservience, inoculation, abortive, desultory, nihilism, casuist, umbrage, torpor, sybarite, neophyte, ancillary, misanthrope, phrenology, physiognomist, escutcheon, assiduously, and Anglomaniacs. As I was already a writer of sorts, I knew the meaning of most of the words, but Scott wanted to be sure.

Some of the volumes that Frances found in second-hand bookshops in downtown Los Angeles were old and shabby-looking. Scott dressed them up in thick red or gold paper and labeled them "Encino Edition." All of my Henry James was in red; *McTeague* still gleams with gold, Scott's favorite gold. He put a new cover on my Morton's *History* and titled it "*Sex in Glasgow* by Pru." There was further information on the front: "*Peg's Paper* 1922–23—Chapter XX—Peg joins the chartists and executes the wicked mill owner Foxy Chamberlain. She marries Hal, the young labor agitator, and becomes class conscious."

To help me enjoy the plays and the poetry, Scott initiated a system of what he called "bridges." He bracketed or underlined familiar or forceful phrases. Passages in *King Lear* are marked on almost every page. He changed a sentence in *Lear* to make the meaning clearer: "... and we'll wear out in a walled prison packs and sects" to "so we'll outlast in a walled prison packs and generations." In the margin of Dante Gabriel Rossetti's "The Blessed Damozel" "... and the lilies lay as if asleep along her bended arm," Scott wrote: "FSF—and Lily lay along his bended arm as if asleep." My real name is Lily and he knew this would make me smile.

Certain phrases and sentences in Shakespeare have been repeated so often that they have become beautiful clichés. These are what Scott would search for and have me learn before embarking on the play or sonnet. In *Julius Caesar*, I first became familiar with "Beware the Ides of March"; "This is my answer: not that I loved Caesar less, but that I loved Rome more"; "This was the most unkindest cut of all"; "Cowards die many times before their deaths: the valiant never taste of death but once"—how often I have said this to myself!—and "Friends, Romans, country-men ..." which Scott had first recited when he was five to his father's friends. "It was my father's favorite piece," he said. When he was twelve he had started a history of the United States "with illustrations." "When a teacher told me that Mexico City was the capital of South America, I knew enough to correct her, although my father told me to agree with her—'You don't have to believe it.' "

In *Macbeth*, many well-quoted lines were highlighted by Scott's pencil for me to memorize: "Nothing in his life became him like the leaving it"; "All the perfumes of Arabia will not sweeten this little hand"; "Out, damned spot! out, I say!"; "Yet do I fear thy nature; it is too full o' the milk of human kindness." And in *Hamlet*, "To be or not to be"— the whole of the soliloquy and all of Polonius's advice to his son and some of Ophelia's speeches. I memorized them be-fore reading the plays and when I came to the lines I knew, I could relax on them—as if I were resting on a bridge over turbulent water. The well-worn phrases were my friends, and, after catching an intellectual breath, I could continue into the unfamiliar areas, helped by words that had served as a secure handrail.

Scott employed a slightly different method with lyric poetry. He would repeat certain lines that he loved. The first time he declaimed, "Hid in death's dateless night," from Shakespeare's sonnet "When to the sessions of sweet silent thought," the words had a hard surface that I could not penetrate. Scott's constant repetition isolated each word, and they opened up for me like the screen in

Laurence Olivier's *Henry V*, which doubled in size as he declaimed, "God for Harry! England! and Saint George!" Scott's repetition of a line from "The Eve of St. Agnes," "The hare limped trembling through the frozen grass," revived the bitter chill of my winters at the orphanage, and it was I who was limping through the spiky grass.

"O for a draught of vintage, that hath been Cooled a long age in the deep-delved earth" from "Ode to a Nightingale" was such swinging poetry that I couldn't refrain from saying it over and over as we walked, holding hands, to Schwab's Drug Store on Sunset Boulevard. "To cease upon the midnight with no pain, While thou art pouring forth thy soul abroad In such an ecstasy"—I say these lines to myself in planes when it gets bumpy and I am afraid. "For them the Ceylon diver held his breath, and went all naked to the hungry shark; For them his ears gush'd blood" (Nicole's family in *Tender Is the Night* had been similar rich parvenus) and "Why were they proud, why in the name of glory were they proud?"—both from "Isabella, or The Pot of Basil." When Scott extracted the best lines from the body of a poem they caused a "tireless ratiocination" in my mind that made me eager to read the whole poem or play.

There is one stanza Scott repeated and I learned that can still make me sad, from Keats' "When I Have Fears": "When I behold upon the night's starred face, / Huge cloudy symbols of a high romance, / And think that I may never live to trace / Their shadows, with the magic hand of chance." Keats knew he was dying when he wrote these haunting lines, as Scott knew when he said them to me until they were in my mind forever.

He did not ask me to memorize the poems, but I was like a girl wanting to please a handsome teacher. "She has a fantastic memory," Scott confided to Frances. I have always been able to remember what I like. I can pick pieces of information from my mind, as a good secretary knows where to look in the filing cabinet. During the concentrated time of the poetry course, when Scott came in the evening I barely gave him time to greet me with "Hello, Precious," "Presh," "Baby," "Sheilo," or "Sweetheart." Then I would stand back a pace and recite what I had memorized that day.

The system for the music was to play each side of the record three times consecutively, or until I recognized the theme to the point where I could sing it. At first all I heard was a cacophony of sound, but after playing the record several times I was able to extract the composer's recurring theme in all its forms. Now, instead of greeting Scott with a poem, I sang the music of the great composers. While before I would sometimes get a popular song on the brain—"Top Hat," "Anything Goes," "Night and Day," "Stormy Weather"—now I was da-da-da-ing to Beethoven, Schubert, Bach, Tchaikowsky, Sibelius, and Brahms. These became "our songs." Scott was soon as familiar with them as I was. He sang them with me, sometimes inventing words to fit the music. He had not cared particularly for concerts, although he had attended some with Zelda and the Gerald Murphys, but now we became regulars at the Hollywood Bowl and the Philharmonic in Los Angeles. It was like finding good friends to hear the live orchestra play the works on my lists.

Scott loved the Mozart minuets, but because they were so dainty he was shy of admitting this to Mr. Kroll. In the privacy of my Hollywood apartment we danced the minuet—Scott's quite elaborate version—to the music of

Mozart, reaching up with our hands, bowing and curtsying extravagantly.

We thought Rembrandt was the best painter, in the same rank of genius with Beethoven, Shakespeare, and Keats. My only knowledge of Rembrandt until I studied the art course with Scott had been a statement from Cecil B. DeMille that he had invented the Rembrandt style of camera work in his films—half in shadow, half in light. When we visited the art galleries, Scott was delighted when I was able to recognize the painters before peering at the names. There were many exhibitions at the Los Angeles Museum and we went several times and tried to evaluate the different techniques of Rembrandt, Frans Hals, Brueghel, Manet, Monet, Degas, Cézanne, Van Gogh, Utrillo, Seurat, Renoir, and Picasso. At that time I described people in terms of painting. Dorothy Parker was a Renoir. Robert Benchley was a Frans Hals, Humphrey Bogart was a character in a Hogarth drawing, Donald Ogden Stewart a Grant Wood. Scott was a Dürer. He called me Botticelli's Venus on the half-shell.

This education was alive. It had bones and flesh and blood. It was filling the emptiness that had been inside me. I was looking outward and inward. I was adding and subtracting. Like all converts, I became more devout than the apostle. When the vital Screenwriters election—the right versus the left—was to take place soon after one of Scott's drinking periods and he was feeling shaky, I told him he would go to vote "even if I have to carry you there." This was miles from not knowing the difference between radical and reactionary. But the real leap forward and the deep contentment did not materialize until the last twelve months of his life.

CHAPTER TEN
1940

HE WAS ON HIS FINAL BINGE. IT HAD LASTED LONGER than all the others combined—on and off all through the summer of 1939—and it was completely out of control by the beginning of November. The rejection by *Collier's* magazine of the first part of *The Last Tycoon* had shattered him. He had counted on the money. He was glad to have had Scottie with him during the summer, but his nerves were worn to a hairline strand and there had been great tension. After she left—he had needed to borrow money from Gerald Murphy to pay for her Vassar tuition—he seemed determined to drink himself to death.

I had come to Encino late in the afternoon to find Scott giving his money and clothes to two disreputable-looking men he had picked up somewhere on the road. When I ejected them, he struck me and shouted, "I'm going to kill you." He searched ineffectually for his gun, which Frances and I had hidden on a top shelf in the cupboard in the kitchen. The nurse Dr. Nelson had sent a few days previously heard the shouting and ran hastily downstairs from his bedroom, where she had been tidying up following his rampage through his clothes to give most of them to his new "friends." When she tried to pacify him—"Mr. Fitzgerald, please be calm"—he screamed all the secrets of my humble beginnings I had told him, believing they would be safe with him. And because he was immediately ashamed of having betrayed me, he turned on the nurse and kicked her violently on the shinbone. She was terrified, believing she now had a madman to contend with, and, giving me a despairing look, fled. I knew Scott too well by this time to be really afraid. He was being "the bad brownie" he told me his mother used to call him when he misbehaved as a boy. But I knew I must be careful. In his frustration he *could* become dangerous, and while he guarded the kitchen door to prevent my escape, I called the police without giving my name and told them to come at once, and then he let me go. I almost felt sorry for him. He was so helpless and childish, but I was so ragingly angry all I wanted was to leave as quickly as possible, and this time I would never ever see him again. Soon after I left, he told me later, he tried to commit suicide with an overdose of sleeping pills, but he had become so accustomed to them it had merely resulted in a long and necessary sleep.

I did not see him again until early January 1940, but I continued my College of One. It had become a way of life for me. It was harder doing it alone, but I had long conversations on the books with Eddie Mayer, Irwin Shaw, Benchley, Buff Cobb, and all the clever people I was seeing again.

When I returned to Scott, it seemed that we had both come of age. We would have almost a year of quiet happiness. There were no more fights, no more swearing, no more drunkenness, although Miss Kroll is sure that, when I went to Dallas in September for the premiere of Gary Cooper's film *The Westerner*, Scott took her brother, Morton,

with her to Victor's restaurant in Hollywood, where he
downed a whole bottle of wine. She is sure it was 1940, "because afterwards we went back to his apartment in Hollywood, where he drank some Scotch and I was terribly upset
because he had been on the wagon so long." Nineteen-forty
was the only time except in the beginning, at the Garden of
Allah, that Scott had an apartment in Hollywood. He had
left Encino in May 1940; we had decided the heat of another
summer in the valley was impossible. "I was worried that it
was the start of another drinking period," Frances told me.
According to Frances, there were some other times in 1940
when Scott drank hard liquor. I am not convinced she has
her dates right. Dr. Nelson assured me that to his certain
knowledge Scott did not drink in the twelve months before
he died. Frances, who adored him, believes that he did. At
Encino she had been made to put the empty bottles in a
burlap bag and drop them over Coldwater Canyon on her
drive home. "When he lived in Hollywood, there was no
reason for me to drive over the Canyon, so the bottles were
put in an ordinary bag and placed with the garbage in front
of the apartment house. He was quite alarmed one evening
when you accidentally kicked the bag as you were walking
to his car. He was also amused and told me he would have
liked to share the joke with you."

So it could be true that he was drinking in 1940. If he
was, he had won a greater victory than I knew. Previously,
once he started to drink, he could not stop. It had been
like that all his life. A few drinks today, twice as much tomorrow, and on and on until the collapse. Then the drying
out period; sober for a few weeks or a few months; then
he started again. But except for the night I was away in
September, I saw him many hours of every day, and he

seemed completely sober. I often wondered whether he would drink again when *The Last Tycoon* was finished, and I sometimes hoped he would go on writing it forever. But if Frances is right, it wouldn't have mattered. It is all right to drink if you can stop when you have had enough. Perhaps he was in control of his drinking then because he had no valid reason to get drunk.

Like Cooper, the "tall mule skinner," Scott had sailed into a harbor of sorts in this last year of his life. He had come to terms with himself for almost the first time. It was a calm year, a year of stability. He was not trying to impress anyone; he could relate to the normal. Being admired was not as important to him as finishing his novel. He was no longer fighting what he could not change. He still wrote loving letters to Zelda; they continued until the week before his death. But he had lost the unbearable guilt that had caused him to drink so fiercely whenever he visited her. He knew he had not caused her insanity, as her family had accused him of doing. He knew she would never get much better, but it was possible, the doctors told him, that she could in time live quietly with her mother in Alabama. He would always take care of her and always love and pity her, but it was over and the knowledge brought him peace.

Scottie was doing better at Vassar. She was off probation. He wrote in March 1940: "I was incredibly happy that the cloud had lifted." He was proud that she had written a play for the college and two short stories for *The New Yorker*, although he did not want her using her name of Frances Scott Fitzgerald. It was too similar to his own, and he was not ready for a "hungry generation" to tread him down. It was understood that she would not come to Hollywood again until the book was finished. He now realized that he was unable to cope with the problems of being a father except at long distance. His misgivings that Scottie would become a delinquent daughter were disappearing; her letters were proof of her growing maturity. He was ecstatic when she became an enthusiastic Democrat in her sophomore year. "She has made the vital leap to responsibility," he exulted.

I had rarely interfered between them except in my role as buffer, but now I told Scott, "You owe it to your talent to stop worrying over Zelda and Scottie. If you want to be among the great writers, you must have more important output. Keats and Shelley died young, but they had written so many wonderful things. You have wasted so much of your life. You have written stories that have embarrassed you. You must give all the time you have left to your writing." He put some of this in a letter to Scottie: "I wish now I'd *never* relaxed or looked back, but said at the end of *The Great Gatsby*: I've found my line—from now on, this comes first. This is my immediate duty. Without this I am nothing." He would, of course, always be concerned about his wife and his daughter, but he did relinquish a great deal of the anxiety.

As for me, he knew I had accepted the fact that in all probability we would never be able to marry. He was a conventional man at heart, and he would have preferred to make me his wife. Stahr had not planned to marry Kathleen at the beginning of *The Last Tycoon*, but he was getting more and more in love with her and this had changed the focus of the novel. Shortly before his death Scott wrote to Max Perkins, asking him to return the chapters he had already sent him, as some of the material was no longer valid and he planned considerable changes. I was no longer "punishing him with my silences." We loved each other, and that was enough for me. If I lived forever, I could never pay my debt to him for the love and education he was giving me. We had enormous respect for each other. What we had together could not be measured by a wedding ring. I was aware of my good fortune. How many women ever have a Scott Fitzgerald? He could never be promiscuous. He idealized women. It was necessary for him to have *the* woman, and, especially in the last year of his life, I was the woman. If we could not marry, it was a comfort to him that he was doing something extraordinarily valuable for me in our College of One. I've heard teachers say, "If I can reach only one of my pupils, I will be satisfied." Scott reached the whole class.

He was annoyed with me once or twice in that last year. He had come to my apartment and discovered I was reading Mortimer Adler's *How to Read a Book*. "But this will make you hate reading," he stormed, grabbing it from my hands. I had to confess that *How to Read a Book* was hard to read. He was sarcastic when I told him that Lew Ayres, the actor, had told me on the set of *Doctor Kildare* that he was plowing through "The 100 Great Books" as lately photographed on three shelves by *Life* magazine. "He won't learn a thing from them," my jealous professor assured me. Without telling me, Scott checked *his* list against theirs: "5 in the first row, 6 in the second, 10 in the third—a total of 21 books." I found this list later at Princeton labeled: "Progress in 100 Books."

He was happier in that last year because of the months working on "Babylon Revisited" and *The Last Tycoon*. He had given up the idea of wanting to conquer Hollywood.

When he had arrived in the summer of 1937, he had been full of dreams that this time he would beat them, he would force them to make films his way. "Movies can be literate as well as commercial," he was sure. He had a daring idea. "Why can't the writer also be the director? One man in control from the inception of the film to the finish." This is quite usual now, but Scott was laughed at when he suggested it in 1937. The system of relays of writers on each film had disillusioned him long before that last year. It was all beyond his control, and what was the use of writing the best he could when the chances were almost certain that someone would rewrite everything he did? With each job, his enthusiasm had diminished.

In the spring of 1940 he wrote to the Gerald Murphys: "My great dreams about this place are shattered." And in September: ". . . I find after a long time out here that one develops new attitudes. It is such a slack *soft* place that withdrawal is practically a condition of safety . . . everywhere there is, after a moment, either corruption or indifference." However, at the end of this letter he felt "a certain rebirth of kinetic impulses—however misdirected." "Isn't Hollywood a dump?" he wrote a friend in the summer of 1940, "in the human sense of the word? A hideous town pointed up by the insulting gardens of its rich, full of the human spirit at a new low of debasement." When *The Last Tycoon* was finished, we would leave Hollywood and never return except for a great deal of money for his stories or scripts. Now, of course, his work is earning the "great deal of money" he once longed for, and at least the irony of these posthumous rewards is softened by the fact that he left a living heir.

Scott was so sure we would leave Hollywood "and

travel" by the time I had graduated from the College of One that early in December he started to worry about a job for Frances Kroll. "What would you do," he asked her, "if we should go away?" Frances was twenty-one and not a bit worried about the future. She has long since married and has two teenage children.

Scott was having minor heart trouble early in 1940, and we did not know about it until December, when it was too late to save him. In a letter dated February 7, to Dr. Nelson, he mentioned that he was being more active "than at any time since I took to bed last March. I suppose that my absolutely dry regime has something to do with it, but not everything. Oddly enough, the little aches around the elbow and shoulder return from time to time whenever I have had a great orgy of cokes and coffee." The aches and pains in his arms had increased when we drove to Del Monte, three hundred miles north, between Los Angeles and San Francisco, for the two weeks of my vacation in June, and we still did not know it was his heart. He was irritable, complained of feeling ill, and remained in his room during the day while I read and read. He would feel a little better in the evening and we could discuss my reading quietly.

I did not know it, but he was poorer then than he had ever been in his life. After his death, there was $706 cash in hand, Frances Kroll wrote Judge Biggs; $613.25 would go for burial expenses: "casket and service $410; shipping $30; city tax $1.50; transportation (to Baltimore) $117.78." His worldly goods consisted of

    1 trunkful of clothes
  . 4 crates of books
    1 carton of scrapbooks and photographs

1 small trunk with some personal effects—the Christmas presents sent him, personal jewelry (watch, cuff links), several scrapbooks and photographs
2 wooden work tables, lamp, radio

Is this how a man ends?—a few crates "dumped to nothing by the great janitress of destinies" (from the brief verse found in his desk after his death).

The cash balance had sometimes been less when he was alive. In July 1940 he wrote Zelda to hold off cashing a check because his credit in the bank was only $11. It might have been at this time that he listed the possible monetary value of his first, sometimes autographed, editions. He expected to realize $25 from nine autographed Mencken books (some firsts); $5 from Tarkington's *Seventeen* (autographed); $5 from Dos Passos' *Three Soldiers* (with autographed card); two books by Charles Norris (autographed), $15; $2 from *Jurgen* (autographed); $3 from *Emperor Jones* (first). "400 books," he wrote, "range 10¢ to $1.50, average 40¢. Probable value of library at forced sale $300."

He seemed better when we were back in Hollywood. The books he loved were still in his apartment, his secretary was available, it was easier for him to work. He thought he could finish the first draft of the book by the end of the year.

During those last months I did my weekend reading on the balcony of his top-floor apartment or in his living room, sitting on what he called his "vomit-green" sofa, while he worked on the desk across his knees in the bedroom. The quietness was sometimes disrupted by the huge woman in the opposite apartment, who earned her living screaming and laughing for actresses on radio. She seemed to be *always rehearsing*—except in the early morning, when she exercised her dog on the roof immediately above Scott, causing him to write an anguished letter to the landlady: "... I know dog racing is against the law in California, so thought you'd like to know that beneath the arena where these races occur, an old and harassed literary man is gradually going mad."

But mostly he was content. He was delighted when Frances Kroll informed him that her younger brother, Morton, and his friends were reading Fitzgerald in college. He had thought he had been forgotten long since by the new generation. He was always very sensitive and easily deflated. When he telephoned Norma Shearer to tell her that Stahr in *The Last Tycoon* was based in part on her late husband, Irving Thalberg, she did not return his call. She had been a good friend on his previous visits to Hollywood. "She doesn't want anything to do with me," Scott said resignedly, after writing her a letter that she did not answer.

His unswerving regard for Hemingway as a writer had diminished after reading *For Whom the Bell Tolls*. "It's not up to his standard," he assured me. "He wrote it for the movies." Nonetheless, it had become a habit to prostrate himself before Hemingway, who had inscribed the copy: "To Scott with affection and esteem." He wrote Hemingway a glowing letter, calling it a fine novel and frankly envying him the financial success that would give him the freedom to write as he pleased. In that last year he complained that "Hemingway has become a pompous bore." Zelda was sure that Hemingway was a homosexual. It had been hate at first sight between them. She was suspicious of a man with such an obsession about physical bravery. She was sure he had been in love with Scott. Scott's time was more limited than

Hemingway's, but Scott had the better end. There was no drinking, no insanity, no suicide. And great hope. Hemingway believed he was finished as a writer. Scott was working on a book. He might have been surprised that critical posterity has placed him on a pedestal as high as his idol's. But he might not have been. He knew that his last book, about Hollywood, would be better than Hemingway's story of the Spanish Civil War.

CHAPTER ELEVEN
LESSONS IN WRITING

IT HAD NOT BEEN ENOUGH FOR SCOTT TO EDUCATE me. He wanted to improve me as a writer and even on radio. "You will never be successful until you have had a success," he said, somewhat ambiguously. I was a disaster on radio, with my early British accent, and the scripts he rewrote for me did not help; they were far too literate for the average listener to Hollywood gossip. Half the time the audience didn't know what I was talking about even when I was talking about Clark Gable. But I was a writer by trade, and in this area Scott believed I could be improved.

He decided I had a good ear for dialogue, which I do not have. I could never be a John O'Hara and get down exactly the way they seem to say it. But Scott was sure I could write a successful play. "We'll do it together," he announced one day. The topic? "It must deal with something you know." I didn't know much besides being a movie columnist. The play, Scott decided, would be about a pretty reporter in Hollywood who was always in hot water with the stars, which in fact I was. We both liked the name Judy. He had used it for his heroine in "Winter Dreams"—Judy Jones. He was under contract to MGM at this time and trying to prove himself a screenwriter. The terms of his contract gave everything he wrote to the studio. Our project must be secret. Scott's cover-up name for the play was *Institutional Humanitarianism*. Realizing I would not understand *Institutional Humanitarianism*, we privately called our play *Dame Rumor*. He was too busy to do more than edit what I wrote. Scott had already written a play, *The Vegetable*, about a postman who dreams he is President of the United States. It had closed in Atlantic City without coming to Broadway. Moss Hart and George S. Kaufman were in the audience at Atlantic City and later they came up with a similar idea—*Of Thee I Sing*. "Someone starts it, then someone else comes along, adds to it, and makes money," said Scott, quoting Picasso. As I knew nothing about playwriting, Scott bought me George Pierce Baker's *Dramatic Technique* and instructed me to study it before starting. "Underline what you consider difficult or important," said my professor. The only paragraph I apparently considered worth discussing: ". . . he cannot write a successful play until he has studied deeply the *psychology of the crowd* and has thus learned to present his chosen subject so as to gain from the group which takes from the theatrical public the emotional response he desires." A pained Fitzgerald disassociated himself from my underlining by writing on the margin: "S.G.'s marking . . . You have marked as advisable the attitude to which you are already prone. Journalism with its accent on circulation has made you cater to 'public taste' in other writing. FSF." I got the message. After a prologue and two dreary acts corrected rather hopelessly by Scott, we abandoned the play.

There was still the hope that with Scott's guidance I could succeed as a writer. My prose was stilted and

conventional, but with practice he was sure I could be
loosened up. I would never be as good as his editing of my
stories when I gave them to him for his approval. The first,
the original "Beloved Infidel," a 5,000-word story written
in the summer of 1939, was something quite different after
Scott's pencil had cut through it. It was about our meeting
and our life together. I had made him a successful painter
in my story, as Zelda had in her fictionalized autobiography *Save Me the Waltz*. His weakness was gambling. He
had a son. Scott changed the name from John O'Brien to
Carter O'Brien. Benchley was disguised as Douglas Taylor.
I had Douglas writing for a smart magazine. Scott changed
it to "He was a child of repeal; once he had done ecclesiastical interiors—now he did modernistic bars with a homey
touch of the ecclesiastical." Carter's wife, Alicia, "was dead
six years now." Carter had been rumored "living with a
brood of native women and children in a South Sea Island."
Scott turned it into "living as a cannibal ..." My name in
the story was Mara Mackenzie and I married Carter. Much
of what I wrote was eliminated by my teacher of English.
Words were added that made a difference. "Carter took
a long time to light a cigarette." Scott inserted "shy" after
"long." Mara, I wrote, had "a cream skin as fine as smooth
notepaper." Scott gave her a skin "like peach-colored notepaper." Where I had Carter say "Like hell I will," Scott made
it "In a pig's eye." It was the same as the real-life story. The
meeting. The mistaken identity. The arrival of his son. The
dancing. The pursuit by Mara, whose "thick yellow-brown
hair tickled his chin." Scott colored her hair "dark gold."
In talking to Carter of her ex-fiancé, George, the Earl of
Mulhaven, Mara "moved her head backwards and tossed
George out of her life." Scott did it more effectively: "She

dropped a match over the table's edge and tossed George out of her life." He cut such purple prose as "... passion dropped them into a delicious whirlpool." I used a line I had said to Scott: "I'd like to walk into your eyes and close the lids behind me." He did not cut that, but he had her *say* it instead of *whisper* it. Instead of " 'I'm going out to-night—now,' he told her defiantly," it was " 'I'm going out,' he said, killing the fly on the pane." I did not omit Scott's joke about having a twin brother. In the cafe at Metro, Scott had confused the waiter by saying, "That was my twin, Irish Fitzgerald." In the first "Beloved Infidel," the twin was Brien O'Brien. Of course Carter gave Mara books to read—"for example, Proust." The ending, a foretaste of Scott's sudden death, can still make me weep.*

After an embarrassing encounter on the studio set with Constance Bennett, Scott advised me to put the incident into a short story, which I titled "Encounter on Parnassus." (It was during my study of Greek history.) Scott considered the title pretentious and substituted "Not in the Script." Reading his corrections, I was grateful, but wondered when, if ever, I would write really well.

Scott could never remain uninvolved when it concerned the written word. When I agreed to undertake a lecture tour in the early autumn of 1939 to tell the people of Boston, Cleveland, Louisville, St. Louis, and Kansas City about Hollywood, I typed out what I thought they would like to know—the glamorous lives led by Loretta Young, Spencer Tracy, Joan Crawford, Robert Taylor, Clark Gable, Carole Lombard, Barbara Stanwyck, etc.; how kind they were, how happy, how charming, and all the latest gossip. I had a story

---

*The story with Scott's corrections appears as an Appendix.

about Gary Cooper; he had had a fight with Sam Goldwyn, who had threatened to sue him for $500,000 if he did not make a certain film, accusing him of throwing hundreds of people out of work. "I'll never forgive him," Cooper said. But he did, and a year later, at the premiere of *The Westerner*, you'd have thought they were the best friends in the world. There was a story about Charles Boyer, then at the height of his fame and his mistrust of press agents and the public. The first time he met the press agent of his current film, he told him flatly, "We are not going to get on." He was startled when the man replied, "No, I don't think so." When a fan-magazine writer asked for his autograph, he replied suspiciously, "Is she going to publish it?" These stories were in my lecture, together with some anecdotes about how certain stars had landed in films. It was all very light and frothy, although I studied up on the technical side of film-making in case I was asked questions at the end. I knew nothing about the actual machinery, cameras, etc., for the making of films.

When Scott read my lecture, he frowned and asked me, "Do you really believe they will be interested in this?" I had to admit that I wasn't sure. And that I was extremely worried. "Then why did you write it?" he demanded. "Here, let me have it." A few days later, he presented me with my lecture. But it wasn't mine. It was all his. He had rewritten it completely. "You can give them the gossip when you answer questions after the lecture. But you are an important person. You are coming to them as an authority on Hollywood. You must explain the part films play in their lives in all areas. They have a kitchen the way it is because that is how they saw it in a Norma Shearer movie; they make up and dress the way they do because this is how

they see Joan Crawford on the screen. I have kept some of
your ideas, such as the difficulty of finding a husband in
Hollywood, but that is far less important than explaining
the enormous value of the director. The stars are merely
puppets who dance to his tune. Without the director, there
would be neither stars nor films. Now, let's rehearse the
lecture. I have written it carefully, and I want you to read it
carefully. If you follow what I have written, you will have a
success." I read it, after several false starts, to the audience
of three—Scott, his secretary and his maid—to encourag-
ing laughter and applause initiated by Scott.

The lecture in full follows. Today it may seem little
more than a series of faded clippings from an old magazine. However, the words are entirely Scott's and they show
how closely he attempted to identify with me and my professional strivings. The careful reader will also discern between the lines and from the selection of details a good
deal about Scott's own attitudes toward Hollywood and the
movies as both craft and industry.

THE LECTURE

A few months ago I visited the enormous back lot of the Gold-
wyn studio. The picture was *The Real Glory*—the scene a Phil-
ippine village on the banks of a swift river. After a minute of
absolute silence there was a quiet command from the man
sitting under the camera. This was echoed through a loud
microphone by his assistant—"All right, we're rolling"—and
then a wild uproar filled the air. Filipinos jumped to the walls
of the village, rifles crackling; screaming Moros rushed from
the jungle; men were catapulted through the air from bent
trees; David Niven died at the feet of Andrea Leeds; and down

the raging stream came Gary Cooper on a raft. "Cut," said director Hathaway quietly. "Print it."

In the sudden lull I said, "It must be wonderful to be back of all this. It must give you a great sense of power." A rueful expression came over Hathaway's face. He reached down and turned up his shoe for my inspection. The sole was worn through to its last layer. "You can have the power," he said. "I'd like time to get a new pair of shoes." (*Pause.*)

On the stage the director is merely the man who says, "Now, Miss Cornell, you cross left at this point. You'll have an amber spot following you."

The duties of the motion picture director are on an infinitely grander scale. From the first day of shooting until the word "printed" is uttered after the last take, he *is* the picture. *He* is its life, its *heart* and its *soul*.

The actors may have to do scenes which have no meaning to them. For instance, they may have to do the last scene before the first because it was more economical to build the set for the last scene first. But the director can *never* be in the dark. He must know at every moment and at all times just where his story is, how it feels, how it looks. He must know just how this scene will dovetail with another scene to be taken on location two weeks hence.

Often the director's work begins long before the first day of shooting. For example, director Henry Koster and producer Pasternak are crosssing the Universal lot. They want a picture for a girl. Koster has read somewhere that three girls are more trouble than a sack of fleas. He says, "Let's make a picture about three girls."

Pasternak agrees and decides that the writer will be Adele Comandini because when Pasternak was a waiter in a studio cafe and she was a secretary, she always left him a dime tip.

The first blow is when the two are told that their leading lady is an unknown little singer named Durbin. (*Pause.*) All they've got now is the idea, the kid, and a budget of $260,000, which is small change in Hollywood.

It might seem that the writer now takes over, but that's not quite the case. A writer's instinct is to think in words. The director has got to work with the writer and turn the writer's words into visual images for the camera. We can do without speeches, but we've got to see, for on the screen, *seeing* is believing, no matter what the characters say.

It's rather interesting to watch the different methods of the different directors. You've all heard of the famous Lubitsch touch? I was introduced to it in a rather unusual way. I was on the set when Lubitsch was directing *Ninotchka.* (*Pause.*) Garbo was home that day with a cold. I said hello to Mr. Lubitsch. Whereupon he kissed me on the cheek. And then, for no reason at all, we both tried to sit on the same chair at the same time. Now, he's a little man, I'm a big girl, and the chair was very rickety—so it was rather a painful experience for both of us. (*Pause.*) I've since wondered whether Lubitsch did the same thing with Garbo, and that's why she laughs so much in *Ninotchka.*

John Ford is inclined to be very sarcastic when he's making a picture. I remember going on the set when he was directing *Mary of Scotland* with Katharine Hepburn. The way those two insulted each other was nobody's business. I enjoyed it thoroughly until he suddenly saw me and said, "And how is little Poison Pen this morning?" It's not all fun being a movie columnist.

When Frank Capra made *Mr. Deeds Goes to Town* he suddenly got the idea that when Mr. Deeds' train pulls out for New York and the serenading band has reached its full pitch, he'd turn his camera on the *band*, move it to a close-up, and there, sending himself off with a *terrific* trombone serenade, show Mr. Deeds. (*Pause.*)

If you remember that, you probably think of it still with amusement. But you probably have forgotten that when the audience *saw* Gary sending himself off, their appreciation was not only hilarious but, from that point on, they felt that they *knew* Mr. Deeds better than they would have from a hundred speeches.

The director must aim for such moments at all times. If at any time during the unrolling of the eight or nine reels of a feature picture the director allows one minute of relaxation to his audience, one minute when they're not emotionally held, he's almost certain that he's directed a turkey—in other words, made an expensive mistake.

When you're reading a book and you come to a dull description or to some difficult technical stuff, you skip; if your husband comes to the part about how beautiful Sally looked in her new coachman's hat, *he* skips. But in a moving picture you and your husband have got to *sit* there. So, there can be no uninteresting parts, nor even any highly complicated parts. Everything has got to be simple, forthright, and compellingly interesting.

While most great pictures like *Captains Courageous*, *Birth of a Nation*, *The Good Earth*, and *Mutiny on the Bounty* have this enormous pictorial quality—we are absorbed in seeing rather than hearing—this accent on the visual need not mean we have to blow up a city or have schooners sailing the seven seas. The focus may be on something as small as the famous "kitten and boots" gag in Harold Lloyd's *Grandma's Boy*. You may remember that Harold Lloyd had greased his boots with a special ointment which proved unexpectedly attractive to cats, and at the crisis of his love affair, sitting on the sofa with his girl, a family of kittens kept licking at his boots. (*Pause.*)

Gone With the Wind had three directors in as many months. First there was George Cukor. He had directed *David Copperfield* and *Little Women* for Selznick, so he seemed a natural choice for *Gone With the Wind*, which was another attempt to put a long novel on the screen.

Now Cukor likes to direct women. In fact, he likes to direct women so much that he's liable to slight the male star—in this case Clark Gable. It was rather funny to hear Selznick telling one of the seventeen writers who worked on the script, "Look, don't let Scarlett romp all over Rhett Butler. George will try and throw everything to her. You and I have got to watch out for Clark."

Shortly after this, George comes suddenly into Selznick's office. He looks worried. He says to Selznick, "Do I understand we start shooting tomorrow?" "Yes," says David. "But we're not ready," says Cukor, adding that he wants new scenes for Scarlett's arrival at Aunt Pitty's in Atlanta. "Then we'll just have to work all night," Selznick replies. One of the current authors on the picture [Scott] groans and telephones his fiancée not to expect him for dinner. The conference begins.

"What worries me," says George, "is the character of Aunt Pitty."

"What's the matter with her?" says Selznick.

"She's supposed to be quaint," says Cukor, who is the brain behind the camera. "That's what it says in the book."

"That's what it says in the script too," says Selznick. He opens the script and reads: "Aunt Pitty bustles quaintly across the room."

"That's just what I mean," interrupts Cukor. "How can I photograph that? How do you 'bustle quaintly across the room'? It may be funny when you read about it but it won't look like anything at all."

They argue about this question for three long hours, and the two writers try desperately to *make* Aunt Pitty funny and not just *say* she's funny. Which are two different things.

By midnight, Cukor and Selznick fire one of the writers. The other writer is sent home and immediately a telegram is dispatched saying that he too will not be needed any more [Scott]. Next day, two new writers come on. By noon George Cukor, having directed the first scene for *Gone With the Wind*, hands in his resignation. (*Pause.*)

Very much perturbed by the whole situation, Mr. Selznick, who grew up with pictures and has very strong opinions of his own, turns to his father-in-law's studio—Metro-Goldwyn-Mayer—and asks for the loan of Victor Fleming, who's a man's director.

Fleming made *Captains Courageous* and *Test Pilot*. He's a huge man, six feet two, and full of immense physical vitality, like all the directors. That is *one* thing that they *must* have. Also they must be iron-nerved, they must sleep at night. Let *actors* get the jitters, let *producers* go up in the air, as Mr. Gold-wyn is so often accused of doing—and does. Let writers go into temperamental fits. The *director* must be the strong man. The organization of victory is *his* fight against time, against human vanities, against luck—which is the story of every big picture. (*Pause.*)

Victor Fleming comes, bringing with him two new writers. The two writers Selznick has engaged only that morning are hastily put out of sight—two more leaves have "Gone with the Wind."

Victor Fleming is a producer's favorite. Because he's so softhearted and good-natured. Producers will beg him to make *just* this *one* picture, and they promise him on their word of honor that next year he can take a whole week off. When Fleming reminds them gently that's what they said last year, the producer sobs. "It isn't for me that I ask this favor. I've got plenty of money. It's for the dear old company."

Whereupon, Victor Fleming sheds a furtive tear, sighs, realizes he's caught. He phones his wife that she might as well go on the trip to Bermuda without him. He will try to get into wireless communication with his children during the next month. And then the studio gates close behind him. (*Pause.*) (*Confidentially:*) I was once in love with a director, but I couldn't get him to marry me. He was *just—too—busy.* At least that's what he said. (*Pause.*)

In the case of *Gone With the Wind*, Victor Fleming was too kind for his own good. After the picture was three months in production, he broke down. The doctor told Selznick that unless Fleming got three weeks of absolute quiet, even this fine adaptable mechanism—which in the morning could direct the action of two thousand extras, and in the afternoon decide on the color of the buttons on Clark Gable's coat and the shadows on Vivien Leigh's neck—even Fleming had fallen a victim of that great Hollywood vice, overwork.

By this time Selznick is almost immune to shock and calls on reliable Sam Wood, a veteran of twenty-six years in pictures. Sam, perhaps, takes things a little less hard than Cukor or Fleming. Sam is what they call a "trouble shooter." He's not particularly intellectual. Directors like Lubitsch and Capra plan every move that a character is going to make long before the starting date of a picture, but Sam Wood doesn't prepare his own scripts. They can always count on him, though, for a thorough, thoughtful job—as witness his fine direction of *Mr. Chips*. (*Pause.*)

He keeps *Gone With the Wind* going until Fleming recovers. For a while the two directors even overlap; then Fleming takes over again completely, without friction or jealousy.

After six months on the sound stages, the first draft of this problem picture is completed. A few more months of re-takes—during which Clark Gable is the chief sufferer, because his hair has to grow way down his neck for Rhett Butler and it's a hot summer and he would like to cut it—well, after re-takes and then more retakes, the picture is finished.

Like all pictures, it has been a community enterprise. Margaret Mitchell wrote the story; David Selznick, perhaps the most competent producer in Hollywood, dedicated himself to the four-million-dollar production; seventeen writers have figured on the payroll; the cutters, technicians, cameramen, designers, music recorders, dressmakers, tailors, all have done their share—but the tensile strength of this great effort has been furnished by the director.

But don't feel too sorry for the director—he has his compensations. (*Pause.*) Capra, Ford, Vidor, Fleming, and the other top directors get from $50,000 to $150,000 a picture. And, in the popular mind, there is another compensation for the director. I quote from William de Mille's book *Hollywood Saga*.

"When I first assumed my duties as director, I was surprised and just a bit startled to discover that my personal attraction seemed to have increased in an amazing fashion. Never had I realized the number of charming and ambitious young women who were willing, nay, *anxious* to pay the price, as they so naïvely expressed it. But my tottering modesty was saved, against its will perhaps, by the inner conviction that all the ladies wanted was a job."

The question I am asked most frequently is: "How can I break into the movies?"—and I'm just the person to come to. Nine years ago, I had a screen test in London. (*Pause.*) I was strongly advised to become a writer. (*Pause and smile.*) However, I always feel that I didn't have a fair chance. (*Smile.*)

There is no royal road to screen success. You can be the daughter of a director and have no luck, like Katherine de Mille; you can be a great beauty and a millionairess in one, like Mrs. Jock Whitney; you can be the wife of a Barrymore, or a glamour girl like Brenda Frazier, and *then* not click in front of a camera.

One of the best ways to get into the movies is to *fall* into them. David Niven had no idea of becoming a screen actor until he fell off a boat. (*Pause.*) He was visiting friends on a British cruiser off California. After a rather gay evening, he had retired for the night. Shortly afterwards, the captain of the boat received orders to sail to Australia. There was the problem of Mr. Niven. They couldn't take him along—even if David wanted to go. For a while the captain considered throwing David to the sharks, but we English—well, that sort of thing just isn't done. So he hailed a ship a hundred yards away. "Can you take aboard a young man who can't travel under his own steam?" (*Pause.*)

The boat hailed was the sailing ship chartered by Metro for *Mutiny on the Bounty*, and the *Bounty* was nothing if not bountiful. The ship was to appear before the camera the next day, but they could put up this lost young Englishman for one night. A launch came alongside. David turned at the gangplank to say "Good-by" to his friends, made a false step, and descended hurriedly into the Pacific, whence he was dragged into the *Bounty*'s launch, a very wide-awake young man. (*Pause.*) David didn't know that it was the beginning of his career. At that moment, he was only trying to survive; he was not looking ahead. (*Pause.*)

Producers never make mistakes about talent—this is a well-known fact. At least if anyone says differently between Santa Monica and Hollywood Boulevard, they'd better start looking for a job outside the movies. Producers sense talent by a sort of second or third sight. For example, when the screen tests were run for a certain young lady in 1930, Carl Laemmle, Junior, who'd grown up in the business, immortalized himself with the remark "She's got no talent, she leaves me cold."

He was right, of course—that is, so far as his own feelings were concerned. However, about a hundred million Americans thought differently and also thought that *Miss Bette Davis* was one of the great actresses of our time. Nevertheless, five years passed from the time of Mr. Laemmle's decision before Bette got her chance in *Of Human Bondage*, and that was only because every other actress in Hollywood refused the part.

The handsome Errol Flynn will tell you that *his* career came to life when he played dead. (*Pause.*) This is literally true. He was first spotted for the big money when, in desperation, he accepted the role of a *corpse* in a picture called *The Case of the Curious Bride.* (*Disparaging gesture.*) It wasn't much of a part. He had no *lines* to speak of. But it was a nice quiet occupation and it didn't require any experience. (*Smile for first time.*)

But while he was lying dead, news came that Robert Donat was too ill to come to America and a handsome actor had to be found to take his place. So a lot of talent scouts were brought in to look at this corpse with sex appeal. And that's how Errol Flynn won the title role of *Captain Blood.*

Then there's always that old feminine trick of fainting in

the producer's office—only this time it was used by a *man,*
who gave it a different twist. Joel McCrea was driving a motor-
cycle outside the Paramount studio. A delivery truck bumped
into him. Before he lost consciousness, Joel managed to stag-
ger inside the studio. When he came to, he heard Cecil B. de
Mille say, "He's good-looking, he ought to be in pictures." Before he was fully awake, de Mille had him under contract, at
fifty dollars a week.

Sometimes personality conquers all. When Clark Gable
was tested for the screen, they dressed him in a sort of sarong,
with a rose in his mouth and a wreath of flowers round his
head to cover his ears. (*Pause.*) Even that couldn't stop Clark
Gable. When you've got it, you've got it.

Again, one can change one's self in order to win friends
and influence producers. Fifteen years ago, Molly O'Day (sister of Sally O'Neil) had a portion of both calves amputated,
which caused somewhat of a scandal and injured her career.
But there were no protests *whatever* when George Brent sacri-
ficed a piece of his nose to make it a little less Roman.

Seriously, it does seem that the best way of making a reputation *for* Hollywood is to make it *outside* of Hollywood. Judy
Garland lived in Hollywood nine years but couldn't make
the movie grade until she sang at Lake Tahoe, where she was
heard by a talent scout. And a girl like Mary Martin had to
sing unnoticed for two years in Hollywood night clubs. Then
she went East, made a hit on Broadway, and was immediately
deluged with screen offers.

I won't depress you by dwelling on the fact that 9,000 extras worked last year an average of 29 days each—for an average pay check of $320 for the year. And that even if you do
click in your first picture that's only *one* hurdle in a long stee-
plechase. For one whole year I used to gape at the exquisite

Hedy Lamarr sitting neglected in a corner at the Hollywood Brown Derby. And then overnight, after the release of *Algiers*, she became the glamour girl of the screen. Three months later, her next picture was abandoned in the middle because of the honest conviction of all concerned that she couldn't act. But she could act in *Algiers*. (*Pause.*)

What is the answer? (*Pause.*) As Bernard Shaw says, "The Golden Rule is (*Pause*) that there are no golden rules." There are no reliable signposts on the road to Hollywood success.

One thing I know you all want to know is "What are the stars like?" (*Pause.*) It's a little hard to know what they are like physically—after the Hollywood make-up experts get through with them. And we haven't much time now to go into it deeply, but we'll take a few of them very briefly.

There's Shirley Temple. Shirley has changed quite a bit in the four years that I've known her. We first met at the hairdresser's when we were both having our hair brightened—a little. She bought me a Coca-Cola. (*Pause.*) She hasn't quite gotten around to buying whiskeys and sodas—yet—but that will come—I hope.

I think Shirley is going to be a prettier girl and woman than she was a baby. She's lost a lot of weight, and she's getting fairly tall for her eleven years. Her mother has wisely decided to let Shirley's hair revert to its near-natural shade. It will soon be black, like her mother's. Shirley's amazingly intelligent. She recently discussed the European war with me, and from the way she spoke, I think she reads *Life* and *Time*. She is currently studying Greek philosophy—or rather that's what her press agent told me.

Charles Boyer—what of him? (*Pause.*) In real life Charles has a much higher forehead than on the screen. But, like Edgar

Bergen and Fred Astaire, he has to wear a little something for the screen. But that doesn't detract from his tremendous personal charm—whether on the screen or in private life.

I understand that the French government has taken him from the Maginot Line with the view to sending him to this country to spread French propaganda among the clubwomen. (*Pause.*) You'd better not let him come, because when Boyer meets clubwoman, the combustion will put America right in the war on the side of France—and Mr. Boyer.

Hedy Lamarr? Is she as beautiful in real life as she is on the screen? I'm afraid she is—in fact she's more beautiful. She has the most perfect complexion I've ever seen, literally as soft and white as a camellia. I could go on like this for hours about her. Luckily for the sanity of the rest of the women in Hollywood, Hedy's figure doesn't match up with her face. Which is why she wears those long skirts.

Hedy is like a bright child. She laughs like a child, and she probably cries like a child. You have a feeling that she ought to be playing with dolls. As a matter of fact, she *is* playing with a doll right now. Her husband, Gene Markey, recently bought her a nice, live, masculine doll—a cute little boy, with whom Hedy is now playing Mama.

Mickey Rooney is practically the same in real life as he is in the movies—except that he doesn't cry as much in real life as he does in the movies. And he's rather serious in real life, except where girls are concerned. Master Rooney appreciates the fair sex. They used to say at one time that it was slightly dangerous for any woman—even a columnist—to be left alone with Mickey. But apart from referring to me as "that dame"—and calling me "honey"—his attitude and behavior has always been very respectful. I'm not his type, I guess.

And now for Ann Sheridan. I feel rather sorry for the "Oomph" girl of the screen. (*Pause.*) Ann is one of the nicest girls out there. She'll do anything they want her to. So when they came to her about a year ago, and said they were going to glorify her via an "Oomph" label, Ann said, "Swell, go ahead." She naturally thought that as the fame of her "Oomph" spread, her picture roles would swell in equal proportion. But they didn't. (*Pause.*) Recently a California gasoline company renamed its product—"Oomph" gasoline. This was the final straw for Ann, and she told her studio, that unless they withdrew the "Oomph" from her name, she'd withdraw from pictures.

I'm going to get very serious, and probably just at the moment when I should be telling a funny story. (*Pause.*)

You remember the Greek orator who was trying to prepare the defense of his city? He kept saying, "Fortify the Acropolis. The Persians are upon us." But everyone yawned. Finally he paused, looked out at his audience, and said (*Pause*): "Once there was a man who fell in love with a frog." Immediately everybody was listening. "That's all," he told them, "but now that you're with me, how about those defense plans?" (*Pause. Smile.*)

I feel like this when I start to talk about education in pictures. Please bear with me. (*Confidential tone.*)

Some years ago, two little friends of mine—they were twelve years old—asked me to take them to a moving picture, to a movie I'd already seen. They won me over by saying that the picture was considered *very educational*. It was *The Story of Louis Pasteur*.

We went and enjoyed it enormously, but coming out of the theater I looked at the faces of the two little girls and failed to recognize the tired look that usually goes with education. I wondered how much of the picture they'd remember.

They spent the night with me, but before they went to bed I asked one of them to look up Louis Pasteur in the encyclopedia. She put up quite a struggle—said she knew all about him, hadn't she just seen the picture? But she finally agreed. Meanwhile, the other little girl had gone to bed.

A month passed. The girls asked again to be taken to a picture. Again they mowed me down by telling me it was an educational and historical subject. Here was a chance to prove my theory. I asked the little girl who had *not* read about Pasteur to tell me something of his life.

She hesitated, then she said: "Well, he went around kinda—well, there was something about some sheep and a mad dog (*Quickly*) and Anita Louise married the young man at the end." Then I asked the little girl—the one I'd coerced into reading up on Pasteur. She frowned and felt she was being put on the spot, but in the end she gave me a fairly *good summary* of Pasteur's life. The reading had reinforced the picture; the picture had made the reading vivid. (*Pause—lighter expression.*) But even she will always think, Pasteur was lucky to look like Paul Muni. (*Pause.*)

But I'd found out something. Because of the extra effort *she* had put in, Hollywood had contributed something to her education.

My conviction is that if anyone invented a system to educate without effort—merely by giving a sugar-coated pill—that would be closer to Huxley's dream of a "Brave New World" than to present-day motion picture realities. So many sorts of pictures loosely called "educational," are really "informative" or "propaganda" pictures. Education is a privilege that *cannot* be got *without effort*.

But let's see what the movie *can* do towards education in a legitimate field, the classroom. The classroom is something you approach in the morning when you're fresh. While the picture house is something we turn to in the evening when we're tired. The Rockefeller Foundation financed a study of human relations as exemplified in motion pictures. It's believed that 175 different situations confront the average adult, and that showing them in the classroom will help the student to take care of himself with the least possible harm when the time comes.

A typical thing would be to show that little bit from *A Star Is Born* where a popular actor is drunk in public—to show how the sympathy of the crowd withdraws from him.

Another example would be from the picture *San Francisco*, when Gable hits a man of God—and the ineffable reproach on Spencer Tracy's face as he sinks down before the fists of his friend. No boy who would see that bit from *San Francisco*—see it in the morning, detached from the flow of the film—would ever again take a delight in being a bully.

The so-called educational shorts that are shown in the theaters are really just informative. We're interested, but what we've come to the theater for is to see the *feature* picture, and we're inclined to put the short out of our mind and save our memories for Clark Gable or Myrna Loy. (*Pause.*)

What about the newsreel in screen education? My idea is that a newsreel is neither more nor less educational than a daily paper.

You pick up a newspaper. The first column is about the war; the second, the escape of a criminal; the third, a speech by the President—and so forth. Each headline drives out what you read in the preceding column. We don't drag along the memory of what was in the first column through our reading of the second. The headline about the crime makes us forget the column about war—to a great extent. As a newspaper-woman, I admit reluctantly that my chief concern is to entertain you first—instruct you only if I can. And this is true of the newsreel.

If you go to a newsreel to look for something—for instance, what a bombardment does—you'll find it. Just as you'd turn to the real-estate section of a newspaper if you want to buy a house. But in general, the voice of the newsreel commentator drives out of mind whatever has passed before our eyes a second before. (*Pause.*) This is as it should be. If we remembered everything we saw, our minds would be like a log jam on the Columbia river. Our machinery for forgetting is as important as our machinery for remembering.

What I'm shooting at is not a disparagement of the newsreel or the program short. I'm merely groping for a better definition of screen education than the present one, which throws everything that doesn't say Boy Meets Girl, or Man Meets Bullet, into a huge bag labeled "Educational."

I'll tell you a story which doesn't exactly illustrate this but has a sort of moral of its own.

Ernest Hemingway visited Hollywood a few years ago. He and two producers were walking across the lot of a certain studio. Both producers were praising his works. Hemingway was naturally pleased and asked one of them which of his books he admired most. The producer looked a little blank, so Hemingway tried to help him out.

"*A Farewell to Arms?*" "Yes," said the producer so eagerly that Ernest grew a little suspicious and asked (*Pause*): "Do you mean the play or the book?" (*Pause.*)

"I mean the movie," the producer said. (*Pause.*)

Hemingway was somewhat disappointed and turning to

the producer on his left he asked, "Is that what you admire—the movie?"

"No," said the producer. "I never got around to seeing the movie—but I heard the song." (*Pause.*)

While I'm sure that the youth of the nation has more intellectual curiosity than these two producers, I still maintain that when you go towards education, you've got to take your book with you.

One type of picture that wavers on the border of the instructive is the propaganda film. The first propaganda films were issued by the British during the last war. They took a picture of the Battle of Loos that was so horrible it was finally put back in the files of the War Department. The first *successful* propaganda pictures were made by Eisenstein and other Russian directors in the middle 1920s (*Pause*)—among them *The Cruiser Potemkin*, and *The Last Days of St. Petersburg.*

Once in Paris I saw these pictures behind closed doors—after showing my British passport to prove I wasn't a member of the French police. (*Pause.*) These Russian pictures certainly had an emotional sway. And this was due to the recognition that the moving picture can convey an *emotion* more easily than a *thought*. Pictures are an emotional rather than an intellectual medium.

That is the reason for the success of Merian Cooper's fine film, *Grass*, which showed the migration of an Asiatic tribe in quest of new pastures. Anyone who's ever felt hunger couldn't help but feel in sympathy with that picture. (*Pause.*)

But it's in the world of fashions and manners that movies have spread their most effective propaganda. It's a commonplace to say that Hollywood has become the style center of the world. The up hairdo was popularized by Danielle Darrieux in her first picture here. Remembering all the untidy necks with straggling wisps of hair that followed, I'm not so sure we have anything for which to *thank* Miss Darrieux.

Joan Crawford was responsible for those heavy, thickly made-up lips that swept the country from coast to coast a few years ago.

Greta Garbo wore a pillbox hat in a picture several years ago. We're still wearing a version of that very same hat.

Hedy Lamarr parted her black hair in the middle and wore an off-the-face turban in *Algiers*. Ever since, the country has swarmed with girls who've worn off-the-face turbans, parted their black hair in the middle, and wishfully believed they looked like Hedy Lamarr.

And American films have acted as a common denominator of customs and even speech in other countries. They are largely responsible for the emancipation of the Japanese woman, who rebelled against her age-long subjection by demanding the delicious freedom enjoyed by American women—as reflected in American movies. (*Pause.*) And American slang, such as "Oh yeah" and "Bump off" and "Scram," is now heard in the best London drawing rooms—and I don't mean maybe. (*Pause.*)

The uneven quality of Hollywood's product, the question of why some pictures were ever made at all—all this is usually blamed on the producer. It isn't quite fair. In the long run, people get the sort of entertainment they demand. But the producer has been the scapegoat for so long that perhaps he can stand one more story about himself—of which I was a firsthand witness.

One of the producers at a big studio wanted to change the tragic ending of *Three Comrades*—he wanted Margaret Sullavan to live. He said the picture would make more money if

Margaret Sullavan lived. (*Pause.*) He was reminded [by Scott, who wrote the script] that Camille had also coughed her life away and had made many fortunes doing it. He pondered this for a minute; then he said, "*Camille* would have made *twice* as much if Garbo had lived." (*Pause.*) "What about the greatest love story of all?" he was asked. "How about *Romeo and Juliet*—you wouldn't have wanted Juliet to live, would you?" "That's just it," said the producer. "*Romeo and Juliet* didn't make a cent." (*Pause.*)

I'd like to drop the production side of the industry and take you, directly and intimately, into Hollywood for a few minutes.

Of course I know that women here have no difficulty in finding husbands—the right sort of husband, I mean. Or in keeping them. And it may seem a little remote to you, and I almost apologize for bringing it up at all, but out in Hollywood (*Pause*) we're up against it. (*Pause.*)

In most frontier towns, the proportion of men to women is such that almost any girl—so I'm told—is overwhelmed with golden nuggets and offers of marriage. But not in Hollywood, where two-thirds of the mining population wear skirts. (*Pause.*)

But if ever a woman needs a husband it's in Hollywood. It's a lonely place for the woman without her own man. And believe me, he's exclusively hers—when and if she can find him. As Lana Turner told me emotionally, "When you do find a good man—hang on to him, sister." (*Pause.*)

Norma Shearer is only just beginning to adjust herself to her loneliness since the death of her husband, Irving Thalberg, in 1936. Not long ago she told me how much she envied couples like Gable and Lombard, and Taylor and Stanwyck. "They have someone they can trust," she said very sadly. Norma still has found no one she can turn to, no one she can quite trust as she trusted Irving Thalberg.

What chance *has* the average film actress of finding a husband in Hollywood? In the old days she could hope to marry her leading men and directors—alternately. (*Pause.*) But nowadays all the leading men and directors are very much married—with the exception of a minority.

There's Jimmy Stewart, who doesn't want to marry an actress; Cary Grant, who's bespoken for Phyllis Brooks; and a few young actors—among them Richard Greene, who recently stated that he wasn't going to marry anyone for two years. Rather discouraging, isn't it? Stay East, young woman, stay East.

Take the case of Olivia de Havilland, who's twenty-four, very pretty, utterly charming, and wants to marry. Olivia is in love—or rather she was when I left Hollywood. (*Pause.*) She's in love with Howard Hughes. But then, so are a lot of other girls. Mr. Hughes is perfectly aware of this pleasant condition. And he wants to enjoy it as long as it lasts.

The normal girl in a normal city does her work by day and sees her beaus in the evening. But the movie actress, when she's making a picture, is usually too tired in the evening to do anything except have dinner in bed and go to sleep at nine. And when she does go out she wants to go home early. That's why in Hollywood you'll see Howard Hughes and Olivia de Havilland having dinner together, but by late suppertime Howard has to find another girl. Which doesn't help Olivia to get the proposal she wants. (*Pause.*)

In other cities, girl meets boy at parties. We have our parties in Hollywood too, and sometimes girl meets boy there. Clark Gable and Carole Lombard are supposed to have fallen in love at a big Hollywood party—but they're the exception, not the rule.

My first party in Hollywood is typical of most of them. It was at Marion Davies' modest shack on the beach (*Look up*)—the cloakroom is about the size of this *hall*. (*Pause.*) It was on a Saturday night, the only night all Hollywood can stay up late. Of course, I knew I was up against pretty stiff competition. I couldn't hope to compete with the richest, most glamorous girls in the world. So, when my escort vanished immediately we were inside the door, I was disappointed but not surprised.

But I *was* surprised to find glamour girls like Loretta Young and Ginger Rogers without the dozens of adoring men I'd expected. Every other girl at that party was a celebrity, but there were three girls to every man, which means that there were times when even the *film stars* were wallflowers! At the long supper table there were usually two women, then one man, then two women. *I*, being a newcomer, was placed between two women. (*Smile.*) My escort was up to his neck in film stars about a mile down the table. And if I wanted to talk to a man I had to do a bit of shouting. Somehow I didn't enjoy that party. (*Smile.*) So you see parties are not awfully helpful to the Hollywood girl who wants to marry.

Rosalind Russell has been in Hollywood five years without finding a man that would do for a husband. Rosalind's motto is "Live alone (*Pause, look up*)—and don't look it."

Mind you, she'd prefer to be married—if she could find the right man. But the right man will have a hard time getting to know Rosalind. She's too particular. She earns more money than the President of the United States. She wants the best man her golden nuggets can buy.

Meanwhile, she's lonely, complains that she doesn't want to marry a producer, a director, a writer, or *anyone* connected with the movies. She'll probably end up by marrying an actor—to get away from it all. (*Pause.*) Anyhow, we can say without hesitation that if the earning capacity of movie stars suddenly vanished, they'd be infinitely less choosy. (*Pause.*)

Let's presume that the loneliness of the solitary life in Hollywood is finally too much even for the successful film actress, and we'll presume that she's been lucky in getting one of the few available free men. What chance has she of "living happily ever after"?

Contrary to popular belief, the number of divorces in Hollywood is not as big as the [number of] happy marriages. I could name you a hundred actors and actresses whose home-life is as satisfactory and even as blissful as anyone could ask for. Seeing Dick Powell and Joan Blondell together is even a little fatiguing—like watching a three-year honeymoon. But one must admit that Hollywood has its divorces like any other big city—they *seem* to be more because every Hollywood divorce is headlined.

Usually, it's the old story of career versus marriage. Bette Davis decided to put her *work* before her home. She has since discovered her mistake—and I'll place a bet with anyone that she remarries within the next six months.

Joan Fontaine recently insisted on an unusual clause in her contract with Selznick—that even though she's in the middle of a picture she'll accompany her husband if he leaves town, no matter for what reason. But I can't help remembering that in 1930 Joan Crawford said, "There comes into a life only one man (*Pause, say solemnly*) and that's Douglas Fairbanks." (*Smile.*)

One cause of divorce in Hollywood is the intense spotlight in which we demand that these people live. We permit them no private life. This spotlight has made Hollywood's social life very much like that of a village. Everywhere the star turns he finds himself on Main Street.

The gossips had a field day recently when Tony Martin left town on a long personal-appearance tour. They fastened their claws on his wife, little inoffensive Alice Faye. Hardly a day passed without amateur reporters calling me up to tell me—in strictest confidence—that Alice was going to divorce Tony.

Sometimes they'd vary the story by saying that Alice was going around with other men or that Tony had fallen in love with a rich Easterner. For additional seasoning, they threw in the erroneous guess that Alice was going to have a baby and wasn't it terrible that the poor child had to be brought into the world under such circumstances!

They almost had me believing them. But time and experience have made me cautious, and I thought it better to wait for something more concrete. (*Pause.*) Alice and Tony are still living together happily in spite of this pyramid of malicious rumor. But it was a narrow squeak. If they hadn't had such faith in each other it would have been another Hollywood divorce. But in this case, *they* have the last laugh.

I won't say that gossip alone ruined Dorothy Lamour's marriage—but it didn't help. Enforced separation from her husband, who worked in Chicago, had as much, perhaps a little more, to do with it. But the continual items in the newspapers and magazines that Dorothy was out with this man one night and another the next couldn't have been peaceful reading for her husband. Mind you, he'd given her *carte blanche* to go out with whom she wanted to, but there's quite a difference in saying, "Darling, I want you to have an amusing time when I'm not there," to reading that his "darling" *was* having an amusing time when he wasn't there. (*Pause.*)

Randolph Scott's marriage is another that went on the

rocks via separation and gossip. His wife preferred horses and Delaware to films and Hollywood. So she lived in Delaware and Mr. Scott lived in Hollywood. Mrs. Scott told Mr. Scott that it was all right with her if he went out with other women when she wasn't there. And Randy, no less generously, told Mrs. Scott *she* could go out with other men when *he* wasn't there.

Mrs. Scott did more. She wired Randy that a girl she knew was visiting Hollywood and would he show her around. Randy, being an obedient husband, took his wife's friend to dinner at the Trocadero. (*Pause.*) Within the next few days, every reporter in Hollywood—and there are nearly four hundred—was informed that Randolph Scott was going places with a pretty woman and that it signified the end of his marriage.

Randy told me that his wife was furious. He reminded her that it was *she* who'd asked him to be nice to the girl. "Yes," she wired back, "but I didn't expect you to be *that* nice to her." "But I wasn't," Randy wired back. They made it up that time, but things were never quite the same. (*Pause.*)

Of course, the happy marriages aren't written up in the papers. It's hardly a news story to say that the Paul Munis are never apart—she's even on the set when he's working; or that the Warner Baxters have been married twenty-one years; (*Pause.*) Even such career women as Myrna Loy have made a pretty good thing of marriage. (*Pause.*)

Only we must consider this—that if a woman star has made a *mistake* in the man she's married, she's not forced by lack of money and lack of opportunity to make the best of it.

(*Pause.*) A lot can happen in a Hollywood day. I'm not trying to say that as much couldn't happen right here in this city, but in Hollywood all the big names, that we know as intimately as the names of our brothers and sisters, give a kind of glow to things. At least they did four years ago, when I first went out there.

I remember a special morning when Robert Taylor called me up and asked me to play tennis. And, believe it or not, though we play the same brand of tennis, I turned him down. That same day William Powell had asked me to dinner at his house. I turned that down too, because a wire had just come from my syndicate asking for an interview with Cecil B. de Mille. This was to take place at his country home—Paradise Ranch, somewhere up in the hills. I was furious. Here I was with an invitation to play tennis with Taylor and dine with Powell. Moreover I'd planned to fly to Catalina that afternoon and learn something of Leslie Howard's new plans.

To be honest, I wasn't absolutely sorry to forgo the Howard engagement because the interview would have to be conducted on Tay Garnett's yacht and I'm one of those *seasick* girls. I'd had another interview before with Leslie under the same conditions and we caught some fish and talked vaguely about life and love. But I'd rather interview Dracula on good dry land. (*Pause.*)

Anyhow, I started out to Mr. de Mille's, who'd been kind enough to invite me for the weekend. I didn't know what to expect. One of my illusions before I went to Hollywood was that the stars lived in fantastic houses and on enormous estates. Usually it isn't so. Even in such Beverly Hills houses as Joan Crawford's, your immediate impression is that any personal taste that might exist has been subordinated to the taste of an interior decorator.

But the de Mille ranch promised to be the exception. De Mille is an individualist. I was going to interview the man who recreated the American bathroom. Abraham Lincoln, in the White House, had the first bathtub with running water in the country, but Mr. de Mille had made the bathroom an exquisite sanctum and if he could do that much with a mere bathroom, what was his ranch going to be like? I still regretted that dinner date with William Powell, but I was game. •

A secretary met me at the door. In a few seconds, she had told me the rules:

1. A husband and wife cannot come there together—a husband alone or a wife alone is quite welcome. This rule is waived only once a year on the birthday of Mrs. de Mille.

2. There's no such thing as getting food before twelve in the morning.

3. Guests must not believe in the rumor that women were frequently murdered in the night. It was just another Hollywood story. This last was to make me feel at home.

I broke loose from the secretary at this point, went outside to where the first meal of the day was being served in the middle of a tennis court. I presented myself to Mr. de Mille.

"Why?" I asked. "Why are you serving steak and soup on the tennis court?" De Mille explained that the tennis court used to be a patio and he liked the view from there, and they used to eat on the patio, and he was dashed if he'd eat anywhere else just because he'd inserted a tennis court. I was getting that Alice in Wonderland feeling.

I listened to de Mille outline the afternoon routine to his guests. "Some of you people have got to clean out the swimming pool. The rest will come with me on a mountain hike. (*Pause.*) We *may* meet a mountain lion."

"You mean we ought to go armed?" asked a timid guest.

"No," said de Mille complacently. "*I* have a revolver. You'll find some *canes* in the hall." The guest looked a little green as he turned back to his steak and soup.

"Don't worry," de Mille assured him. "Your sticks will come in useful if we meet rattlesnakes." I don't remember the name of that guest, but something tells me he chose to stay and clean out the pool.

This was my introduction to Paradise Ranch. I asked where the telephone was and called up William Powell. "I think I'll be free for a late dinner," I said.

Now I have to confess to a complete hiatus in my memory of that afternoon—except that I didn't go mountain climbing and I didn't clean the pool. I'd been up till three the night before, covering the Academy Dinner. So after lunch I tottered to the room assigned me and fell into a deep sleep. (*Pause.*) Perhaps I had a confused dream of playing tennis with Robert Taylor in the middle of a patio. (*Pause.*) Perhaps the peacocks screaming on the terrace made me believe that guests *were* murdered in their sleep. (*Pause.*) Perhaps in my dreams I heard the field mice on the bureau eating away at my purse, for there were really field mice, and it was—or had been—a real purse. (*Pause.*) But my dream couldn't have been as weird as the reality to which I presently woke up. I looked out the window. It was about seven o'clock.

Men in Russian blouses were hurrying across the patio. Had the Revolution come? I pulled myself together. I must be on the spot to report it. I fixed myself up quickly at the mirror and dashed downstairs just in time to see a strange ritual. Cecil B. de Mille was mixing a cocktail. He wore white gloves, like the white rabbit in Alice in Wonderland. Upon the cocktail shaker, as if the ice inside wasn't enough, there were bells, which with every motion of his elbow played "My Country, 'Tis of Thee."

Being from England, where the same tune is used for "God Save the King," I stood stiffly to attention until I was rudely brought back to mobility by the whispered advice—this time from a de Mille yes-man—that until eight o'clock the women had to be subservient to the men.

"If this seems difficult," he said, "remember you'll each get a present from that tree."

I looked at the tree. It was a sort of Christmas tree loaded with all kinds of presents from imitation jewelry to huge bottles of Chanel Number 5. But meanwhile, the process of women being subservient to men had begun. The women were helping the men be seated at table very much as a mother puts a child in a high chair. It was all right, I was assured; in another half-hour when de Mille gave the word at *eight* o'clock, the world was going to be all for women again. But I can't report upon that because this was the exact moment when William Powell's car came for me. By this time, I was honestly sorry to leave. Some day I'm going back—just after eight.

That was three years ago, and I still feel a little like Alice in Wonderland. (*Pause.*) In talking to you, I've tried to be very practical and very serious. (*Pause.*) I've tried to tell you something about the director as the great vitalizing force in pictures. (*Pause.*) I've tried to tell you how people break into movies. (*Pause.*) Also I've discussed impartially the question of if, when, and how motion pictures are educational. And I've tried to tell you a little about the personalities of Hollywood and their problems.

But it's impossible to crowd into an hour all that I know or think or guess about Hollywood. After four years out there, I'd be silly not to admit that I'm a little person circulating about a great medium. It's too big for me—too big for any of us, too big for most of the people who direct its destinies.

Once in a while a great figure has appeared on the horizon and led it through a mighty exodus. Griffith was one,

Thalberg was another. There is no such person now in Hollywood—no single person whom we, of the movie industry, believe capable of controlling this vast art in all its many manifestations. But there's some boy growing up in America now who by some combination of genius and luck will answer Hollywood's great problem.

Now that we have every device of nature itself—nature's color, nature's sound. And technicians have made experiments in nature's three dimensions so that figures on the film will seem to have the corporeal reality of life itself. Now that we have all this—what are we going to do with it? Now that we've a way of saying in pictures almost everything that used to be said in books, how far do you want us to go? And what do you want us to say?

I regret to state that I was a dismal flop as a lecturer in Boston, the first stop. I was so intimidated by the Boston clubwomen that I was afraid to raise my eyes from the written page. I grew more confident going west, and by the time I hit Kansas City, I had them rolling almost literally in the aisles. A cocktail party had preceded the lecture, which I could now give from memory with only a casual glance at the papers. I felt I had done extremely well and Scott was delighted when I telephoned him with the good news, before flying back the same night to Hollywood.

When I called him the next morning, I was in tears and read him the scathing attack on my lecture by the Kansas City stringer for *The Hollywood Reporter*. This was when Scott asked John O'Hara to be his second for the duel he threatened with the editor of the *Reporter*. When John O'Hara declined, Scott mumbled something about his being a coward and he would get Eddie Mayer, who

was warned by O'Hara and spent the morning compos-
ing excuses. Luckily the call never came. I vowed no more
lectures in a letter to Johnny, after I told him, "It took me a
long time to get over my short lecture trip. I lost too much
weight and my nerves got jangled. I think I'm too high
strung for that sort of work."

Among the several short *short* stories I wrote under
Scott's tutelage was one called "Ostrich." Remembering
how the Duchess de Guermantes had hastened to a party
in advance of the time when she expected word that a relative had died, for then she would be unable to go, I wrote
on similar lines, about a debutante whose grandmother
was expected to die and who rushed to an important party
before receiving the dreaded telegram.

I planned a plot for a story, "Janey," a thinly disguised
version of Scottie and her father. He was amused when I
showed it to him; it was so exactly what was happening at
that time in their lives. The notes for the story were in my
"Scott" folder.

Description of Janey

[This of course was almost a life-size description of
Scottie.]

Weight 110 pounds
5 feet 4½ inches

golden hair with a flame behind it. Wide apart blue
eyes, the blue of a summer day with a hint of thunder,
flecks of yellow around the pupil like a bright sun in
the sky.

A little mouth that when she is cross looks like a short "u" upside down . . .

Perfect teeth

A forehead that is a combination of the best in Priscilla Lane and Ginger Rogers.

Complexion—a soft piece of finely woven creamsilk— dipped in a pink-gold dye.

She is *vivacious* and *so busy*—can't sit still—always getting things up—and leaving them for others to finish. A terrific prevaricator (except on fundamental things)

Her athletic accomplishments—a superb diver.

She is trilingual—German, French, Italian—her father having lived in Europe until she was 14 (this is why she is still "Janey"—thinks she is still the ideal American girl)

Plot

Story of a girl, 17, daughter of a middle-aged professor, a man who in early 20's was the literary mouthpiece of flaming youth.

His daughter has read all the stories—and loved them—she is surprised that he has such knowledge and understanding of the hot, sweet, exciting problems of youth—can hardly believe he wrote them because he now seems such a timid old soul. He can't believe he wrote them either—and wishes he never had. He now dislikes so much the type of wild heroine he used to write about so prolifically.

The story that makes him writhe most is "Janey"—(his *Josephine* series)—about a girl just the age of his daughter and her complete counterpart in looks—no wonder—"Janey" was her mother (she died when the girl was 8) who breaks every rule—and just manages to get away with it without paying.

The daughter read "Janey" when she was 13—and has never forgotten it. She is now, at the age of 17—"Janey" to the life—but this type of girl is no longer fashionable.

The story deals with the father's determination to kill the "Janey" in his daughter—without her being aware of it—and the daughter's determination to be "Janey"—only more so. Both the father and the daughter win—in their own fashion.

The story could open at a debutante dance with the girl having a hot necking session with a Yale boy—à la Janey. She is a fascinating little minx with the looks and line of Scottie. (Her father doesn't know she is at the deb dance—thinks she is at Bryn Mawr College), but you'd never guess this from the girl's conversation. To hear her talk, you'd think she could twist papa around her little finger (like Janey does).

After the dance, a swift heady drive back to college with

the daughter, a little intoxicated, driving. (At one bend they skid right round three times.) She gets back to the college to find her father waiting for her. (He had come up unexpectedly to see her, finds she has gone to the dance—and is VERY ANGRY.) She is furious because he bawls her out in front of the boy (with whom she is madly in love). The boy is secretly on the father's side. He is a quiet, serious, ambitious youth who drinks—but just a little—is in love with the girl, is fascinated by the Janey side of her, but also irritated by it.

"You told me to write about what I know," I reminded Scott.

He laughed somewhat ruefully. He had recently tried to reach Scottie by telephone at Vassar on a Saturday afternoon and learned that instead of studying—she was behind in her grades—she had taken off somewhere to see a football game. After telephoning all over the Eastern Seaboard, he had tracked her down at the home of her close friend "Peaches" Finney in Baltimore. He was very angry with Scottie, bawled her out for ten minutes without repeating himself, and slammed down the receiver after predicting she would come to a bad end.

CHAPTER TWELVE
WHAT I LEARNED

HOW VALUABLE WAS SCOTT FITZGERALD'S education for me in actual fact? Scott's death prevented my graduation from his College of One. But in a sense I have had my diploma through my daughter, Wendy, who graduated *magna cum laude* from Bryn Mawr. Her honors paper was titled, "F. Scott Fitzgerald: The Tragic Experience of the Creative Hero." She has her M.A. and is now studying for her Ph.D. My son wrote a book when he was sixteen about his experiences in Russia, Poland, and Czechoslovakia the previous summer. *The New York Times* rated his *Journey Behind the Iron Curtain* with the 100 Best Books For Children in 1963. The reviewer for the *Times,* comparing Robert's book with five others on the same subject written by adults (including John Gunther's two books culled from his *Inside Russia*), stated: "Of the books here, the best introduction to Communism by far is teenager Robert Westbrook's ... The point that comes through in young Mr. Westbrook's tale—and which escapes much other and more learned literature in this field—is that communists are people too— good people and bad people, pleasant people and boors . . ."

The torch has been passed. The seed Scott planted with his dying years will bloom forever in the dust of his bosom.

Of course I have not remembered everything I learned in our College of One. If I had to take my examination now, twenty-six years later, I would have to bone up for several months, as any college graduate would have to do. Following Scott's habit of grading his knowledge, I would say that in the areas in which I studied I know as much as any fairly bright college graduate who has forgotten some of what she has learned. Perhaps I know a bit more of poetry and literature. I have the same amount of confidence and assurance in participating in discussions on the subjects I studied so assiduously as the sole student in Scott's college.

A two-year course or even four years cannot educate you in the complete sense of the word, but it gave me, as I said at the beginning of this book, a key. It widened my horizon. I know where to look. I know how to evaluate. I am curious. I am open for new ideas and facts. The politicians and biased historians cannot fool me any more. To understand the present and future, you must know something of the past. I can relate today to yesterday. I am involved. I make up my own mind. I ask questions.

I have discovered that the more people know, the more they enjoy telling you about it. Not long ago in Paris, for example, I had a fascinating discussion with Edmund Wilson on where you put the comma. I didn't retain it all, but I found the conversation exhilarating. When I first met Bernard Shaw with C. B. Cochran, I wouldn't have dared talk with him and even in the year after Scott's death I was not too confident in discussing my new knowledge. But I continued with my reading. Recently, for example, I have enjoyed *John Keats: The Making of a Poet* by Aileen Ward; *William Shakespeare* by A. L. Rowse; W. A. Swanberg's *Dreiser*; and *The Letters of Oscar Wilde*, which I am sure

Scott would have enjoyed as much as the Turnbull book of his own letters. I have read Salinger and Camus and Yeats and Dylan Thomas, whose prose (though not his verse) and addiction to hard liquor were so much like Scott's.

It isn't only what you learn as a student, it's what you do with it in the unshepherded world where there are no familiar tracks, where there is no longer a teacher to pressure or to prod you into reading so many pages a day. With the right groundwork, you can go on by yourself, receiving pleasure from books and ideas for the rest of your life, which was the case with Scott and which has been true for me. And one of these days soon I am going to read *Finnegans Wake* and Spengler.

"If you learn to like poetry, it will give you pleasure all your life," Scott promised me. It has. And the joy of music. Recently I underwent some serious eye operations and had to lie flat on my back for three weeks with both eyes bandaged, with sandbags around my head to prevent the slightest movement. I could reach for my bedside radio and turn the knob fixed at the music station—Beethoven, Chopin, Schubert, Schumann, Brahms, Stravinsky—hour after hour. Time turned back and I was in the living room of my Hollywood apartment listening to the familiar themes of the great composers.

The books. They are still warm and alive for me. Not long ago when I was moving from the West Coast to the East, and the books were ready for the packing cases, I decided to take some of them with me on the plane so I could put them on my shelves as soon as I arrived. I opened Matthew Arnold's *Essays in Criticism*. On the flyleaf I read again: "For Sheilah, with love (and annotations) from Scott. 1940." What if I crash? I thought. No, it was too dangerous to take the books with me. I hastily removed from my suitcase Arthur Rimbaud's slim *Season in Hell*. I couldn't risk losing that, or Ernest Hemingway's *The Sun Also Rises* with the inscription from Scott: "For Sheilah, from Boris Karloff. Boo!" or Upton Sinclair's *The Jungle*. Not a first edition, but *The Jungle* couldn't fly with me either. Keats. What was I thinking of? All the books would have to come by Railway Express as they always had. If anything happened to me in the plane, *they* would be safe.

As a good student of the College of One, I have been able to help my children. I am not outside the circle when they discuss books and current events with their college friends. They are not embarrassed by me. My daughter Wendy always asked my advice about the long papers she had to write in high school and college. When she was preparing one paper in high school on the tragedies of Shakespeare, we discussed the project in detail. Afterward she said, "Mother, you know so much." It was like getting my B.A. Not long ago Wendy and Robert invited a group of graduate students at Columbia to dinner. I decided to make myself scarce and went to a movie, coming back when I thought dinner would be over. They were still eating when I returned, and they insisted that I join them. They asked me questions about Scott Fitzgerald and I was glad to answer them. We discussed politics, poetry, the war in Vietnam. Afterward Wendy said with affection and, I must admit, some surprise, "Mom, you contributed."

I had not read much of Virginia Woolf before Wendy chose the aspect of unity in her writings as a thesis for her master's degree at Columbia. We discussed the project and I became as enamored of that author as my daughter was.

Like Scott Fitzgerald, my son has always been less

interested in the prescribed studies in high school and college. He prefers the dreamlike world of ideas rather than hard facts. I was his editor for *Journey Behind the Iron Curtain* and he has respect for what I can do in my own area of work. His appreciation of music is far more advanced than mine. The unusual in poetry and painting delights him. The film as a form of art is his special subject. He is twenty years old and searching for new answers in all forms of creation. He is the future. I wish Scott could have known Wendy and Robert, the children of my marriage to Trevor Westbrook. They would have been at ease with each other.

It is now two and a half decades since the death of the founder of the College of One. I believe he would be pleased that I, his pupil, his guinea pig, have put his ideas on education between the covers of a book. I hope I have communicated his enthusiasm for the project. As Scott was a perennial Princetonian, I am a lifelong standard bearer for the Fitzgerald system of learning. I am immensely grateful that a charming, intelligent man with an inherent magic that could "illuminate old shapes" decided to give me the benefit of what he had learned from books, and from life.

APPENDICES

APPENDIX 1:
THE CURRICULUM

POSSIBLE LINES OF STUDY

French Drama (with some instruction) One play of Corneille, two of
Racine, five of Moliere and two of Beaumarchais.

6 weeks

Outline of Music (with Records)

6 weeks

Greek and Roman History

3 weeks

Medieval History (500-1500)

3 weeks

History of France (100 B.C. to last World War)

3 weeks

Eli Faure's Ancient and Medieval Art
                (with Architecture and drawing)

6 weeks

Eli Faure's Renaissance and Modern Art
                (with Architecture and drawing)

6 weeks

Decorative Art and Furniture

3 weeks.

Readings in Foreign Literature (excluding
                French and Russian
        (Greek, Roman, Italian, Spanish, German)   6 weeks

Cushman's Philosophy, with Readings

12 weeks

Spengler and Modern Philosophers
        (The above course is a pre-requisite)

12 weeks

To the time given these courses one-third must be added for
relaxation reading--unless two fairly easy courses are chosen
that can be taken simultaneously.

The total on the other side is sixty weeks. It would amount to
about a year and half's work.

The Novel
English

Bleak House) Dickens
Tale of Two Cities) *GREAT*
Henry Esmond)
The Virginians) Thackeray
Vanity Fair)
Pendennis)
Alice in Wonderland) Carrol
Alice Thru the Looking Glass)
Tess of the Durbervilles, Hardy
The White Company, Doyle
Tono Bungay, Wells
The Pretty Lady, Bennet
Youth's Encounter)
Sinister Street) McKenzie
A Portrait of the Artist, Joyce
Nocturne, Swinnerton
A Passage to India, Forster
The Moon and Sixpence, Maugham
The Sailor's Return, Garnett

The Short Story

Youth)
The Heart of Darkness) Conrad
Puck of Pook's Hill, Kipling
Dubliners, Joyce
Seven Men, Beerbohm
Lady into Fox, Garnett
The Woman who Rode Away, Lawrence
Christmas Garland, Beerbohm

Drama & Poetry

Macbeth
The Country Wife, Wycherly
Importance of Being Ernest, Wilde
The Playboy of the Western World, Synge
Man & Superman)
Heartbreak House) Shaw
Androcles & the Lion) - *Pamela*
Lyrics of Keats, Shelley, Marvel, *Browning*
Byron & Dowson *[handwritten notes]*

Wells' Outline of History
Morton's People's History
Byron, the last Journey, Nicolson
Colvin's KEATS
Arnold's ESSAYS
Charnwood's LINCOLN
Wilde's INTENTIONS

American
The Novel

Roderick Hudson)
The Europeans) James
Portrait of a Lady)
The Aspern Papers)
Sister Carrie)
The Financier) Dreiser
The Titan)
The Octopus, Norris
The Custom of the Country, Wharton
The Jungle, Sinclair
The Lost Lady, Cather
The Enormous Room, Cummings
A Farewell to Arms) Hemingway
The Sun Also Rises)
The Maltese Falcon, Hammet
Sanctuary, Faulkner

The Short Story

Daisy Miller) James
The Reverberator)
Perfect Tribute, Andrews
Lardner Stories
The Cabala, Wilde
Three Lives, Stein

Drama & Poetry

Pulitzer Plays
Lyrics of Poe, Masters, *Whitman Emerson Eliot Frost*
Lafargue's Property
Browne's Stranger than Fiction
Book of Daniel Drew
Ten Days that Shook the World, Reed
Flaubert & Mme. Bovary) Steegmuller
Ben Johnson)
Life of Wilde, Harris
Artmasterpieces, Craven
Van Loon's The Arts
Wilson's ESSAYS

French
The Novel
Les Liasons Dangereux, Laclos
Le Rouge et Noir, Stendahl
Notre Dame de Paris, Hugo
Peau du Chagrin)
Le Pere Goriot)Balzac
Eugenie Grandet)
La Cousine Bette)
Mme. Bovary, Flaubert
Thais   )France
Le Lys Rouge   )
Aphrodite, Llouys
A La Recherce de
  Temps Perdu (7 books) Proust
Cheri, Colette
La Condition Humaine, Malraux

The Short Story
La Succube, Balzac
Trois Contes, Flaubert
The Morceau de Ficelle   )
The Collier des Diamants)Maupassant
Le Maison Tellier   )

Poesy & happenes
by ... of Villon, Verlaine, Rimbaud

General
Renan's Jesus
Shelley by Maurois
Proust's Life

Other Literatures
The Novel
The Idiot   )
Crime and Punishment   )Dostoievski
The Brothers Karamazov   )
Anna Karenina)Tolstoi
War and Peace)
Smoke   )Turgenieff
Fathers and Sons   )
The Song of Songs, Suderman
GROWTH OF THE SOIL, Hamsun

The Short Story
The Decameron, Boccaccio
The Cloak, Gogol
The Darling, Chekov
Death in Venice, Thomas Mann
The Natural Woman, Maupassant

Drama *+ Poetry*
The Doll's House)Ibsen *The Wild Duck*
Hedda Gabbler   )
The Cherry Orchard, Chekov *Uncle Vanya*
Plays of Molnar
The Seagull

General
The Apologia)Plato
The Phaedo   )
Song of Solomon)
Ecclessiastes   )
Job   ) The Bible
Mathew   )
Mark   )
Luke   )
The Working Day, etc. Marx
Communist Manifesto, Marx & Engels
New Russia's Primer

Reading List

Well's Outline		159-184	Vanity Fair,	Thackeray
"	"	185-205	Man and Superman,	Shaw
"	"	205-226	The Red and the Black,	Stendhal
"	"	226-252	Bleak House (1st half)	Dickens
"	"	252-295	Seven Men,	Beerbohm
"	"	295-302	Bleak House (2nd half)	Dickens
"	"	302-322	Androcles & The Lion,	Shaw
"	"	322-344	Henry Esmond,	Thackeray
"	"	344-375	The Dolls House,	Ibsen
"	"	376-387	Sister Carrie,	Drieser
"	"	388-412	The Red Lily,	France
"	"	412-435	Youths Encounter,	McKenzie
"	"	435-454	Sinister Street,	McKenzie
"	"	455-480	The Kreutzer Sonata,	Tolstoi
"	"	480-501	Death In Venice,	Mann
"	"	501-523	Madam Bovary,	Flaubert
"	"	524-546	Custom of the Country,	Wharton
"	"	546-565	Brothers Karamazov,	Dostoevski
"	"	565-597	Tone Bungay,	Wells
"	"	599-617	Roderick Hudson,	James
"	"	617-634	The Pretty Lady,	Bennet
"	"	635-667	Tess of the Daburvilles,	Hardy
"	"	667-698	How to Write Short Stories,	Lardner
"	"	699-732	Cheri,	"Colette"
"	"	733-751	My Antonia,	Cather
"	"	751-778	The Sailors Return,	Garnett
"	"	778-803	The Financier,	Drieser
"	"	803-825	The Titan,	Drieser
"	"	825-866	The Lost Lady	Cather
"	"	867-893	The Revolt of The Angels,	France
"	"	893-928	"Ariel" or The Life of Shelley,	Maurois
"	"	929-955	The Song of Songs,	Suderman
"	"	956-991	The Sun Also Rises,	Hemingway
"	"	991-1025	Growth of the Soil	Hamsun
"	"	1025-1050	Byron: The Last Journey,	Nicholson
"	"	1051-1076	Southwind,	Douglas
"	"	1076-1101	Man's Fate,	Malraux
"	"	1102-1128	The Woman Who Rode Away,	Laurence
"	"	1128-1152	The Cabala,	Wilder
"	"	1152-1170 &Chronology	Tender Is The Night	Shakespeare

Renan's   Life of Christ

Joyce's   Portrait of an Artist

Stien's   Three Lives

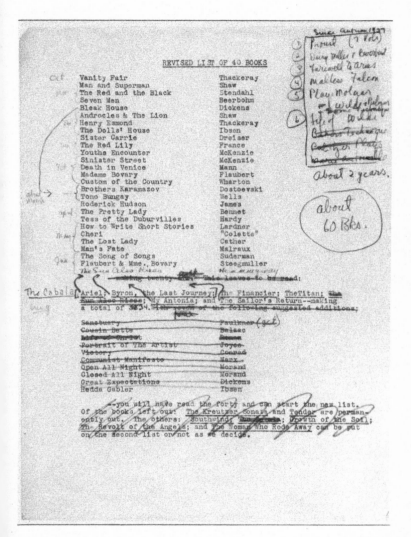

REVISED LIST OF 40 BOOKS

Vanity Fair	Thackeray
Man and Superman	Shaw
The Red and the Black	Stendahl
Seven Men	Beerbohm
Bleak House	Dickens
Androcles & The Lion	Shaw
Henry Esmond	Thackeray
The Dolls' House	Ibsen
Sister Carrie	Dreiser
The Red Lily	France
Youths Encounter	McKenzie
Sinister Street	McKenzie
Death in Venice	Mann
Madame Bovary	Flaubert
Custom of the Country	Wharton
Brothers Karamazov	Dostoevski
Tono Bungay	Wells
Roderick Hudson	James
The Pretty Lady	Bennet
Tess of the Duburvilles	Hardy
How to Write Short Stories	Lardner
Cheri	"Colette"
The Lost Lady	Cather
Man's Fate	Malraux
The Song of Songs	Suderman
Flaubert & Mme., Bovary	Steegmuller

making twenty-five of the leaves to be read;

Ariel; Byron, the Last Journey; The Financier; The Titan; The Sun Also Rises; My Antonia; and The Sailor's Return--making a total of 34. With some of the following suggested additions;

Sanctuary	Faulkner (get)
Cousin Betty	Balzac
Life of Christ	Renan
Portrait of The Artist	Joyce
Victory	Conrad
Communist Manifesto	Marx
Open All Night	Morand
Closed All Night	Morand
Great Expectations	Dickens
Hedda Gabler	Ibsen

--you will have read the forty and can start the new list. Of the books left out: The Kreutzer Sonata and Tender are permanently out. The others: Southwind; The Sorrows; Growth of the Soil; The Revolt of the Angels; and The Woman Who Rode Away can be put on the second list or not as we decide.

Substitute List of Good Novels

Virgin Soil) Turgieneff
Liza   )

London Venture, Winesburg
Some People

The Ambassadors   )
The Spoils of Poynton) JAMES
The Americans   )
The Princess Cassimessa)

Innocence of Father Brown

Ethan Fromme   )
The House of Mirth)Edith Wharton
Summer   )
Silas Marner
Jude the Obscure   )
The Mayor of Casterbridge)
Far from the Madding Crowd)HARDY
The Return of the Native   )
A Pair of Blue Eyes   )

Carnival   )) Compton McKenzie
Flashers Mead)
High Wind in Jamaica - Hughes

Jennie Gerhardt - Drieser
Barchester Towers, Trollope

Mr. Polly   )
The New Machiavelli)Wells
The Passionate Friends)

Dos Passos' Trilogy
The Spanish Farm, Mottram

Wuthering Heights, Bronte
William Miester, Goethe
Les Crois des Bois, Dorgelles
L'Abbe Constantin (in French)
South Wind, Douglas
Tartarin of Tarascon (in French)
The Wrong Box, Stevenson
A Sentimental Education, Flaubert
The Call of the Wild, London
Kennilworth, Scott

The Flirt)
Alice Adams)Tarkington
Women   )

Whom God has Joined, Bennet

The Arrow of Gold, Conrad
Some Do Not, Ford
Revolt of the Angeles, France
Theron Ware, Frederick
Une Vie, Maupassant
The Lord of the World (Benson)
Colette's Novels (in French)
Patience by Gilbert
Le Cousin Pons

A SHORT INTRODUCTION TO POETRY (with interruptions)

Preliminary: A Discussion of Prosody and the most familiar meters.

                The Eve of St. Agnes (Keats)
COLVIN'S KEATS Chaps. I-VIII inc.
                The Pot of Basil (Keats)
COLVIN'S KEATS Chaps IX to End
                Bright Star (Keats)   _dead_
                When I have Fears (Keats)
                On First Looking Into Chapman's Homer (Keats) _Reread Wilder._
                        Chapman's Odyssey--One Page
                        Butcher and Lang's THE ODYSSEY, Books 1-3

ARNOLD ON POETRY
                Poe's To Helen
                Tennyson's Now Sleeps the Crimson
                Christina Rosetti When I am Dead
                Lindsay's General William Booth (from the New Poetry)
                   "   The Congo

                        Chapman's ODYSSEY--Book 4
                        Pope's ODYSSEY--Book 5
                        Butler's ODYSSEY--Book 6

EVERYBODY'S AUTOBIOGRAPHY, Stein pps. 1-165
                Swinburne's The Garden of Proserpine
                   "   The Hounds of Spring (From Atlanta in Calydon)
                   "   A Forsaken Garden (From Oxford Book)
                   "   Laus Veneris

EVERYBODY'S AUTOBIOGRAPHY, Stein pps. 166 to end.
ARNOLD'S "ON WORDSWORTH"
                Behold her Single (Wordsworth)
                Ruth
                Kubla Khan (Coleridge)

                        Butcher & Lang's THE ODYSSEY, Books 7-9

PREFACE TO BROOKE (JAMES)
                The Voice--Rupert Brooke
                Tiare Tahiti "   "
                The Great Lover "   "

                        "On the Odyssey" by Lang (a poem p. 830 Oxford Bk).

                        Butler's ODYSSEY, Books 9-12

ESTHER WATERS--Chaps. 1-16
                Browning's Room after Room
                   "   The Lost Leader
                   "   Rabbi Ben Ezra
                   "   The Laboratory
                   "   Love Among the Ruins
ESTHER WATERS--Chaps. 17-29
                Elizabeth Browning's I thought once) from Sonnets
                                     If there must   ) from The Portugese
                                     How do I   )

ESTHER WATERS--Chaps. 30-to the End.

                        Butcher & Lang's ODYSSEY, Books 13-15

-2-

CHARNWOOD'S LINCOLN Chapters 1-5 (inc.)
                              Chapman's ODYSSEY - Book 16
                              Pope's ODYSSEY - Book 17
                              Butler's ODYSSEY-Book 18
                                west wind
CHARNWOOD'S LINCOLN Chapters 6-9 (inc.)
                              Butcher & Lang's ODYSSEY - Books 19-21

CHARNWOOD'S LINCOLN (to the end)
                    Whitman's My Captain
                           When Lilac's Last

                              Butler's ODYSSEY - Books 22-24
                    Menelaeus and Helen (Rupert Brooke)

GREAT EXPECTATIONS ~~Chapters~~
                    When in Disgrace - Shakespeare
                    Let me not
PORTRAIT OF MR. W.H. (Wilde) in part, and (or) Shaw's DARK LADY
                    When to the Sessions - Shakespeare
                    They that have Power
~~GREAT EXPECTATIONS - to end.~~ *Passages from Julius Caesar + Henry V (1)*
                    Ballad of Dead Ladies (Villon. See Lewis p. 348)
                    L'Allegro (Milton)
UNCLE VANYA (Chekov - in vol. with Cherry Orchard)
                    Where like a Pillow (Donne)
                    Portrait of a Lady (Eliott)   *Blake & Tagorigos*

GROWTH OF THE SOIL - 1st Half
JOSEPHSON ON RIMBAUD - P. 397 New Republic Anthology.
                    Il pleure dans ma coeur (Verlaine) Mary Colum's Trans
                    Claire de lune   "
                    Chanson D'Automne   "
                    Le Bateau Ivre (Rimbaud) - with
FROM THESE ROOTS (Mary Colum) pps. 289-360
A SEASON IN HELL (Rimbaud)
GROWTH OF THE SOIL - 2nd Half
WILSON'S "IS VERSE DYING" (From the Triple Thinkers)
                    The Waste Land (T.S. Eliott) - with
T.S. ELIOTT (Wilson) from Axel's Castle
                    Song (W.H. Auden) From New Republic Anthology
                    The Treasure (Rupert Brooke)

SOME TERMS

‾ a stressed or "long" syllable
◡ a slighted or "short" syllable

as ◡alo‾ne or ‾mon◡key or tee◡pe‾e *& English or*

The French language has no exact equivalent for this. We either
stress or slight every syllable.

‾‾word
◡◡◡

We break verse into "feet". According to the stress, we give these
"feet" different names. The most important is the iambus. Alone is
called an iambus. Also Oh Yeah! Five iambuses form a line of
iambic pentameter *(which means five feet in Greek)*

Example
But still/ the house/ affairs/ would call/ her hence

(Othello)
Shakespeare is all written in unrhymed iambic pentameter (except
his songs). He takes liberties with it of course adding an extra
syllable sometimes or dropping one or inverting a foot. At the
end of a scene he sometimes rhymes a couplet (2 lines)

Other types of "feet"

‾ ◡◡ =	a dactyl. Ex:	‾Per◡lmut◡ter
‾ ◡	a trochi Ex:	Feeble
◡ ◡ ‾	an anapest Ex:	on a bat
	spondee Ex:	Oh God (which can also be an iambus ◡‾)
		or a trochi, as pronounced.)

a trochaic line:
‾Come and/ ‾kiss ◡me / ‾sweet and/ ‾twenty

Song of Shakespeare's

a dactylic meter
‾This is ◡the/ ‾forest ◡pri◡meval

Longfellow
dactylic
(The song "Little Wooden shoes" is trochaic--so are many waltzes)

TYPES OF POETIC WRITING

Rhymed Verse	has metrical pattern (feet) and rhyme.
Blank Verse	has metrical pattern but no rhyme (Ex: Elizabethan blank verse.)
Free Verse	has a very loose metrical pattern which it neglects at will. No rhyme. Like Whitman or Master's "Anne Rutledge"
Ogden Nash Verse	Free Verse that rhymes
Prose Poetry } Polyphonic Prose}	Loose terms to denote anything from Butcher's & Lang's Odyssey to mere flowery language.

TYPES OF POEMS

Ballad	Short narrative
Epic	Long narrative
Dramatic	Shakespeare
Didactic	Instructive
Lyric	A song
Ode	An address
Serenade	Night song
Madrigal	Morning song
Elegy or Threnody	A lament
Pastoral)	
Bucolic)	Country Life

Ecologue and Epode--I never knew

SOME USUAL FORMS

Couplet	Two lines rhyming.
Heroic couplet	Two rhymed iambic pentameter lines like Pope's Odyssey.
Triolet	Three lines rhyming
Quatrain	Four lines Rhyming once or twice
Sonnet	Fourteen lines (8 and then 6) in iambic pentameter with a complete rhyme scene
Alexandrine line	rhymed six-foot couplet. Used in French Poetry (Racine and Corneille)
Hyperbole	exaggeration.

<u>THIRD LIST</u>

<u>Religion</u> and <u>Fiction</u> (1? Readings)

Ecclesiastes
       Portrait of a Lady
                Plates 67-71 (Dutch)

Book of Job
       Anna Karenina
                Plates 84-86 (Spanish) plus
                                45-46 (late Italian)

Gospel of St. Mark
       The Cherry Orchard
                Plates 96-106 (Hogarth-Turner)

Renan (Chapters I-VIII)
       Alice Through the Looking Glass
                Plates 87-95 Fouquet-Corot and
                      116-120 Delacroix-Courbet (French)

Renan (Chapters IX-XIX)
       Playboy of the Western World (Synge)
                Plates 121-128 (From Manet)

Renan (Chapters XX-XXVIII)
       Pendennis
                Plates 129-138 (Cezanne-Grosz)

Preface to Androcles and the Lion
       Sanctuary
                Plates 107-115 (Copley-Bellows) plus
                139-144 (Sloane-Wood)

Short History of the Jews after 100 A.D. (Strange man Fiction)
            Alice B. Toklas

<u>FOURTH LIST--(Part I)--Philosophy, History, Fiction, Drama</u>
                  Part I (30 Readings)

1. Check Well's dates to 359 B.C.; Jowett's Life of Plato
                                              pps. 7-20
   2. THE DARLING (Chekov, Russian Stories)
3. Plato: The Apologia. Vol. III (101-134)
      4. APHRODITE (Pierre Louys) *Pan di Caprie*
5. Plato: Phaedo. Vol. III (214-243)
   6. NOCTURNE (Swinnerton) *Sophronele*
7. Plato: Phaedo. Vol. III (243-271)
      8. THE ASPERN PAPERS (James) *Read Nuclear*
      9. BURLESQUE OF JAMES (Beerbohm) in Woolcott Reader
10. Lafargue's Evolution of Property--Chaps. 1-3 inc.
         11. PEAU DE CHAGRIN (Balzac) The Wild Asses' Skin *Nocturne*
12. Well's dates, 359 B.C.-312 A.D. Prentice's Heritage of
                       The Cathedral, Chaps. 11-7 inc.
         13. THE PEARL NECKLACE AND THE PIECE OF STRING
                                          (Maupassant)
14. Morton's Peoples History Chap. I, Well's dates 312-407
      15. KIPLING: PUCK OF POOK'S HILL: pps. 1-16 and
                                          pps. 135-224
16. Morton: Chaps. II & III, Well's dates 407-1215
   17. CONTES DROLLATIQUE: THE SUCCUBUS
                                          (Balzac)
18. Morton: IV, Well's dates 1215-1381 *Decline of Feudalism*
      19. THE WHITE COMPANY (Doyle)
20. Morton V, Well's dates 1381-1485 *End of the middle Ages*
      21. THE DECAMERON: TEN Stories (Boccacio)
22. Morton VI, Well's dates 1485-1567 *Bourgeois and peasantry*
      23. O Rare Ben Jonson (Steirmuller)
24. Morton VII, Well's dates 1567-1640 *Surgery Revolution*
      25. The Dark Lady of the Sonnets (Shaw)
26. Morton VIII, Well's dates 1640-1649 *The English Revolution*
27. THE COUNTRY WIFE (Wycherly)
28. Morton IX., Well's dates 1649-1692 *Commonwealth + Empire*
      29. LES LIAISONS DANGEREUX (Dangerous Acquaintances) --
                                          Le Clos
30. Morton X, Well's dates 1692-1788 *Whig England*

FOURTH LIST (Part II) History, Economics, Fiction, Drama
Part II (31 Readings)

      1. THE VIRGINIANS (Thackeray)
2. Morton XI. Well's dates 1788-1815   *The Industrial Revolution*
      3. A TALE OF TWO CITIES
4. Lafargue : Chaps. 4 & 5 inc.
      5. LE PERE GORIOT (Balzac)
6. Morton XII. Well's dates 1815-1832
      7. CRIME AND PUNISHMENT (Dostoievski)
8. Morton Chap. XIII. Well's dates 1832-1875
9. Das Kapital. Chap. 10. The Working Day. Sec. 1-3 inc.
      10.
      11.
12. Das Kapital Chap. 10. Sec. 4-7 inc.
13. Morton Chap XIV.
      14. FATHERS AND SONS (Turgeniev)
15. The Communist Manifesto. Well's dates 1875-1914
16. The Book of Daniel Drew (White)
      17. THE OCTOPUS (Frank Norris)
      18. THE JUNGLE (Upton Sinclair)
      19. THE HEART OF DARKNESS (Conrad) in "Youth" volume
      20. BURLESQUE OF CONRAD (Beerbohm) in Woolcott Reader
21. Morton Chap. XV
      22. HEARTBREAK HOUSE (Shaw)
      23. BURLESQUE OF SHAW (Beerbohm) in Woolcott Reader
24. Morton Chap. XVI and Chap. XVII thru section 2.
      25. THE ENORMOUS ROOM (Cummings)
26. The Ten Days that Shook the World (Reed): Finish Well's Dates
27. Reed's Early Life (from New Republic Anthology)
      28. A PASSAGE TO INDIA
29. New Russia's Primer
      30. THE WOMAN WHO RODE AWAY (Lawrence)
31. Morton: Epilogue
32. Wilson: The Triple Thinkers: Chap. on Lenin and Literature

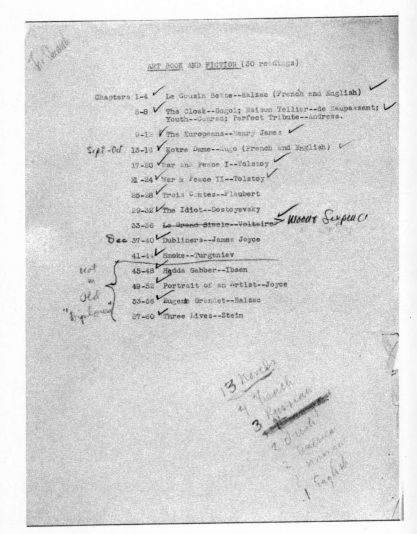

ART BOOK AND FICTION (30 readings)

Chapters 1-4   Le Cousin Bette--Balzac (French and English)

  5-8   The Cloak--Gogol; Maison Tellier--de Maupassant;
        Youth--Conrad; Perfect Tribute--Andrews.

  9-12 The Europeans--Henry James

Sept-Oct 13-16   Notre Dame--Hugo (French and English)

  17-20 War and Peace I--Tolstoy

  21-24 War & Peace II--Tolstoy

  25-28 Trois Contes--Flaubert

  29-32 The Idiot--Dostoyevsky

  33-36 Le Grand Siecle--Voltaire   *Proust Swann*

Dec 37-40 Dubliners--James Joyce

  41-44 Smoke--Turgeniev

  45-48 Hedda Gabber--Ibsen

  49-52 Portrait of an Artist--Joyce

  53-56 Eugenie Grandet--Balzac

  57-60 Three Lives--Stein

13 novels
4 French
3 Russian
2 Dutch
America
England

SIXTH LIST

AN OUTLINE OF MUSIC; GRAECO-ROMAN HISTORY; TEN NOVELS

FREDERIC FRANCOIS CHOPIN (Chapter X – Ewan)
Mazurka, C Sharp Minor, Opus 50, No. 3
Etudes C Sharp Minor, Opus 10, No. 4
G Flat Major ("Black Key") Opus 10, No. 5
Polonaise, A Flat Major, Opus 53

CLAUDE ACHILLE DEBUSSY (Chapter XVII – Ewan – in part)
Iberia
Prelude a L'apres-midi d'un faune
Le Plus que Lent

NIKOLAI RIMSKY-KORSAKOV (Chapter XIV – Ewan – in part)
The Flight of the Bee

(1.) Greek Forms, Review Wells – Chapter XX . *Solon and Lycurgos/Pericles*

~~DISTINGUISH ET XPORES THE COMMENTED (Seiums)~~
            M^c TEAGUE (Frank Norris)
CARL MARIA VON WEBER (Chapter VIII – Ewan – in part)
Invitation to the Dance
Der Freischutz: overture

FRANZ PETER SCHUBERT (Chapter IX – Ewan)
Symphony B Minor ("Unfinished")
String quartet – Death and The Maiden

FELIX MENDELSSOHN-BARTHOLDY (Chapter VIII – Ewan – in part)
A Midsummer Night's Dream: overture
Concerto, Violin and Orchestra, E Minor

(2.) Review Wells – Chapter XXI

            THE DEVILS (The Possessed) Dostoyevsky

MAURICE RAVEL (Chapter XVII – Ewan – in part)
Bolero
IGOR STRAVINSKY (Chapter XIX – Ewan)
Le Sacre du printemps
Petrouchka
SERGEI PROKOFIEV (Encyclopedia)
Love for Three Oranges

(3.) Pericles (Plutarch)

        ~~THE EGOTIST (George Meredith)~~ *Bridge of St Louis Re*
        ~~Decline and Fall (Evelyn Waugh)~~
LUDWIG VAN BEETHOVEN (Chapter VII – Ewan)
Kreutzer Sonata
Symphony No. 3 ("Eroica")
Moonlight Sonata

(4.) Alexander – from Bolitho's "Twelve Against The Gods".

        ~~THE WAY OF ALL FLESH~~ (Butler) *Egotist*

JOHANN SEBASTIAN BACH (Chapter III – Ewan)
The Well-tempered Clavichord: Preludes and Fugues
Toccata and Fugue in D.
GEORGE FREDERIC HANDEL (Chapter IV – Ewan)
Water Music

(5.) Roman Forms, Wells Chapter XXV (Section 1 – 4 inc.)
        ~~THE C.....~~
        ~~NOSTROMO (Frank Norris)~~   *DECLINE AND FALL*
        ~~THE WAY OF ALL FLESH~~   *(Evelyn Waugh)*
            (MORE)

Page 2.

RICHARD WAGNER (Chapter XII - Evan)
Siegfried Idyl; Lohengrin, Preludes to Act I & III
Die Gotterdammerung: Daybreak and Rhine Journey
Die Meistersinger: Prelude
FRANZ LISZT (Chapter XVIII - Evan - in part)
Hungarian Rhapsody No. 2, C Sharp Major, Piano

> (6.) Zama (From Bullon's Battles); Fabius (Plutarch);
>   and comparison of Pericles and Fabius (Plutarch)
>
>   THE BOSTONIANS (Henry James) — or ~~Way of All Flesh~~
>   VICTORY (Joseph Conrad)
>   With Preface to "Nigger of the Narcissus"

MODEST MOUSSORGSKY (Chapter XIV - Evan - in part)
Pictures for an Exhibition
ALEKSANDR SCRIABIN (Chapter XIV - Evan - in part)
PIOTR ILICH TCHAIKOVSKY (Chapter XV - Evan)
Nutcracker Suite
Concerto, Violin and Orchestra D. Major

> (7.) Revolution in Sparta (Postgate) New Republic Anthology P.514
>   Julius Caesar - Froude (Chapters I-XV inc.)
>   LE DIABLE AU CORPS (Raymond Radiquet) - or
>   ~~HIGH WIND IN JAMAICA (Richard Hughes)~~

FRANZ JOSEF HAYDN (Chapter V - Evan)
Symphony No. 94 ("Surprise")
Quartet, Strings D Major ("L rk") Opus 64, No. 5
WOLFGANG AMADEUS MOZART (Chapter VI - Evan)
Symphony, D Major
Concerto, Violin & Orchestra A Major

> (8.) Julius Caesar - Froude (Chapters XVI to End)
>   THE BRIDGE OF SAN LUIS REY (Thornton Wilder)
>   ~~HIGH WIND IN JAMAICA (Richard Hughes)~~

ROBERT SCHUMANN (Chapter XI - Evan)
Concerto, Piano and Orchestra A Minor
Quartet, Piano and Strings, E Flat Major
Carnival - Piano
CESAR FRANCK (Chapter XVI - Evan - in part)
JEAN SIBELIUS (Chapter XX - Evan - in part)
Violin concerto
En Saga

> (9.) Wells: From section 6, P.473 to end of 1st paragraph P.474
>   Anthony and Cleopatra (Shakespeare)
>   ~~DECLINE AND FALL (Evylyn Waugh)~~
>   THE BOSTONIANS (Henry James)

JOHANNES BRAHMS (Chapter XIII - Evan)
Variations on a Theme by Haydn
Concerto, Piano and Orchestra, No. 2, B Flat Major
GIUSEPPE VERDI (Encyclopedia)
Aida: "Ritorna Vincitor"

> (10) Preface to Modern Library Suetonius
>   Life of Nero - Suetonius
>   JUDE THE OBSCURE or
>   LOOK HOMEWARD ANGEL (Wolfe) - or
>   BREAD AND WINE (Silone)

(MORE)

Page 3.

CHARLES FRANCOIS GOUNOD (Encyclopedia)
RICHARD STRAUSS (Chapter XVIII - Emn - in part)
Der Rosenkavalier
ANTONIN DVORAK (Encyclopedia)
Slavonic Dances
EDVARD HAGERUP GRIEG (Encyclopedia)
Anitra's Dance

    (11.) Gibbon's Rome - Chapters I & II
          Wells' Dates 180A.D. - 476A.D. (with my new markings)
          Willa Cather's "In the Palatine (Dark Ages)"
          The New Poetry.

POLITICAL DEVELOPMENT OF THE GRAECO-ROMAN ("CLASSIC") WORLD

(Adapted from Spengler - to be studied
in connection with readings in Sixth List)

PRE-CULTURAL PERIOD. PRIMITIVE FOLK. TRIBES AND THEIR CHIEFS.
AS YET NO "POLITICS" AND NO "STATE".
The Three Legends, Legens of the gods
Mycenean Age (1600-1100 B.C.)

CULTURE. NATIONAL GROUPS OF DEFINITE STYLE. THEY BECOME "NATIONS".

I. Early Period. The two prime classes (noble and priest).
   Feudal economics; purely agrarian values.

(a.) Feudalism. Spirit of countryside and
     countryman. The "City" only a market or
     stronghold. Chivalric-religious ideals.
     Struggles of vassals amongst themselves
     and against overlord. *Beowulf & Odysseus*

(1100-650)
The Homeric Kingship
Rise of the nobility
(Ithaca, Etruria in Italy,
Sparta)

(b.) Crisis and dissolution of patriarchal
     forms. From feudalism to aristocratic
     State. *Aesop & Sapho - the Greek Colonies*

Dissolution of kingship
into annual offices
Oligarchy
Orphic Religion

II. Late Period. Actualizing of the matured State-idea.
    Town versus countryside. Rise of Third Estate (Bourgeoisie).
    Victory of money over landed property.

(c.) The State adopts a fixed form.

Aeschylus 525.
Socrates
Phidias and Acropolis

Athenian Period (650-300)
6th Century. The Early
Tyrants. (Cleisthenes,
Periander, Polycrates in
Greece, and the Tarquins in
Rome) The City-State.
Popular Culture

(d.) Climax of the State-form ("Absolutism")
     Unity of town and country (The "three
     estates") *Plato 427*

The pure People (absolu-
tism of the Crowd.)
Crowd politics
Rise of the tribunate
Themistocles, Pericles

(e.) Break-up of the State-form (Revolution
     and Napoleonism). Victory of the city
     over the countryside (of the "people"
     over the privileged, of the intelligent-
     sia over tradition, of money over policy)
     Aristotle 384

4th Century. Social re-
volution and late Tyrannies
(Dionysius I, Jason of
Pherae, Appius Claudius
the Censor) Alexander

CIVILIZATION. THE BODY OF THE PEOPLE, NOW ESSENTIALLY URBAN IN
CONSTITUTION, DISSOLVES INTO FORMLESS MASS. MEGALOPOLIS
(LIKE ROME, LONDON, NEW YORK) AND PROVINCES. THE
FOURTH ESTATE ("MASSES"), INORGANIC, COSMOPOLITAN

(a.) Domination of Money ("Democracy")
     Economic powers permeating the political
     forms and authorities.

     EPICURUS - ARCHIMEDES

300-100. Political Hellen-
ism. From Alexander to
Hannibal and Scipio royal
all-power; from Cleomenes
III and C.Flaminius (220)
to C.Marius, radical dema-
gogues.

(b.) Formation of Caesarism. Victory of force-
     politics over money. Increasing primitive-
     ness of political forms. Inward decline of
     the nations into a formless population.
     Gradually-increasing crudity of despotism. *(VIRGIL - HORACE - PETRONIUS)*

100 B.C.-0-100 A.D. From
Sulla

Caesar, Tiberius

(c.) Maturing of the final form. Private and
     family policies of individual leaders
     The world as spoil. History less stiff-
     ening and enfeeblement even of the imperial
     machinery, against young peoples eager for
     spoil, or alien conquerors. PRIMITIVE HUMAN
     CONDITIONS SLOWLY THRUST UP INTO THE HIGHLY-
     CIVILIZED MODE OF LIVING.

100-300 Trajan to
Aurelian

Trajan, Septimius Severus,

Reading 1 covers this period for Greece;
the first part of Reading 5 for Rome.
Reading 5 for Rome.
Readings 2 & 3
Reading 4
Reading 6
Readings 7, 8, 9, 10
Reading - 11

POLITICAL DEVELOPMENT OF THE ANGLO-EUROPEAN WORLD

PRE-CULTURAL   (500-900)
  Anglo-Saxons in England. Franks in France--Charlemange.
  Siegfried, Arthur, Beowulf and Charlemang, legends
  [Fermined by the Scalds]

CULTURE   National Groups become "Nations"

I Early Period

(a) From Canute to the Crusades. The struggles between church
    and state. (900-1200)
       Epic Poems fashioned from the above legends

(b) The great Rennaissance towns like Florence and Venice. The
    struggle between king and nobles in England and France (King
    winning with the Tudors) *Dante to Villon -- the Flying Buttress*
    II Late Period

(c) Dynastic family power balanced by great bourgeoise leaders
    (Cromwell in England, Richelieu in France, Wallenstien in
    Germany) (1500-1650)

       Shakespeare
       Descartes
       Michael Angelo - to Bach

(d) Ancien Regime in France--Stuarts still struggling for that
    idea in England (which is eighty years ahead politically)
    (1650-1775) ←   *William of Orange -- Frederick*
       Voltaire   *The Great - Franklin*

(e) End of XVIII century. Revolution in America and France
    (Washington, Fox, Mirabeau, Robespierre (1775-1815)
       Kant

Napoleon

CIVILIZATION

(a) 19th century. From Napoleon to the World War. "System of
    the great powers", standing armies, constitutions.
       MARX - DARWIN

(b) 20th Century. Transition from constitutional to informal
    sway of individuals. Annihilation wars. Imperialism.   *Freud and Einstein Whee oredions*

       [TOLSTOI - LAFORGUE - JOYCE *in literature*]

(c) ? ? ?

APPENDIX 2:
SHORT STORY: "BELOVED INFIDEL"

Columbia Carter [handwritten annotations]
throughout
[handwritten]

Sheilah Graham
1443 N. Hayworth Avenue
Hollywood, California

" BELOVED INFIDEL "

by Sheilah Graham [handwritten]

"I'm having a few people in for drinks," Doug told

him apologetically in the elevator. "Drop in."

John O'Brien hesitated, then said, "Sure -- thanks --."

His dislike of Douglas Taylor dated from their Freshmen days at

Yale. They lived in the same apartment building overlooking the

East River. ~~They were~~ continually meeting in the elevator. It

was simpler to keep up a show of friendship.

Douglas was thirty-nine, fat, popular at parties

because of his reputation for wit and his booming laugh. He ~~wrote~~
of Repeal; once he had done ecclesiastical interiors — now he did modernistic [handwritten]
~~a smart, but brief piece for a smart, weekly~~ magazine. He was
with a homey touch of the ecclesiastical. He was [handwritten]
never tired of telling that he had not tasted liquor or kissed

a woman until he was thirty-one. Nowadays he did ~~too~~ much of

both.

John O'Brien was thirty-eight, but looked thirty,

particularly when he smiled. It was a charming, slow smile that

lingered in his thick~~ly~~ lashed ~~blue~~ eyes several seconds after

his mouth had reverted to its normal, rather sad lines. He had

the build of a lightweight boxer, ~~broad well-developed shoulders;~~
and he [handwritten]
~~narrow hips, strong, well-shaped legs.~~ He walked like a fighter

with his head slightly tucked into his neck, his arms swinging,

and fists closed as though ready to strike. *He had* [handwritten]

~~He had~~ been the best looking man of his class at ~~Yale.~~ *New*
~~If you wanted to annoy him in those days, you called him 'Beautiful'.~~
Haven. The lines and coloring of his face ~~was~~ *were* still like a masculin~~ized~~ *e*

edition of Priscilla Lane.

Explain to your typist difference between dash + hyphen in short [handwritten]
[illegible] One is — ; the other (on the typewriter) is — [handwritten]

2.

At twenty-one he had ~~been persuaded to~~ exhibited his
drawings at Knoedler's New York Galleries. He ~~was the first~~ had gone
~~American artist to go no~~ further than home -- Virginia -- for
(West)
his models. ~~The critics raved over his~~ a pictorial weekly brutal, realistic portrayals
~~of decayed Virginia gentlemen, their land, their negro servants.~~
~~The magazine used~~ his picture on the cover and ~~used~~ used six pages to
eulogize and reproduce his work.

Shortly afterwards, he married beautiful, ~~auburn~~
~~haired~~ Alicia Sanders. They were the most popular couple of
The early Thirties. ~~that crazy decade. You didn't count unless you knew them --~~
~~or said you did. No party of the intelligentsia or rich Long~~
~~Island set~~ was considered a success ~~unless~~ John and Alicia
O'Brien ~~were there.~~ He was glamour boy number one and his gay
vivid wife trailed happily along in the cloud of his glory.

Alicia ~~had died~~ was dead six years ~~ago~~ now. Since then, John had
been variously reported as dying of tuberculosis, living ~~with~~ on a
cannibal ~~brood of native women and children~~ in a South Sea Island, shot as
a spy by Franco's soldiers in Spain, and running an opium establishment in China. He had turned up in New York six months ago,
taciturn, unobstrusive, with an unexpected line of defeat round
his sensitive mouth.

He decided not to go to Taylor's cocktail party. But
he went.

"You must have guessed I'd be there," Mara Mackenzie
told him later.

There were not many people in the room. "It's a small
party," Doug explained, ~~with his habitual air of apology.~~ John
sat down in a corner, took a long shy time to light a cigarette, and
through the smoke glanced acutely around the room.

3.

~~Usual bunch of dull people, he decided.~~ There was
a bald movie actor, who laughed in between the pauses of Douglas'
anecdotes. Another painter whom John knew slightly. Three women
he did not know ~~-- hard masculine types~~. A ~~short, slender~~ Frenchman who discussed the ~~high~~ *awful* prices of New York ~~very~~ earnestly with
an Englishman -- and, listening to them with an expression of
fascinated interest in her vaguely up-slanting eyes, a blonde girl
of about ~~21~~ *twenty-one* with a ~~cream~~ skin ~~as fine as smooth note paper~~ *like peach-colored note paper.*

~~Douglas thrust a drink into John's hand. He put it on
a table and wondered why in hell he had come.~~ One of the hard,
masculine women tried to draw him out:

"Are you living in New York now?" she asked with sterile
vivacity.

He said, "Yes," -- ~~And "No," when she wondered whether~~ *and after ten minutes*
stood up ~~he had seen the Linders lately.~~

"You're not going, ~~John~~," Douglas said with a great
show of disappointment when John walked towards the door.

"I'm expecting a long distance call," he lied ~~glibly~~.

"Come back afterwards," said Doug by the door. "We'll
wait for you."

~~--In a pig's eye I will,~~ said ~~John~~ to himself ~~and escaped.~~

~~He called Doug from his apartment, but Doug wouldn't
accept his excuses.~~ *called him immediately in*

"Come on, we're all going out to dinner." And he
mentioned ~~a feminine~~ name *Ruth Somebody -- a* that seemed to belong to the ~~attractive~~
~~blonde girl~~ *An* unexpected flicker of anticipation ~~touched~~ John. *peach-colored note paper*

"All right~~, he said~~, I'll be right over."

But Ruth turned out to be one of the hard, masculine

4.

women. And the ~~blonde~~ *other* girl had gone. He had a miserable evening that was not bettered in retrospect when he heard a few days later ~~from Eddie Barnett, one of the few men he still liked,~~ *from Lady Barrett* that Ruth was dining out on the lie of how J~~oh~~hn had ~~tried to seduce~~ *made passes at* her, and of how she had repulsed him.

"There was a lovely blonde girl at Doug's party," J~~oh~~hn told Eddie. "Round face, ~~questing lips~~ *extraordinary skin*, Mongolian ~~looking~~ eyes -- "

Sounds like Mara Mackenzie, Eddie laughed.

"Anything wrong with her?"

"No -- she's going to marry Lord Mulhaven -- or rather the Earl of. Doug was giving the party for them."

"Oh," said J~~oh~~hn and would have dismissed her from his *thoughts* ~~mind~~ -- but Eddie said:

"He went back to London the day after the party -- I'll call her and see if she's free tonight."

She was not free.

"Put off your concert," Eddie persisted on the telephone. "A friend of mine -- J~~oh~~hn *Carter* O'Brien -- ~~wants to meet you~~ -- Oh, you won't come for me -- but for him --" Eddie laughed, put the receiver down -- "She's coming ~~-- you made a hit with her too.~~"

They went to the Stork Club.

~~She's~~ "She's passionate, X J~~oh~~hn decided, ~~enjoying her glowing face~~. Her slanting eyes weren't grey after all, they were green, rimmed with gold.

He asked her to dance. *She was*

~~Mara was~~ about *half a foot* ~~six inches~~ shorter than J~~oh~~hn and when she jerked her head back, her thick, *dark gold* ~~yellow-brown~~ hair tickled his chin.

5.

"Is it getting in your mouth?" she asked him once with
a soft ~~giggle~~ *chuckle* and quick throw-back of her head. She stared con-
fidently ~~into his oval eyes. He~~ *at him and he* smiled, enjoying her coquetry.

"I like your nose," he told her.

She self-consciously touched it, and opened her mouth
with a quick intake of breath ~~that made John want to kiss her.~~
Their eyes held together and the smile left both faces, leaving
behind a faint anger.

~~"I'm sorry my fiance had to leave -- I'd like you to
have met him," Mara said breathlessly.~~

"When are you getting married?" he asked absently.

"In about three months." ~~The words had a sobering
effect on her. Why did George leave her exposed to attractive men
like this? She must watch her step.~~ *Watch your step.* A working girl didn't have
a chance to be a Countess every day. She followed ~~John~~ *they* as ~~he~~
weaved in and out of tables ~~until they reached~~ *to* their own.

Mara looked at her diamond and platinum watch, *a* gift
~~from~~ *of* George *Mulhaven.*

"Don't go yet," John ~~pleaded.~~ *pled.*

"One more highball," Eddie ~~said~~ *objected* and went ~~to~~ *off* the bar.

~~When she looked at John again, his smile had a warm,
friendly quality.~~

"I ~~could talk to you and you'd understand,~~" she said.
~~and~~ Under his almost ~~naive~~ questioning she told him the highlights
of her existence. How she had been married at eighteen ~~to an
american~~ *to an* Army officer -- ~~that they~~ were divorced five years later.
that she was now twenty-seven and for the past four years had
worked for Conde Nast. She was now assistant editor of ~~Vogue a~~
~~a fashion magazine.~~ *been an* *two fashion magazines.*

6.

"Eddie says you're very clever and make a fabulous salary," John said with the smile that started in one corner of his mouth and travelled with his head in a semi-circle towards her.

"I've been lucky -- and clever," she ~~laughed~~ said. "The fabulous ~~salary is~~ *make* $150 a week."

"Where do you live?"

"Just around the corner -- ~~55 East~~ *on* 54th Street. *Will*

~~"Alone?"~~

~~"I have a day maid --~~ will you come to see me?"

"When?"

"Tomorrow?"

"About six o'clock?"

~~Eddie re-joined them, and Mara suddenly felt extremely tired and they took her home.~~

The next day, Mara's maid awakened her ~~at nine o'clock~~ with a telegram. From John. He was going away, didn't know when he would be back.

"The man's lying," she said aloud, and was surprised at her disappointment. She broke every rule in her code ~~on how~~ *by* ~~to deal with men. She~~ telephon~~ed~~*NG* him.

He was embarrassed, but insisted he _was_ going away.

"I'm meeting my son --" he ~~mumbled~~ *said*.

"When will you be back?" she persisted.

"Friday." It was now Tuesday.

"Let's all have dinner on Friday -- I'd like to meet your son." She was amazed at ~~her persistence~~ *herself*.

7.

He hesitated, then agreed.

"She's damn ~~sure of herself," he said after replacing the receiver. He smiled. Then sighed.~~

Mara called Eddie.

"Let's have dinner tonight," she said ~~very~~ authoritatively.

Eddie was suspicious.

"What do you want?"

She affected to be hurt.

"To see you, of course."

"You're a fake, Mara, but ~~a delightful fake.~~ *seven-thirty.*" ~~Seven-thirty?"~~

There was nothing subtle about Mara when she was on the track of information, and they were barely seated at Voisin's when she plunged into the subject of ~~John~~ O'Brien. ~~Eddie was willing to talk. Most people were about John O'Brien.~~

"He wasn't just a success -- he was a legend. Once I saw him almost kill a man, ~~who~~ *It was*

~~"How and why?" breathed Mara, her eyes alight.~~

~~"It was Harrison --~~ ✓John Harrison -- the actor. He was drunk and ~~slightly~~ unpleasant to Alicia, John's wife, *who died.*" ~~There wasn't much left of him after they scraped him away from John."~~

~~"Don't tell me men still fight over their women," said Mara skeptically.~~

~~"They don't, dearie -- this was ten years ago."~~

"What was his wife like?" Mara asked casually.

"Very much like you," Eddie said.

"Oh."

~~Eddie glanced at her quickly, then looked away.~~

"I warned him against you." *he said*

8.

~~Mara threw her head back and laughed.~~

"What did you say?"

"That you were ~~fickle, unreliable, and --~~" *kind of a tramp, he teased her*

"*Shut up*" Does he like me?"

"Yes, ~~you little devil.~~"

"I like him -- tremendously."

"Leave him alone, Mara."

"~~But~~ Why? Can't a girl have a ~~nice~~ friendship*?" she threw back his head and laughed.* ~~She opened her eyes widely and pouted her lips into a soft pout.~~

"Not when you look like that. What about the Earl?"

"Oh, him?" She ~~moved her head backwards~~ *dropped a match on the folder* and tossed George out of her life. "I don't see myself as a belted Countess, do you?"

Eddie looked at her with a regretful smile ~~on his homely face.~~

"I'm not sure what I a e you as, darling. I only know I love you."

She pressed his hand sympathetically, started a speech that began with, "Eddie --" and trailed off into distressed silence.

II

Carley's ~~John's~~ son was a smaller replica of his father -- *he* ~~except for his hair, which was a rich auburn.~~ He had the same quiet charm that would suddenly transfigure his face, and the same ~~twisted~~ smile. ~~He had inherited his father's oval blue~~ eyes. *and rain-blue* *There* ~~There~~ was another good-looking boy and two ~~nondescript~~ girls, ~~aged around~~ fifteen.

"We'll go to the Louvre. The kids want to dance," said *Said* the older John. ~~"There's a good band there."~~

9.

The younger ~~John~~ Carter was suddenly solemn.

"No gambling, Dad."

"I'm merely a looker on," said Carter loyally. Mara

~~"That's not your business." Mara was surprised at the~~
~~irritation in John's voice. She~~ suddenly remembered now some fantastic
stories she had heard of John's gambling ~~sprees~~ -- one of them was
said to have lasted two weeks without John leaving the roulette
table night or day. ~~But like most of the legends about John, she~~
~~supposed it had been exaggerated.~~ She rather hoped he would
~~gamble~~ play tonight. ~~It would be exciting to watch.~~ but when she
suggested ~~this~~ he shook his head emphatically.

~~"I've sworn off gambling."~~

~~Mara found~~ The evening was always a strain. John was less exciting
in the role of a father. ~~He seemed nervous, and~~ too watchful of
his son. He forced ~~the~~ conversation while the The four youngsters talked
"down" to Mara and John, ~~and~~ they only seemed ~~completely at ease~~ natural when
they were dancing.

"They make me feel old," Mara told John when they were
alone at the table. She

~~"Me, too," he~~ confessed.

~~She praised John Junior and his father was pleased.~~
~~But Mara felt dull.~~ She was glad when he suggested taking her
home.

"Don't be late," John cautioned his son. In the taxi, she
avenged herself for her feeling of dullness by painting for
for John a ~~Mara told John of the numerous~~ detailed picture of the men she had been in love with and
was annoyed at his refusal to be shocked. At

~~"Good-night," Mara said coolly~~ at the door of her
apartment. she said good night cooly - then looked
~~"Good-night," John said just as coolly.~~ at him once more.

10.

Mara looked up quickly. He was smiling. The shadow
of the door made deep holes under his high cheek bones. ~~The~~ *out all the*
outlines of his face were lost. ~~She smiled at him challengingly~~ *She smiled back instinctively*
and put up her face ~~to be kissed.~~

"You look like a ~~rose~~ blue rose," he ~~told her~~ *said his*
softly. ~~His voice was like a low-toned song.~~

~~His~~ *own* face ~~came~~ *coming* out of the shadows ~~and he~~ kissed her
warm lips. ~~gently at first, then hard as passion dropped them~~
~~into a delicious whirlpool.~~

She pulled him gently inside the room. The curtains
had been left open and the light from the street softly illuminated
the grey and pink Marie Laurencin over the fireplace, ~~and the wide,~~
~~dark green settee.~~

"You couldn't get away ~~from me~~," Mara *she* boasted exultantly.

~~"I was doomed from the second I saw your lovely face --~~
~~let's sit down."~~

Holding hands tightly, they found the settee. ~~Mara was~~
~~excited and happy, as always when she made a conquest.~~

"I believe I'm in love with you," she ~~told him~~ *whispered.*

"You sound surprised," ~~she shifted her body from the~~
~~uncomfortable position in his arms.~~

"It's unusual," she sighed breathlessly and found her
handkerchief to wipe the lip rouge from his face. He put her
hand aside, and kissed her eyes.

~~She let him go at two o'clock.~~

~~A great content remained with Mara during her sleep,~~
~~and she woke up smiling.~~

III

They were married at the City Hall two weeks later. ~~It~~

~~Was a quiet effair~~ with two strangers for witnesses. They walked
round the square afterwards, ~~the~~ *with the* love ~~in their hearts~~ flowing
around
~~between~~ them like a great friendly river.

John pressed her arm and smiled ~~widely~~ into her bright

face.

"You beautiful girl."

She smiled exultantly.

"I am beautiful, aren't I?"

"I love you, Mara."

Passers-by were stopping to stare and grin. Mara

giggled.

"We'd better go home."

Then ~~They~~ drove *out* to the Connecticut farmhouse they had

rented for the summer. ~~John was a fast driver, swinging crazily~~
~~round corners, hooting loudly.~~ *There were*

~~She liked the~~ lofty eucalyptus trees shading the square

wooden house with its blue painted shutters. On one side was a

~~wide~~ stone flagged terrace with a blue and white awning and ~~green~~
and under   *bloomed a newly painted*
garden chairs. ~~Under~~ a large tree ~~was a~~ ping-pong table ~~that had~~

~~been newly painted.~~

~~An~~ *extremely black negress* ~~had been bequeathed them by~~
H P Latukey
~~Stephen Brooks, the sculptor-owner of the house.~~ ~~They~~ followed *all*

~~her~~ up the polished wooden stairs. John's bedroom was starkly

white, ~~with big comfortable mahogany furniture.~~ ~~A brief passage~~
was painted
~~opened into Mara's bedroom which was painted in a pale~~ salmon
with white
pink. ~~White~~ rugs ~~were~~ strewn haphazardly on the dark wooden

floor.
                                    She
~~She~~ Obediently entered the circle of his arms. Over

12.

her shoulder John ~~shouted~~ *said* to Lucy. "Leave everything now -- we'll
ring when we want you." A double row of milk white teeth shone
dazzlingly on the black face.

~~"Come on," said John quietly.~~

Mara was the first to awaken. She lay still, afraid to
interrupt John's steady soft breathing. ~~it made a precious~~ *There was*
~~symphony with the~~ muted bird cries outside. *in the gathering* ~~It was getting~~ dark *NLED*
and a faint chill came in through the open windows. She ~~felt~~
~~suddenly depressed~~ and moved closer to John, *find him* He was awake *and whispering.*

"Such a sweet face to wake up *to* ~~and find~~," he said ~~languidly~~ *whispered.*

"I'd like to walk into your eyes and close the lids
behind me," *Mara said.* ~~she whispered and kissed them.~~

~~They faced each other in the candlelight across the~~
~~big table in the cool, dark-panelled living room. Lucy was an~~
~~exquisite cook. They were not hungry, but to please Lucy, took~~
~~two helpings of the baked chicken and found room for the wedding~~
~~cake fashioned with Lucy's own black hands, the day before.~~

"I'm going to make you glad you married me," John
told Mara. A sympathetic sigh emanated from Lucy in the kitchen.

~~III~~ *IV*

Monday meant work again. Mara was to continue with her
job. ~~If~~ John had wanted her to give it up she would gladly have
done so, but he preferred ~~that she~~ should have outside interests.

"Alicia," ~~he told her,~~ "would have been happier if she'd
had some ~~way of expressing her personality.~~"

Mara was glad he talked so easily of Alicia. It brought
Mara into his past. She wanted to possess every thought, every
memory of his life.

13.

"he, that was the least possessive woman in the world!"
Mara told Eddie when he visited them two Sunday's later. They
had asked half a dozen friends to a belated wedding celebration.
There was a young couple --the girl had been to Spencer with Mara,
Eddie, Paul Maxwell, the writer, who brought the wife from whom he
had just legally separated. They were extremely polite to each
other -- embarrassingly so. Stephen Brocks had come to see how
his tenants were doing. And there were a couple of intellectuals
who would marry when the man's wife got the divorce. They were
very much in love and quarrelled most of the afternoon.

John insisted on everyone drinking champagne with
lunch. He was utterly charming, and fascinating, drawing them all
into bright conversation, making everyone, even Mrs. Maxwell,
seem witty and important to themselves. His blue eyes were almost
feverish in their sparkling gaity.

Mara was vaguely worried. She wished John would slow
down a little. He didn't have to work so hard to amuse them. Or
was she being wifely and apprehensive through wanting him to shine.
That must be it, she thought, looking at the others who were now
laughing hysterically at something John had said.

John organized a ping-pong tournament. He was very
funny, looking one way and hitting the ball the other. He lost
all his games. Mara won the tournament. The intellectual couple
were drunk. Mara watched John apprehensively. Was he drunk too?
She kissed him suddenly. There was no smell of liquor. He smiled
gratefully for the kiss.

Paul Maxwell said, "We must go." His ex-wife nodded
grimly. But John said "No" very decisively. He took Paul upstairs

14.

to see some sketches, Mara made forced conversation with the ex-
wife who didn't listen.

"Let's go and get them," she finally suggested. Mara
pretended she had something to show John in the garden and took
him to the window. While his back was turned, Paul said "Goodbye."
John didn't turn round or reply. He stared at a fly zooming on
the window-pane.

"What's the matter, darling?" Mara asked. He came back
from his inner nightmare, took her tenderly in his arms and kissed
her passionately.

"Oh, Mara, I love you."

"What's the matter, dearest?" she persisted.

He looked at her with his head sideways, a cynical grin
flooding his handsome face.

"I didn't sleep here last night," he told her.

She didn't believe him. He was playing one of his
practical jokes.

"I drove to town about two o'clock."

"When did you get back?" she asked derisively.

"About six."

"I don't believe you." But she did.

"Why -- where?" The solidity of her existence was
smashed.

"I went to the Louvre -- I lost two thousand dollars."

She felt cold, but relieved.

"I'm going again tonight, -- now," he told her defiantly.

She didn't understand, but it was all right when John
kissed her again tenderly. Now she wanted the others to stay for
supper -- but they seemed uncomfortable and made excuses,

15.

except Eddie. While they were going, Eddie whispered to Mara:

"What's the matter with John?"

"He's been gambling," she told him. Eddie's face

lengthened. "That's not so terrible," she insisted.

He didn't reply and John came back. The golden brown

of his face had pinkened against his high, white , woolen sweater.

"You and I," he said firmly to Eddie, "are going to

drive into town."

"I'll come with you," Mara said quickly.

"No, just Eddie," John said.

"If that's what you want." Mara turned and ran inside.

The day had been a strain and she didn't want to cry in front of

Eddie.

John came to her bedroom, kissed her gently. "I'll

only be gone a little while."

She kissed him passionately, tried to hold him, but

felt the resistance in his body. They walked down the stairs

together.

"When do you want supper, Mrs. O'Brien?" Lucy's voice

roused Mara from her brooding reverie. She looked at her watch.

Nine o'clock. Two hours since they had gone. She was suddenly

furious with John. It was cruel of him to leave her behind.

"I'm not hungry," she told Lucy.

"Can I go and see my boyfriend then?" Lucy giggled.

Mara nodded and smiled absently. But when she was alone her anger

returned.

"Damn John, damn him, damn him," she walked up and down

the big living room. She turned on the radio. A "blues" singer

16.

was moaning frustratedly. She snapped the voice off.

"I'm an idiot," she said with a short laugh and went
into the garden and slowly picked up the ping-pong balls. They
looked like stars on the dark ground.

"I'm a fool to worry," she said and went to bed.
She must have fallen to sleep immediately.
At two o'clock and stumbled into his room.
He had not yet returned. She sat on his bed and sobbed. "I
should have gone with him. Why did I let him go?" She rocked
herself miserably to and fro.

At five o'clock she telephoned the Louvre. A cold
impersonal voice said he didn't know whether Mr. O'Brien had been
there, but he certainly wasn't there now. She called him a liar
and slammed the receiver down. She was very angry now.

She was telephoning for a taxi when she heard voices
outside.

"Steady, sir," She tripped down the last three stairs
and twisted a toe on her unslippered feet.

"Donal"

A young man was helping John out of a taxi. His white
sweater had been cut all down one side. His coat was over his
shoulders like a cape.

"It's my arm -- I've broken it."

"Oh, darling," was all she could say. They helped him
into the living room.

"What happened?" she asked tenderly.

John grinned suddenly. He extricated a wad of notes
from his coat pocket and

17.

~~threw them on the floor.~~

"The wages of sin," he ~~chuckled.~~ said "Help yourself," he
said to the boy. "Take a hundred dollars -- go on," as the ~~boy~~ other
hesitated.

"No -- don't." Mara protested sharply.

"Give him a hundred dollars," John told her. She shrug-
ged her shoulders and counted out the money. "Go away," snapped
John. The boy ~~grinned.~~ ~~They~~ heard the taxi drive off. Then said
hastily:

"Don't say anything," ~~John said hastily.~~

"But your arm -- "

"I've been to a hospital, had it ~~set~~ -- it's my left,
~~luckily~~ -- so I can work ~~a little.~~ I'll get a nurse to help me
~~dress and bathe.~~

"I'll do that." He dress you and bathe you.

"Not on your life."

~~"I'll telephone for a nurse," said Mara quietly.~~

He wept unexpectedly and Mara was by his side.

"Your arm -- it hurts," she began.

He shook his head. and muttered.

"Your feet -- your poor little feet -- you'll catch
cold." He wanted to rub them.

~~She kissed his twisting mouth,~~ and slowly they walked
up the stairs to his bedroom. He took a strong dose of sleeping
~~medicine~~ and slept until two in the afternoon.

He was ~~furious~~ annoyed when he saw Mara with a tray of food.

~~"The~~ nurse can do all that," he said.

Mara obediently turned the tray over to the ~~quiet-mannered~~
~~pretty~~ nurse -- she had insisted on a pretty nurse.

18.

"Oughtn't you to be at your office?" John said *suggested* ~~peevishly.~~

"How can I?" Mara's voice trembled and she looked quickly away.

"Come here," he commanded. She went to him. "Look," he said quietly, "I don't want to be ~~baby-ed~~ *babied*. ~~This is my fault,~~ ~~and~~ I'm going to get out of it by myself, with the nurse to help. I don't want you to worry about me. ~~Understand?~~"

She nodded and kissed him.

"But it's too late to go to the office today," she said ~~shakily~~. "Can I read in here? I won't bother you."

"Of course, ~~darling~~," *he said after a moment.* "Sit at the end of the bed where I can see your sweet face."

IV *V*   *it had ever spent*

That summer was the happiest ~~of Mara's life~~. ~~Occasionally~~ *Sometimes* in the evening they went to a movie in Stamford. They saw ~~very~~ few people and didn't want anyone. The weather was beautiful, the heat cut off by the big trees. John worked ~~four hours a day~~ *hard and she* loved the way he twisted his hair to a turnip-like point while he painted. She was back by six-thirty, and he showed her the work he had done during the day and talked about her job, as ~~eager~~ and enthusiastic for her as for himself.

Before her marriage to John, Mara's standards of right and wrong had fluctuated according to how she personally was affected. Her horizon had been limited to "what do I get out of this?" Looking at life through John's eyes, she saw a new world ~~in which self mattered least, integrity most~~.

~~He gave her a new appreciation of art.~~ On Saturdays they ~~usually~~ lunched in town as a prelude to spending the afternoon

19.

in a museum or ~~picture~~ gallery. Under John's ~~eager teaching~~, Mara discovered the greatness of ~~Cellini~~, Velasquez, Goya, and Manet. ~~She had always~~ considered herself well read because she ~~liked~~ Dickens, Thackery, and ~~Tennyson~~, and had been able to discuss the best ~~sellers~~ of the day, but John's ~~wide knowledge of literature~~ made her feel inadequate for the first time in her ~~self-satisfied~~ life. Her new reading ~~course~~ included Shelley, ~~Joyce~~, Dostievsky, and Proust. ~~The latter was~~ hard going at first, but when she finished the ~~last of~~ "A la Recherche du Temps Perdu," it was hard to ~~tell who was the prouder, she or John~~. He was her Bible and her encyclopedia -- anything she wanted to know, right from wrong, history, politics, architecture, John knew the answer.

Eddie was one of the few visitors that summer. Mara walked round the garden ~~with him and~~ gloated, "You thought I couldn't stick to any one man, didn't you? I'll be faithful to John the rest of my life."

Eddie kicked a small stone. Then casually, "How's the gambling?"

"What really happened that night?" she asked. He evaded a direct answer.

"It's like liquor ~~with some men~~. John just can't take gambling. ~~And~~ Alicia was worse, ~~he laughed~~. ~~She~~ once ~~tried to~~ give ~~them~~ her clothes when they had no more money left. ~~She was arrested and John fought the entire police department of Monte Carlo~~. ~~But~~ don't worry, I've never known him so happy ~~and content~~. You're good for him."

"Who's good for who?" John had heard the last words. He hated to be discussed, Mara changed the conversation immediately.

20.

But she was glad when Eddie had gone. There was no room for a third
person in their paradise.

In September, John's son returned from a tour of Europe
with five St. Paul's boys and a master from the school. He was to
stay with them two weeks before entering Yale.

Mara heard the two John's quarrelling in the garden one
evening. She caught the word 'liquor' and then young John said
angrily. "If you can ruin us with your gambling, I suppose I can
drink." She longed for him to leave.

The following evening, the boy went to New York. There
was a telegram from him next day. He had decided to visit a friend
in Georgia. "I was afraid you wouldn't let me go," he explained.
Mara had never seen John so angry.

The glorious peace of the summer was gone. John had
promised a mural for the State Capital at Albany. But Monday came
and the job was at a standstill. Young John's trip abroad had cost
$1500 and new bills poured in for clothes that John had already given
his son money to pay for.

"He's like me." John said in the softness of the evening.
He showed Mara the stack of bills. "I've never had a money sense."

And then just as life looked peaceful again to Mara, a
letter came from young John stating that he had definitely decided
against Yale and with or without his father's permission would get
a job instead.

"What are you going to do?" Mara asked apprehensively after
reading the letter twice. She dimly remembered the time when she was
the centre of John's universe. Now she was a shadow eclipsed by a
willful boy of 16.

"I'm not sure." John kissed her absently and said, "Let's

21.

forget him."

the committing

She ~~was relieved and~~ went slightly comforted to her train, *till in the afternoon*

But he ~~he called~~ her at the office ~~as she was about to leave.~~

"I'm coming in -- we'll dine in town," he said.

"It's hot, darling. I was looking forward to the country."

"I'm coming in."

"All right. Where shall I meet you?"

"The Louvre."

The gambling rooms were invisible to those who dined and danced in the ~~blue and~~ silver restaurant. But there were always four or five phlegmatic foreigners, standing aimlessly in the egg-shell blue ~~entrance~~ foyer.

John was already there when Mara arrived.

By last
"He's a gangster," he said in a stage whisper after intro-ducing her to the pasty, dark-haired manager. Mara looked at the 'gangster', expecting an answering smile. But his features were as *Curtis* blank as an unrelieved wheat field. ~~John~~ wore a dinner jacket with a stiff shirt. His face looked freshly laundered. His chin seemed more pointed than usual and more impudent.

Curtis
When the waiter said, "Good evening, Mr. O'Brien," ~~John~~ replied ~~coldly;~~ *tilkey:*

Brian O'Brien
"I suppose you mean my twin brother, ~~¶~~ ~~The waiter stared~~ ~~at him.~~

"The likeness is remarkable," he said slowly. ~~Jennie noting~~ *had refused for a minute that* was so good ~~even~~ Mara ~~was ready to believe~~ he had a twin brother. He was like a little boy in his delight when the waiter, convinced, gave *imaginary relative* him a message of regards for the non-~~existent twin brother.~~

approvingly
They danced. John looked at Mara ~~intimidatingly.~~

"New dress?"

12.

Mara glanced ~~down~~ at the blue and white print ~~dress~~.

"I've had it a year."

dancing "Then it's you that's new tonight." He held her closer,
~~He danced~~ in a loping, collegiate way, ~~looking at her with a non-
explainable smile on his thinned lips.~~ *Mara brushed his ear*

"I love you tonight," Mara whispered in his ear ~~and brushed~~
~~it with her~~ *There* ~~warm~~ mouth. He danced her out of the restaurant; *They*
were in the foyer again. A ~~large~~ fat man *led* ~~took~~ them through an unexpected doorway, through a thin ~~passageway~~ cluttered with trays of dirty
glasses and silverware. An elevator at the end took them up to the
gambling rooms.

~~Mara was intensely disappointed.~~ The room into which they
were admitted by the two men who guarded the elevator ~~exit~~ was supremely
drab. Not even the ~~three~~ heavy crystal chandeliers suspended from a
~~the~~ high white ceiling could impart elegance to the bored croupers
chanting in nasal ~~American~~ sing-sing, "Place your bets." There were
four trente-et-quarante tables, Three Bird-in-Cages, two craps tables,
two roulette wheels. ~~and~~ Around them were *tense they-wish* ~~dull, ugly people, making~~
silent or discordant noises as they placed their bets. John ~~grinned at Mara~~
~~and~~ steered her into a small adjoining room.

A haze of smoke gave a watery outline to the men and
women -- there were about thirty ~~mostly men~~ slumping on thin-
backed chairs around the oval green ~~baize~~ topped table. There was
no other furniture in the room.

John's ~~way~~ "Hello, ~~everybody~~ *Suckers! fellow*," was like the crashing of
glass. Mara ~~smiled~~ *felt* apologetically for him. A few heads nodded. ~~But~~
most of them ~~continued~~ *remained* to frown into ~~their~~ cards. John seemed taller
and broader. He filled the air with glowing vitality, making every-
one else seem dark and sallow. There ~~was no place for him to sit~~

23.

down, and Mara followed him round the ~~backs of the chairs~~. He ~~"bango-ma"~~ a wizened bald man, ~~and~~ won $500. ~~The old man shook his head.~~ Mara thought it would never stop. ~~John~~ crammed the chips into her hands.

His face had changed. His eyes ~~were~~ faintly bloodshot. And he had difficulty in making his lips meet. ~~His pastel complexion coarsened.~~ Tiny crystals of perspiration covered his nose and ~~upper lip.~~ He was aware of her scrutiny and turned quickly from her.

Two players left, and John and Mara sat in their chairs.

"You're not to play," he ~~commanded~~.

On the right of Mara was a middle-aged woman with a grey crepe complexion and skeleton hands. She stared at the ripeness of Mara's bloom and gave her what was meant to be a friendly smile. John won steadily from the crepe-faced lady and from the man on his left. ~~Soon there was~~ a pile of $100 chips in front of him. ~~It was~~ fantastic but terrifically exciting. Mara calculated there was $10,000 worth at ~~least. Now~~ was surely the time to ~~transfer~~ them into cash and go ~~home~~. Her head was splitting, but when she told this to John, he ~~was calling~~ to her pain for the first time since they had met.

"You ~~can't~~ go." ~~His voice had the abruptness of cold water.~~

His luck changed. He lost to ~~his left-hand neighbor,~~ a pencil thin Italian ~~with a beak~~ profile.

She took advantage of this to urge, "Let's go now -- it would be a pity to lose all this money." ~~He turned his back to her.~~

Over his shoulder he said, "~~Maybe you had better go,~~" and ~~twisted round angrily.~~ Her face crumpled and he softened, "Stay if you like, but behave," She nodded and tried to smile brightly.

When the "shoe" came to the ~~Italian~~ on John's left, the

24.

Italian won from the man on his left, 9 and 5. John ~~triumphantly~~
turned up 9 and 8. The Italian had two nines. John stood up suddenly
and scattered the cards on the floor.

"I want new cards, ~~--~~ this ~~damned wop~~ is cheating," ~~he said.~~

There was a quick arrested movement in the room. The
Italian grinned and a couple of men who had been nebulous as background, were now behind John's chair. One of them gently touched
his arm. John swung at him and the man slid noisily to the floor.
Mara pulled the other man's coat as he was about to hit John. He
pushed her ~~roughly~~ and she fell hard against the table.

"You --"shouted John. His fist banged against the man's
mouth, drawing blood. And then John collapsed. Mara thought he had
fainted. Then she saw a ~~little~~ pistol that ~~was smoking~~ in the Italian's
hand. Magically, the room was empty except for herself and John.
She felt passionless and unfeeling. John had been ~~shot~~. How absurd.
~~And why wasn't she upset?~~

"~~A doctor,~~ get me a doctor," John whispered. She looked
blankly at his white face, ~~with~~ its delicate texture ~~again~~ restored.
~~And~~ a hot tearing at her heart made her feel pain again.

She shouted, "~~Get a doctor,~~ Someone get a doctor. Come
back someone, and help me."

Three men -- one of them had been playing chemin-de-fer--
came back into the room. They dragged John towards ~~a concealed~~ door,
His blood stained the grey carpet. Mara begged them to stop.

"You'll kill him -- he shouldn't be moved!"
~~They~~ continued to drag him.

"Stop it, stop it!" ~~Mara screamed,~~ pulling first at one man,
then another. ~~She might as well not have been there for the notice
taken of her.~~

John's car was in the alley outside. They slumped him into it.

25.

One of the men put his face close to Mara's. "This didn't happen here, ~~you understand?~~ It wasn't a query. ~~It was a statement.~~ She would deal with them later. She mustn't say anything now -- they might stop her getting to a hospital. She drove slowly so as not to jerk John. He was smiling when she looked at him.

"Cigarette?" she asked ~~tenderly~~. He nodded. She lit *one* ~~hungry~~ and put it between his lips.

"We'll soon be at the hospital," ~~she told him weeping.~~ The cigarette dropped from his lips and smoldered on his coat. She threw it out the window. John was whispering something. She bent her head.

"I'll make this up to you somehow -- "

"Sure," she said jerkily, "Sure."

His smile left a small glow on his pale face.

He was dead before *they reached* the hospital, ~~was reached.~~ Mara remembered saying to the surprised porter, "I'm going to faint." She did not know how much she had lost until three weeks later and the doctor told her she ~~was~~ all right now. *He was quite*

AFTERWORD
WENDY W. FAIREY

WHENEVER I TEACH *THE GREAT GATSBY,* AS I HAVE
so many times in my forty years in the college classroom,
I always wonder if I will tell the students my story. It's
my mother's story, really. But it's mine, too, the story of
a personal link to the author of the book that tinges every professional comment I make about themes and nar-
rative voice and structure and the other facets of fiction
that English professors train their students to look for. I
care about all these, to be sure, but I have an intensely private as well as professional understanding of the novel at
hand. Or rather, the private and professional strands are so
intertwined that I can't really say where one ends and the
other begins. In class I present them as separate. I tell the
personal story when I've proven to myself that perhaps I
don't have to, when I feel we have satisfactorily "covered"
the "material," as we call it, with professorial dispassion
and dispatch. Perhaps the revelation comes in an impulsive
moment of warmth for the group of young people before
me—I want to be closer to them, to give them something
they might find special. Or perhaps there's been a little sag
in classroom energy and I turn to the story to reinvigorate
us.

"Here's a personal connection that may interest you. My mother actually knew F. Scott Fitzgerald. It was in the last years of his life in Hollywood."

I see mild interest in their faces. "She was involved with him," I say. A variant of this, if the group seems more sophisticated, perhaps a class of graduate students, might be: "She was his lover." Interest at this point increases, usually mixed with a bit of understandable anxiety that an aging female professor, talking about her mother's lover, has become unpredictable.

"Yes, they were together for three and a half years. He died in her living room—stood up and dropped dead of a heart attack. A few days before Christmas 1940."

Now I've made it vivid.

"But what interests me the most," I say, "is that he devised for her an education. The F. Scott Fitzgerald College of One. It was an entire college curriculum—with history and art and music, and even a little economics. But above all poetry and the novel: Dickens, Thackeray, Henry James. We had the books from the College of One in our library when I was a child. Those were the books I read growing up."

My private relation to F. Scott Fitzgerald is that he bought the books for my mother that I have loved all my life, the books, it's fair to say, that turned me into a professor of English literature. I loved the volumes in the College of One, inside and out—their bindings, their pages, their print, their stories—and I lived in them more fully than I can remember living in the world around me. Thus, *my* F. Scott Fitzgerald story is less that he was my mother's lover for those three and a half years before I was born, dying dramatically in her living room, releasing her to go forth and be with other men and become my mother, than that he shaped my life's reading by having bought her those books. Long before I even knew of her connection to him, they lined the shelves along opposite walls of our den, there for me to take down and carry upstairs to my bedroom and immerse myself in stories that transported me to other times and places. The palm trees and eucalyptus of dusky Southern California gave way to the imagined bustle of Thackeray's London or the green landscape of David Copperfield's Suffolk downs. And as soon as I finished one book, perhaps *Tom Jones* or *Bleak House*, I would ask my mother to recommend another, thus building the shadow world that I would live in, have lived in all my life.

So reading and teaching *The Great Gatsby* entails for me, always, not only the themes of the great American novel with its tragic dreamer hero, believing in the wrong dreams, but also the subtext of my mother's relationship with Fitzgerald, my mother herself looming as a kind of female Gatsby, a woman who emerged from a Jewish orphanage and made herself up as Sheilah Graham, London chorus girl and Hollywood columnist, suppressing her Jewishness and her early poverty, believing anything was possible, and awesome in the energy of her self-creation, to which she proved faithful to the end. And I also understand Gatsby as myself, someone who has wed her dreams to people, starting with my mother, whom I wanted to believe in as golden and magic. But I am Nick Carraway as well, awed by Gatsby but able to judge him; the levelheaded spectator, who ultimately turns away from a gaudy world to seek something else, a more solid if more ordinary existence. And I link, too, with Fitzgerald, in our shared love for my mother. And with him as a pedagogue, devising his syllabi for the F. Scott Fitzgerald College of One, joining with me in our shared love of Victorian novels. Everything is all mixed together.

The story of how Lily Shiel, born September 15, 1904, in Leeds, England, and placed in an East End of London orphanage at age six, transformed herself into glamorous Sheilah Graham is one that my mother recounted in no less than eight published works of autobiography. Some focused on her time with Fitzgerald, some were more concerned with her childhood—its poverty and her eight years, from ages six to fourteen, in the orphanage—others drew on her remarkable thirty-five-year career, stretching from the late 1930s into the '70s, as one of the "unholy trio" of Hollywood columnists along with Hedda Hopper and Louella O. Parsons. No book tells quite the whole truth—I'm sure there are many buried secrets even now. My mother had emerged from her orphanage with the contradictory qualities of courage and secrecy, optimism and wariness that would guide her to the end of her life. Of all her books, though, *College of One* seems to me the best and perhaps the most truthful because it conveys the full truth of her love of literature and learning, and at least the essential truth of her love for the man who I believe was her life's great love and teacher.

As one of my mother's two children born some years after F. Scott Fitzgerald died, I came to know her story in pieces and over time. When I look back to my own childhood, I marvel at how lacking I was in curiosity about her earlier life. She was a single parent (having divorced our almost incidental father early on), working to stay at the top of her profession and to raise me and my younger brother, Robert. We lived in an elegant Spanish-style house in Beverly Hills, with pets and bicycles and a Ping-Pong table on the back veranda. I remember the orderly life of the house, the reassuring points of reference in the people who worked there: my mother, whom I always sought out after school, never afraid to interrupt her on my way to play in the high-walled backyard; the housekeeper in the kitchen, making pastry dough or ironing laundry; the secretary typing out my mother's column in the bookcase-lined den; the Filipino gardener working shirtless among the hibiscus. This was my early life and all the past I ever knew. An avocado tree in the backyard. Family friends. A series of cherished dogs. Then Malibu in the summers for children, dogs, and servants. And our mother, our only relative, the prime mover of it all.

I learned of my mother's Dickensian childhood as well as her relationship with Fitzgerald only when I was a teenager and she published the first of her books, *Beloved Infidel* (1957), which drew its title from a poem Fitzgerald had written for her. The movie version, starring Gregory Peck as Fitzgerald and Deborah Kerr as my mother, appeared two years later. "I had only one life to give my producer," quipped my mother, "and Jerry Wald ruined it." She thought the casting all wrong: Peck, too stiff for Fitzgerald (she would have preferred Richard Basehart), and Deborah Kerr, much too ladylike. A better choice, she asserted, would have been Marilyn Monroe, who, if I think about it, had a lot in common with my mother—from their bleak childhoods and savvy reliance on sexiness and wit to their aspirations to be taken seriously and their relationships with major American writers, which were so important to both of them. But however much she embraced this parallel, my mother was in no way ready to reveal all. Neither the book *Beloved Infidel* nor the movie made any mention of my mother's five older siblings or of the fact that her family had been turn-of-the-century Jewish immigrants from Ukraine, in flight like so many others from the pogroms. She had to tell Robert and me about her family in 1959, because one of her brothers, upset at the family's erasure from her history, revealed the "real Sheilah Graham story" to a London tabloid. I was sixteen. Raised Episcopalian (indeed, one of the few children left in my Beverly Hills public school on Jewish holidays), I was intrigued to find myself, as I put it, "half Jewish," and went around informing my friends. My mother begged me to show some discretion, though in her later years she gradually became more open, at least among her close friends, about her background.

Once we children knew about the members of her family, she relished talking to us about them. She also renewed contact with her older sisters—"the thin sister" and "the fat sister," she dubbed them—who lived two miles from each other in Brighton, England. Beginning in 1960, Robert and I were taken to visit them on our trips abroad, but since these sisters were not on speaking terms with each other, we would have lunch with one and tea with the other. My mother loved them and loved their Jewish cooking. By then, two of her brothers were dead, and she wouldn't see the one living brother, who had betrayed her to the press.

Strangely, I never knew the names of my mother's parents until after her death in 1988, though I had seen their pictures and knew something of their stories. I found her birth certificate among her papers, attesting that Lily Shiel's father and mother were Louis and Rebecca Shiel.

Their names leapt out at me, somehow making those distant figures more substantial. I knew how much my mother had cherished the one photograph she had of her father, a dignified-looking tailor, whose death when she was a baby left his family impoverished. He died on a trip to Berlin to consult doctors about his tuberculosis and is buried there in the Jewish cemetery. My mother visited his grave in the early 1930s and told us about the German children who came around throwing stones and shouting *"Juden, Juden."*

The family moved to Stepney Green in the East End of London, where my grandmother, who hardly spoke English, worked cleaning the public lavatories. As was not uncommon among families in such straitened circumstances, she put my mother and her next youngest child, Morris, in the institution we had known only as "the orphanage" while my mother was alive but that I was able to identify after her death as the Jews' Hospital and Orphan Asylum in the neighborhood of Norwood. Entering Norwood at six, she had her golden hair shaved to the scalp as a precaution against lice, and to the end of her life she was haunted by the degradation of this experience. When she "graduated" at fourteen, she had established herself as Norwood's "head girl": captain of the cricket team and recipient of many prizes, including both the Hebrew prize and a prize for reciting a poem by Elizabeth Barrett Browning. The orphanage wanted her to try for a scholarship to become a teacher, but her mother, who was by then dying of stomach cancer, needed her at home.

It is revealing of the times that all six Shiel children adopted unmistakably "English" names: Heiman became Henry; Esther changed to Iris; Sarah became Sally; Meyer—the "bad" brother who had taken my mother on his thieving expeditions when she was small—took the name of Jack; Morris became Maurice, the owner of a successful ladies' clothing shop.

And Lily? After her mother's death when she was sixteen, my mother left home to move into her own little flat in the West End. She had a job in a department store demonstrating a toothbrush that cleaned only the backs of the teeth. When the toothbrush company folded, she looked up one of the many gentlemen who had left their cards. At eighteen, she married John Graham Gillam, a kindly older man who proved impotent, went bankrupt, and looked the other way when she went out with other men, but under whose Pygmalionesque tutelage she improved her speech and manners, enrolled in the Royal Academy of Dramatic Art, and changed her name. She became a chorus girl, one of Cochran's Young Ladies, the English equivalent of the Ziegfeld Girls.

My mother started writing professionally during her period on the stage. She came home one day to find her husband trying to write an article for the newspapers about Easter eggs. When she suggested he might be wasting his time, he challenged her to think of a better topic. She promptly sat down with a pencil and yellow notepad and wrote "The Stage Door Johnnies by a Chorus Girl." *The Daily Express* ran it and paid her two guineas.

By the time she left England in 1933 to try her fortune in America, my mother had earned a modest reputation as a freelance journalist. She had also written two unsuccessful novels, a credential that allowed her to bluff her way into jobs as a New York staff reporter, getting scoops and writing eye-catching features such as "Who Cheats Most in Marriage?," a breezy inventory of the men of Western nations. Then, in 1936, she landed the opportunity to go to Hollywood as a nationally syndicated columnist, a position she held for more than thirty-five years.

On July 14, 1937—Bastille Day—my mother went to a party at her friend Robert Benchley's bungalow in the Garden of Allah, where she met F. Scott Fitzgerald, with whom she soon fell in love. Because their time together and her Hollywood years in general are well documented, I will note only what seems salient for this remembrance. One day in 1938 Fitzgerald found my mother struggling to read the first volume of Proust. He took her in hand and drew up the two-year plan of study that became the College of One. My mother spent hours each day reading books and discussing them with her teacher. The curriculum had history in it—the aim was to work up to reading Spengler—and art and music, but above all it was the study and appreciation of literature. Nineteenth- and early-twentieth-century authors were the favorites. Keats, Shelley, Swinburne, T.S. Eliot, Dickens, Thackeray, Tolstoy, and Henry James. Fitzgerald and my mother recited the poems together and pretended to be characters of their favorite novels—Grushenka and Alyosha from *The Brothers Karamazov*, shortened to "Grue" and "Yosh"; Natasha and Pierre from *War and Peace* (my mother had rebelled against being cast as the worldly, jaded Hélène); Swann and Odette from Proust; Esther Summerson and Mr. Jarndyce or the Smallweeds slumped in their chairs from *Bleak House*; Becky Sharp and Rawdon Crawley from *Vanity Fair*, or, for a change, Scott would become fat Jos Sedley.

It is the story of the education that has brought my mother and Fitzgerald together alive for me, along with a few other of her shared memories of little things: Fitzgerald looking at her "with such love," with his head cocked to one side, the two of them lying at opposite ends of a sofa with their shoes and socks off and massaging each other's toes, the two of them at Malibu scooping into buckets the tiny fish called grunion that come onto the beach at night to spawn.

My mother told Fitzgerald the truth about herself— not just about the poverty and the orphanage, but also about her Jewishness. But it's as much a part of the story that Fitzgerald abused her trust as that he had first won it. As she puts it in *College of One*, during his great drinking binge of 1939, he screamed "all the secrets of [her] humble beginnings" to the nurse taking care of him. That same day, my mother and Fitzgerald grappled over his gun, and she made the pronouncement of which I think she was rather proud, "Take it and shoot yourself, you son of a bitch. I didn't pull myself out of the gutter to waste my life on a drunk like you." What Fitzgerald had screamed to the nurse, my mother eventually told me, though she never brought herself to write it in any of her books, was that she was a Jew.

She forgave him, he stopped drinking, and they had a final deeply calm year, immersed in the education project, before he died. Dying in my mother's living room, twenty-one months before my birth, his death made way for me— for surely there would have been no me if he had lived, and he hovered over our lives as our own personal guardian angel and, strangely, our ghostly progenitor. I read the books he had bought for the College of One and absorbed his politics, which had converted our mother from a conservative to a liberal "in a day." When we moved east in 1959—my mother restless after a short bad marriage and convinced

she could write her column even from a cottage in Connecticut—the library came with us to line the shelves of
the den in our new house in Westport. A Fitzgerald scholar
once visited to do research on the author's reading. "Are
these Fitzgerald's underlinings?" he inquired, excited to
find such keys to the writer's intellect and sensibility. "Well,
some are Fitzgerald's," I replied, home from my nearby
boarding school. "And some are mine." The scholar was
horrified, but I had no sense of transgression. The books
seemed mine, too, since I had loved and lived in so many of
them through all my reading history. They still do, though
I no longer enjoy their physical proximity. In 1968 they left
their last home with us, my mother's New York apartment
on the Upper East Side. Seeking, I think, to be recognized
for her important and "legitimate" contribution to F. Scott
Fitzgerald's life and work, she donated the College of One
collection to Princeton.

My mother died on November 17, 1988, two months and
two days after her eighty-fourth birthday. Six months earlier she had suffered a massive heart attack following a hip-
replacement operation at New York's Hospital for Special
Surgery—for years she had suffered from bad arthritis. After this, her heart half destroyed, she betook herself to her
apartment in Palm Beach—her last home of many in her
perpetual search to feel at home—hired round-the-clock
nurses, and, ever someone to face life's exigencies with
courage and without complaint, she summed up her life
as a good one and declared herself ready for death. Often
when I spoke with her over the phone, she would quote to
me lines of poetry that she and Scott Fitzgerald had read

and recited together. She loved the line from Keats's "Ode to a Nightingale," "I have been half in love with easeful Death," drawing out that wonderful adjective "easeful" as she intoned it. Another of their favorites that also seemed to give her solace was Swinburne's "The Garden of Proserpine," especially its second stanza:

> I am tired of tears and laughter,
> And men that laugh and weep;
> Of what may come hereafter
> For men that sow to reap:
> I am weary of days and hours,
> Blown buds of barren flowers,
> Desires and dreams and powers
> And everything but sleep.

My mother's love of poetry, the way its words and cadences suffused her thoughts and emotions and became part of her expression of self, is one of my fondest memories of her. I can only hope that among the many students I have taught over the past forty years, there are those who have found the kind of lifelong joy and enrichment in English prose and poetry as did F. Scott Fitzgerald's best and only pupil in the College of One.

THE NEVERSINK LIBRARY

THE NEVERSINK LIBRARY

THE MADONNA OF THE SLEEPING CARS
by Maurice Dekobra

978-1-61219-058-7
$15.00 / $17.00 CAN

THE BOOK OF KHALID
by Ameen Rihani

978-1-61219-087-7
$15.00 / $17.00 CAN

YOUTH WITHOUT GOD
by Ödön von Horváth

978-1-61219-119-5
$15.00 / $15.00 CAN

THE TRAVELS AND SURPRISING ADVENTURES OF BARON MUNCHAUSEN
by Rudolf Erich Raspe

978-1-61219-123-2
$15.00 / $15.00 CAN

SNOWBALL'S CHANCE
by John Reed

978-1-61219-125-6
$15.00 / $15.00 CAN

FUTILITY
by William Gerhardie

978-1-61219-145-4
$15.00 / $15.00 CAN

THE REVERBERATOR
by Henry James

978-1-61219-156-0
$15.00 / $15.00 CAN

THE RIGHT WAY TO DO WRONG
by Harry Houdini

978-1-61219-166-9
$15.00 / $15.00 CAN

A COUNTRY DOCTOR'S NOTEBOOK
by Mikhail Bulgakov

978-1-61219-190-4
$15.00 / $15.00 CAN

I AWAIT THE DEVIL'S COMING
by Mary MacLane

978-1-61219-194-2
$16.00 / $16.00 CAN

THE NEVERSINK LIBRARY